UNEQUAL CURES

Unequal Cures

Public Health and Political Change in Bolivia, 1900–1950

ANN ZULAWSKI

Duke University Press   Durham and London   2007

© 2007 Duke University Press
All rights reserved
Printed in the United States of America on
acid-free paper ∞
Designed by C. H. Westmoreland
Typeset in Adobe Garamond by Tseng
Information Systems, Inc.
Library of Congress Cataloging-in-
Publication Data appear on the last printed
page of this book.

Duke University Press gratefully
acknowledges the support of the Committee
on Faculty Compensation and Development
at Smith College, which provided funds
toward the production of this book.

To the memory of my parents,

GLADYS KIDWELL LACHENBRUCH

AND DAVID LACHENBRUCH

CONTENTS

ILLUSTRATIONS

ACKNOWLEDGMENTS

The research and writing of this book were made possible by two fellowships from the National Endowment for the Humanities, a Fulbright American Republics' Grant and financial assistance, and sabbatical leave from Smith College.

I thank the directors and staff of the Archivo and Biblioteca Nacional de Bolivia in Sucre; the Archivo Histórico de La Paz; the Archivo de la Casa de la Cultura "Rosendo Gutiérrez," of La Paz; the library of the Universidad Mayor de San Andrés of La Paz; and the Rockefeller Archive Center in Sleepy Hollow, New York. Most especially I would like to thank the staff at the Hospital General in La Paz for giving me access to their records when they were not at all set up to accommodate researchers. I am also grateful to Rolando Costa Arduz and Alberto Vázquez for allowing me to work in their private libraries. I thank the individuals who very graciously allowed me to interview them for this book. Their names are listed in the bibliography.

I owe a great deal to many people who have helped me at different stages of this project but, first and foremost, I must acknowledge my debt to Cecilia Arauco de Machicao, indefatigable research assistant and valued friend. I have also received important advice and assistance in doing the research for this book from Claudia Heckl, Carola Echalar, Laura Escobari de Querejazu, René Arze, Ximena Medinacelli, Alfredo Caballero, and Rossana Barragán. I also sincerely thank Brooke Larson, Clara López Beltrán, Laura Gotkowitz, Lesley Gill, Seemin Qayum, María Lagos, Agustín Echalar, Elsa Echalar, Marcos Cueto, Mauricio Mamani, Jimmy Salles, and Sinclair Thomson, for various types of help with the project.

Laura Gotkowitz, David Sowell, and an anonymous reviewer from Duke University Press read and commented on the entire book manuscript. Diego Armus, Brooke Larson, my colleagues in the Latin American and Latino/a Studies Program at Smith College, and the members of the New York City Latin American History Workshop read and offered suggestions on sections of the book. I thank them all sincerely for their time and effort and hope that the final product is better as a result.

Janira Bonilla did the arduous work of transcribing taped interviews, and Marta Schaaf produced statistics from quantitative hospital and cemetery records. Jon Caris of the Environmental Science and Policy Program at Smith College prepared the maps. My longtime friend Ruth Elwell did the index.

Two chapters of this book are expanded, revised versions of articles I previously published elsewhere. I thank *Latin American Research Review* for permission to use my article "Hygiene and the 'Indian Problem': Ethnicity and Medicine in Bolivia, 1910–1920," 35:2 (spring 2000) and Duke University Press for allowing me to use "Mental Illness and Democracy in Bolivia: The Manicomio Pacheco, 1935–1950," which originally appeared in 2003 in *From Cholera to AIDS: History and Disease in Modern Latin America*, edited by Diego Armus.

At Duke University Press Valerie Millholland was a responsive and supportive editor, and Miriam Angress and Mark Mastromarino kindly and efficiently got me through the production process. I also thank members of the Duke production staff whose names I don't know but who were helpful and efficient when I had questions.

Finally, I am grateful to a number of people who were less immediately connected to this book but whose presence and friendship vastly improved my life while I was working on it: Judy and Peter Valdez, Donna Lazarus, Mario and Lourdes Sarabia, Rodrigo Muñoz Reyes, Patricia Plaza, Arturo Yarish, and Carolina Avila. Most of all I thank my husband and *querido compañero*, Dan Zulawski.

INTRODUCTION

Throughout the first half of the twentieth century, Bolivia presented formidable public health problems: tropical and even temperate zones were plagued by malaria and yellow fever; yaws and hookworm were endemic in low-altitude zones, while whooping cough, typhus, and typhoid were especially common in high altitudes; and people in all parts of the country suffered from TB, smallpox, venereal disease, and illnesses generally associated with lack of pure drinking water and with malnutrition. Silicosis was accepted as an occupational cost for workers who mined tin, the country's most important export. Everywhere infant morality was very high.

In 1900 Bolivia had a population of 1,633,610 people, and by 1950 it had grown to almost 3,000,000. Yet its health statistics and most common illnesses remained substantially the same throughout the half century, and, despite concerted campaigns against specific diseases in the 1930s and '40s, some health problems became worse. By the early 1950s, although control measures had reduced malaria in

Map 1 Bolivia, showing area lost to Paraguay during Chaco War (1932–35). Prepared by Jon Caris.

some zones, in others the disease had spread unchecked. Tuberculosis had become much more prevalent in the preceding decades and was considered the most serious health threat in the country in 1951. Smallpox was still common because vaccination was generally done only after epidemics broke out.[1]

Bolivia's health problems would have been daunting even with substantial resources; the country's great geographic diversity meant that doctors had to deal with diseases of the tropics as well as those more common in high-altitude and temperate zones. The altitude of the capital city of La Paz is over 12,000 feet above sea level, and a vast high-altitude plateau stretches for 800 miles between the two ranges of the Andes mountains. Yet part of Bolivia lies within the Amazon basin, and fully two-thirds of the country is in the lowlands. There are also temperate zones in mountain valleys, and tropical microclimates wedged in valleys near Andean peaks. Throughout the period studied, Bolivia's health system remained particularly unequal to the task of providing care to people in this challenging geography. Areas, especially in the lowlands, were often inaccessible due to flooding during the rainy season, and medical professionals were pathetically few in number. In 1900 there were 142 doctors in the major urban areas and virtually none in the countryside. Bolivia was poor even by Latin American standards, and funding for public health was inadequate. In 1931 only 1.5 percent of the national budget went to the Dirección General de Sanidad Pública (responsible for administering public health on the national level; see chapter 2).[2] By 1951 there was still an acute shortage of medical facilities in small towns, and doctors generally tried to stay in the capitals of departments (Bolivia's equivalent of U.S. states) because there was so little governmental or private support for medicine in the countryside. Many people in cities, as well as in rural areas, relied on various types of healers who were not academic doctors—some within the Western medical tradition, others who practiced Andean spiritual or herbal techniques.

Health problems affected almost every aspect of national social and economic life. Infant mortality caused policy makers and social critics to worry about lack of population growth. In malarial areas many previously productive agricultural zones were depopulated, and when some inhabitants remained they were often so enervated

from malarial anemia that they could barely work. Epidemics of typhoid and typhus frequently decimated the workforce of the agricultural estates that provided food for the capital city of La Paz. The
paralysis and mental degeneration of late-stage syphilis and malarial
psychosis sent significant numbers of patients to the national mental
hospital. Botched illegal abortions and unintentional miscarriages
were the leading causes of maternal death.

One purpose of this book is to provide an account of these major
medical problems that Bolivia faced during the first half of the twentieth century, and to examine their social and economic causes and
what was done to ameliorate them. Another aim is to analyze the
political and social significance of the writings of doctors and policy
makers about medicine and health during a volatile period that
began when the country was a political oligarchy and ended on the
eve of a revolution that ushered in universal suffrage, agrarian reform, and nationalization of the country's tin mines. In this study
I ask: How did thinking about medicine change as a result of the
major ideological and social transformations that took place in those
years? What significance did ideas about public health, hygiene, and
sanitation have for national debates about what kind of country
Bolivia was or should be? In what ways did political change affect
the professional status of university-trained doctors, and how did
doctors participate in the new populist politics of the era?

Ethnicity and gender are central to this examination of medicine and political change. In the first half of the twentieth century,
Bolivian ruling groups were still struggling with a question that had
been at least partially resolved in other Latin American countries:
could Bolivia, a country in which Indians made up approximately
half of the population, be progressive and civilized? Between 1900
and 1950 intellectuals made many proposals for roles the country's
indigenous people would, or should, play in a modern nation. Although in different terms, policy makers also addressed the question of women's citizenship and participation in the state. Most of
the contributions to these debates in one or more ways touched on
health, medicine, and biology. Doctors, who often were writers and
politicians as well as physicians, intervened in the discussion as experts on everything from illegal abortions to the psyche of the Indian
to the need for socialized medicine. Thus, this book explores the
ways in which medicine, far from representing an independent sci-

entific truth, was influenced by and intrinsic to the most important social debates in Bolivia.

This discussion of what selected, privileged Bolivians thought about public health and nation building cannot be separated from an overview of national health conditions and how the majority of Bolivians, who were mostly poor, lived. So the story of public health and political change in Bolivia is also the story of housing and working conditions, how people's lives were affected by political and armed conflict, and how different social groups organized to improve their lives materially and to achieve the rights of citizenship. Furthermore, the first five decades of the twentieth century saw major advances in medical knowledge, and these advances at least potentially offered Bolivians new treatments for many of the diseases that plagued them. Consequently I try to always keep theoretical discussions of medicine linked to this more down-to-earth analysis through the use of (among other sources) hospital and cemetery records, censuses, doctors' assessments of patients' conditions, newspaper accounts, and interviews with people about their health and medical treatment during the period.

Frameworks

This book is the intellectual product of a new history of medicine that has gained momentum and practitioners (including myself) in the last twenty years or so. It is also indebted to recent historical studies of Latin America, and Bolivia in particular, that from differing theoretical viewpoints examine the type of states that developed after independence in the nineteenth century, and the means by which Latin Americans struggled to bring democracy and greater social justice to those nations. Finally, this story could not be told without the perspectives and some of the tools of the now not-so-new social history. Analysis of quantitative sources, while not the main part of this book, provides a solid base of information about health in Bolivia generally and particularly about which classes and social groups were most likely to fall prey to particular maladies.

Unequal Cures shares several fundamental approaches with other recently published works on the history of medicine in Latin America. Most basic is the assumption that scientific research and medical treatment are part of the social and political realm, and cannot be understood as some type of "hard" truth exempt from critical inquiry. Like other authors of studies of medicine and science, I have avoided uncontextualized accounts of medical triumphs and scientific breakthroughs or standard biographies of eminent physicians.

A few recent studies have looked at older medical traditions or the conflict between, or blending of, modern biomedicine and other European healing systems, such as homeopathy, humoralism, and spiritism.[3] However, most work on Latin America has concentrated on the fairly recent history of medicine, when advances in parasitology and bacteriology created new understandings of the causes of disease and new methods of fighting them. For this period, documents for the study of medical history are abundant (journals, treatises, theses, etc.), and academic medicine gained greater intellectual prestige and had somewhat broader availability. Biomedicine also had an important association with modernity and progress, which Latin American countries were keenly pursuing in the late nineteenth century and early twentieth. In my case I chose to begin around 1900, after discovering that nineteenth-century medical documents are quite scarce. By the beginning of the twentieth century even a poor country such as Bolivia could potentially apply some of the new medical techniques; it also had a few laboratories, professional organizations, and medical journals.

Historians of medicine generally (but not always) have left the study of Native American and African American curing, and the syncretism of folk and scientific medicine, to medical anthropologists.[4] This tendency is probably due, at least in part, to the difficulty in finding documentation on non-European curing in the periods historians study, although for more recent studies researchers are sometimes able to do oral history interviews. Although *Unequal Cures* is primarily about Western medicine in Bolivia, I include information about Andean healers and other nonacademic curers whenever it is available and relevant. This is essential because throughout the period I study (but especially in the first decades of the twentieth century), university-trained doctors were far from holding a monopoly on medical care and were very concerned with elevating their professional prestige by proving their skill was greater than that of other practitioners. The competition doctors faced was formidable. In this period they were challenged not only by native

Andean healers of several different traditions but also by various types of practitioners in the Western medical tradition.

Although recent historians of medicine in Latin America share certain general approaches, there is still much variation in interest, themes, and theoretical orientation. Several authors have written important studies that examine the research of Latin American doctors and scientists, their proposals for improving public health in their countries, and the often limited international recognition they received even when their original research led to new knowledge about the etiology of disease.[5] Some of these researchers and physicians were motivated by nationalist sentiments and the desire to prove that scientific excellence was possible outside of Europe, despite Social Darwinist assumptions about Latin American intellectual capabilities. For instance, Julyan Peard has demonstrated that the research of a group of doctors in nineteenth-century Bahia sought, at least in part, to prove that it was possible for the population of tropical countries to be healthy and that geography and climate did not necessarily relegate Brazil to illness and backwardness.[6] While there were certainly physicians in Bolivia who dreamed of making their mark in the international scientific community, they were prevented from doing so by a variety of factors. Marcos Cueto has written about medical research in Peru as an example of "excellence in the periphery." Unfortunately Bolivia was peripheral even to other Latin American countries, and its doctors did not have the government support, financial resources, core of trained researchers, or connections with the scientists abroad that would have allowed them to engage in original primary, or even applied, research.

The idea of Latin America as a periphery, of course, was taken from dependency theory, which, especially during the 1980s, some researchers used to examine how medicine and scientific research were employed as means of social control, or as adjuncts of U.S. foreign policy in Latin America. This approach was in keeping with other historical scholarship at the time that explored the causes of underdevelopment in a period when social and revolutionary movements in Latin American countries were attempting to eliminate U.S. domination and create social equality. These studies were also influenced by important work on imperialism, medicine, and colonial doctors in Africa and Asia.[7] While recognizing that Latin America's situation in the late nineteenth century and in the early twentieth was different than that of British colonies—most of the region had been independent since the beginning of the 1800s, and the majority of doctors there were citizens of the countries in which they worked—authors still argued convincingly that medicine had been used to make Latin America safe for foreign investors and national elites and to guarantee a relatively healthy workforce for various enterprises.[8]

The medical missions of the Rockefeller Foundation (RF) in Latin America have generally been understood as part of the U.S. effort to extend its political and economic hegemony in Latin America, and clearly this was often the intention of the Foundation's International Health Division (IHD) and its overbearing representatives.[9] Yet some new studies on the RF indicate less chauvinism on the part of some foundation personnel, and a range of reactions to the programs in Latin American countries according to political and social conditions. In other words, the intentions of the IHD, the nature of its programs, and the relationships between professionals in host countries and RF administrators have turned out, upon close examination, to be varied and not always simply the imposition of a U.S. model of public health from above.[10] In the case of Bolivia, in the early twentieth century the country was not considered of great enough economic or scientific importance for the United States or other nations to warrant medical intervention. Not until the 1930s did the Rockefeller Foundation begin a program there, mostly because of fears that yellow fever would spread from Bolivia to neighboring countries.

With a theoretical perspective presumably opposing the metanarrative of Marxism or dependency analysis, yet ultimately advancing a similar argument about medicine as a vehicle of social control, are studies of Latin America that have used a Foucauldian framework. While in these works power may be more diffuse and harder to identify—the culprit is not international capitalism and its manifestations in peripheral areas—the result is still to view medicine as an instrumental agent of "normalization" and discipline.[11] Although not necessarily reaching Foucauldian conclusions about power and modernity, much of the new history of medicine does reflect a "linguistic turn" in historical research,[12] as many researchers in the field analyze texts for social meaning, sometimes to the exclusion of other types of historical sources. In extreme cases this can lead to dehistoricized exegesis that could be equally applicable to Iceland, Japan, or Ecuador. However, when placed in a broader historical perspective, this use of literary analysis can be highly revealing. A case in point is Diego Armus's skillful use of tango lyrics and other popular texts about young women succumbing to tuberculosis to examine changing gender roles in Buenos Aires between 1910 and 1940.[13]

My own roots in social history are too strong to allow me to think that I can offer a satisfying version of the past by only reading (even if against the grain) various types of texts. The writings I have used for this book provide fascinating information on what policy makers, doctors, and other relatively powerful people thought about connections between medicine and a variety of issues considered urgent at the time: ethnicity, gender, citizenship, the future of Bolivia as a civilized nation. But, as anyone who follows the news knows, even today, when much more of the public is literate, there can be a considerable gap between the writings of politicians, intellectuals, and scientists and the experiences of less educated, less prosperous, unconsulted citizens. So, I do what most historians of medicine have done (although perhaps not as self-consciously): I combine the sources and methodologies of intellectual history with those of social history. It is my hope that in the process of playing these sources against one another, rubbing them together so to speak, I will tell a fuller story and provide a more useful interpretation of the past.

Many recent works on the history of public health in one way or another examine the role of scientific medicine in state formation in postcolonial Latin American societies, where political institutions were considered to be weak and governing elites saw racial and cultural heterogeneity as impediments to the development of democracy. Scholars have looked at the role of Western medicine in varied projects of state building, from nineteenth-century liberalism to twentieth-century revolutionary regimes. Some of these studies show that there was a clear tendency for political modernizers to collaborate with academically trained physicians. In other instances neither the politicians' nor the doctors' hegemony was complete. Popular resistance, conflicting political and religious views among those with access to power, or particular alliances during revolutionary periods made the connection between medicine and the state complex. Both modernization and biomedicine experienced uneven success, and in many cases forms of medical pluralism continued to exist, often with the tacit support of the state.[14] One important finding of my research is that in the case of Bolivia, the democratic-populist politics that developed in the 1930s and 1940s helped consolidate the professional position of university-trained physicians. Doctors benefited when reformist politicians argued that modern medical care should be accessible to all Bolivians and made public health a base for their state-building program.

A good number of the studies about medicine and the state focus on gender, since in the late nineteenth century and early twentieth women were viewed as inextricably linked to biological reproduction and therefore responsible for improving the national racial stock, and increasing population size—major concerns in many Latin American countries at the time. Anxieties about declining or unfit populations led governments to propose programs for women and children's health, regulate prostitution, and discuss means of combating venereal disease and alcoholism. These efforts, as well as more drastic proposals, became part of eugenics movements in many Latin American countries in the early twentieth century.[15]

Surprisingly few studies have specifically analyzed the political linkage of medicine with ideas about ethnicity or race, although racial heterogeneity was an issue that Latin American countries with large indigenous or black populations were attempting to resolve in a variety of ways. National policies often alternated between encouraging immigration and various eugenic solutions to "whiten" their population, on the one hand, and embracing an ideology that claimed that racial mixture or *mestizaje* was the basis of nationhood, on the other. Doctors were often at the center of these debates about race and nation, yet, thus far, little of this fevered concern has appeared in works on the history of medicine, even those dealing with countries with large nonwhite populations. Nor has much been written about how public health professionals viewed the medical problems of different ethnic or racial groups, or the reactions of nonwhites to often intrusive public health campaigns.[16]

In Bolivia in the first half of the twentieth century, ethnicity or race (*race* was the term used at the time)[17] was everywhere. Intellectuals cited the latest international writings on eugenics and Social Darwinism, and they were aware of the racist, segregationist policies in the United States. Although ethnicity was sometimes euphemistically covered with other terminology, as in references to "rural migrants" or "popular classes," in general it was openly discussed because intellectuals considered the problem of race to be the biggest one the nation faced. Ethnicity and race were frequently discussed in medical journals, theses, prescriptive literature on health, and newspaper accounts of health problems. Data on race and color appear in hospital and cemetery records. Race is evoked in medical discourse about mental illness, typhus, infant mortality, TB. Consequently, ethnicity is a salient topic in every chapter of this book. And, whenever sources permit, I examine the responses of indigenous and other nonwhite Bolivians to Western medicine and to public health campaigns.

For all the unabashed use of ethnicity or race to explain national problems in Bolivia, racial terminology and identification could be surprisingly fluid and it changed over time. How this worked will be illustrated throughout the book, but at this point it is useful to clarify how some key terms were generally used in the writings analyzed here. During the period I study, Bolivian writers tended to refer to the upper class as white or *criollo* and to use the terms *mestizo* or *cholo* to refer either to people of mixed ethnicity (white/Indian) or to acculturated Indians who generally lived in urban areas. Although *mestizo* and *cholo* were often used interchangeably in this period, the term *cholo* might denote a greater proximity to Indianness and, as used by the elite, had a distinct class bias.[18]

If the new history of medicine has provided a means of "looking at old problems in new ways,"[19] this would not have been possible without a body of historical scholarship that, broadly defined, examines the complicated process of creating nations in Latin America after the end of colonial rule.[20] This field is diverse both in topic and methodology and includes the contributions of many researchers that together provide a multilayered picture of such topics as liberalism, positivism, Native Americans' struggles for land and citizenship, mestizaje, populism, gender, and women's rights. I discuss here a sampling of works—mostly about Bolivia—that provides a general historical framework and broader methodological context for my story.

While most countries in Spanish America became independent nations in the early nineteenth century, scholars have shown that it was primarily a small, privileged sector of Americans of Spanish heritage who benefited politically and economically from the separation from Spain. There were few or no immediate changes in social or political life for the majority of people.[21] Thus political independence has been viewed as only the first stage in a long struggle to determine whose interests and welfare would be represented and protected by the new states. Inevitably, the process of forging national identities, especially in the multiethnic countries of the Andes, proved contentious.[22] Liberal parties, which developed in most Latin American countries in the nineteenth century, at least initially offered a more dynamic, individualistic approach to economic life than did the conservatives, who often clung to many of the hierarchical, corporatist structures of the colonial period. Liberals also were on record as supporting constitutional government and individual rights.

Although some historians maintain that early-nineteenth-century Latin American legal codes gave nonindigenous women expanded citizenship rights,[23] whether or not women gained more political freedom under liberalism is still being examined. For instance, Kristin Ruggiero has recently argued that despite the espousal of democratic principles, Argentine liberals found ways to use modern scientific theories (positivism, Lombrosian criminology) to justify women's inequality.[24] If the jury is still out on the effects of liberalism on white (or near white) women, most historical studies have shown that liberalism's impact on Native Americans was primarily negative. Liberal land laws, often put into effect when there was increased demand for agricultural products, were designed, in theory, to create a class of enterprising small- and medium-sized agriculturalists. Yet, by outlawing the communally held properties of Native American communities, the liberal laws often ended up threatening the survival of indigenous people. Rather than becoming small proprietors themselves, which liberals maintained would make them more civilized and progressive, many Indians, despite long struggles to prove that they in fact held title to lands, were left landless and often forced to become hacienda laborers.[25] Historians of Bolivia have also demonstrated that it wasn't just communally held property that liberals opposed. Rhetoric to the contrary, many were not in favor of extending to the Aymara- and Quechua-speaking population the individual rights and freedoms that liberals championed: full legal citizenship, education, individual property rights, access to markets for their goods, civil liberties, or even physical mobility.[26] Thus, as explained by anthropologist Tristan Platt, in many instances native people not only lost whatever minimal protections they had under colonialism—when the payment of tribute to the state generally guaranteed continued access to land—but also were denied the benefits of a liberal political system.[27]

However, as Florencia Mallon has shown for Mexico and Peru, liberalism could be interpreted in a more "communitarian" fashion to include citizenship rights for those generally denied them as well as equal access to property and resources.[28] There is certainly a long, well-documented history of struggles by native people in Bolivia to keep or regain their lands and demand education and other perquisites of the new political system.[29] By the 1920s and '30s other movements that challenged many of the tenants of liberalism altogether emerged: miners and other workers, including women, were forming unions, and socialist and anarchist parties were organized.[30] Intellectual historians have called our attention to the proposals of early twentieth-century writers and policy makers for modernizing Bolivia and integrating Indians into the body politic. In the first decades of the century, many writers favored limiting education and occupational options for indigenous people, attempting to restrict men to farming, mine labor, and serving in the army and women to domestic service and petty commerce.[31] In fact, the desire to limit schooling and control professional possibilities for native people reflected elite anxiety about growing geographical mobility and the diversity of social roles indigenous peoples were assuming. By the 1930s and '40s native Bolivians' political networks; their alliances with socialists, anarchists, and organized workers; and a changing international situation forced open doors to more professional opportunities and political participation to broader sectors of the population.[32]

Despite some changes in the legal status of women during liberal regimes in Latin America, until at least the 1930s Bolivia's policy makers (and those in some other Latin American countries as well) operated as if women's only citizenship function was to produce healthy children and educate them for appropriate social roles according to a hierarchy of class, gender, and ethnicity. Even with this obvious connection between gender discrimination and the state, it was only fairly recently that Latin American historians began to examine, as Joan Scott invited researchers to do in 1986, the ways in which studying gender expands our comprehension of political history.[33] The title of Elizabeth Dore's and Maxine Molyneux's 2000 edited volume, *Hidden Histories of Gender and the State in Latin America*, indicates that long after women's history became a significant academic field, politics and the state were not generally examined from the perspective of gender. There were undoubtedly a number of reasons for this, but of fundamental importance were the research interests of Latin Americanists between the 1970s and the early 1990s. This period saw a turning away from an older institutional political history that often seemed divorced from issues of class, race, and social conflict, and a concentration on such issues as the causes of Latin American underdevelopment, debates about the nature of "peripheral" capitalism, and the means for bringing greater economic equality and social justice to the region. With these questions in mind, many scholars interested in women and gender examined economic issues such as women's reproductive labor in the household, women in the international division of labor, and women and agrarian reform.[34] These were important studies, and of course implicitly political, but a limited vision of what was "political" prevented scholars from exploring how gender ideologies were intrinsic to state formation and perpetuation.

A recent revival of interest in the state and a tendency to view it less exclusively as a vehicle for class rule and more as contested territory—where subordinate groups have some role in determining political, juridical, and social outcomes—has led to work linking the state to popular movements and cultures.[35] This approach, which finds the political even in cultural and social events that are not always seen as related to state formation, has inspired scholars to also raise questions about gender in political realms where it was often ignored or considered to be irrelevant. As Sueann Caulfield writes, "What is new is a focus on the interaction between the meaning of gender in everyday life and the role it has played in political formation, institution building, and power relations in general."[36]

Studies on Bolivia have tended to follow the same general trajectory as women's history internationally. Some important basic work concentrated on recapturing women's pasts by publishing essential primary sources for women's history, examining women's roles in national historical events, and uncovering the origins of the Bolivian feminist movement.[37] There have also been a number of pioneering studies on women in the labor movement, particularly those asso-

ciated with the anarchist movement in the first half of the twentieth century. These works indicate that female union members raised
what would now be called "gender-based" demands along with those
related to their class positions as workers.[38] Some scholars have also
taken on the task of examining the complicated interactions of
gender, ethnicity, and power. For instance, anthropologist Lesley
Gill studied the unequal, dependent relationships between Aymara-
speaking household servants and their female employers in the city
of La Paz. Marcia Stephenson has used literary criticism and the
methodologies of cultural studies to analyze overlapping elite dis-
courses on motherhood and nationality, clothing and housing, and
hunger and appetite that are used to domesticate and subordinate
native Bolivian women.[39]

A few scholars have looked more specifically at issues of gender,
citizenship, and ethnicity. Rossana Barragán has written about the
legal principle of *patria potestad* and what it meant in the late eighteenth century and in the nineteenth century, when only a few creole
men were considered citizens and beneath them was a descending
staircase of those with fewer rights and less legal control over their
lives and those of their children. The use of the legal system by lower-
and middle-class *cholas* is the focus of an article by Laura Gotkowitz about insult and injury cases. She argues that as women went
to court to defend their honor in the face of public insults, they
also managed to create a space where they exercised civic authority
despite lacking most formal citizenship rights. Gotkowitz has also
looked at questions of women, ethnicity, and citizenship by studying
the changing meanings of the commemoration of a national patriotic event: the defense of the city of Cochabamba against royalist
forces by mestiza market women during Bolivia's struggle for independence in 1812.[40]

The questions of citizenship for Native Americans and women
in Latin America that have been explored in recent work on the
state are important for the historical examination of medicine. Debates about public health in Bolivia first emerged in the early twentieth century among intellectuals concerned about the integration
of Indians into the nation and its implications for the spread of epidemic disease. As the oligarchical state was challenged by indigenous and working-class militants, health care became an arena in
which different political projects contended. Even though medical

care was not a primary demand raised by social movements of the period, changing conceptions of individual rights and the nation's responsibilities forced doctors to confront the grossly unequal access to medical services in the country and the connections between illness and poverty. If in the first decades of the twentieth century medical campaigns were primarily seen as means of containing epidemic disease and the sectors of the population that were presumed to spread them, by the 1940s more people were prepared to argue that it was the government's responsibility to actively support the health of all its people. This new conception of the role of the state helped bolster doctors' prestige and advance their position vis-à-vis other types of healers. Somewhat ironically, however, this more progressive politics did not always lead doctors to consider women and Indians as equal members of society. In fact both were often still singled out as being the cause of national health problems.

Public Health and Political Change in Bolivia

The chapters of this book examine different realms of medicine in Bolivia between about 1900 and 1950. Each chapter explores a different aspect of public health in the context of the political history of the period. Several major analytical themes recur in the chapters and weave them together. Among these are how medical appraisals of Indians and women reflect and are part of debates about the nature of a modern Bolivian nation; the ways in which ideas about the delivery of health care changed (whether it is a charity or a right) as war and social movements forced a radicalization of Bolivian politics; and how doctors attempted to consolidate their professional position and establish themselves as national policy makers when the frequent failures of Western medicine, the inadequacy of the public health system, and the popularity of other medical traditions undermined their authority.

Chapter 1 examines the proposals of two prominent doctors for improving the health of indigenous Bolivians in the context of debates about culture, difference, and Indians' eligibility for citizenship. In the first decades of the century, Bolivia's elite debated options for incorporating the country's indigenous population into the political and social life of the nation. Hygiene was of paramount importance, as business owners realized that they needed a minimally healthy workforce for their enterprises, and as people in cities became afraid of the possibility that epidemic disease might be spread by a more mobile Indian population. Doctors' policy proposals were therefore extremely pertinent; their assessments of native Bolivians' health problems expose issues of identity that the nation's elite confronted. The chapter also examines Bolivian medical pluralism and the doctors' attempts to discredit medical competitors.

Although there were challenges to their hegemony from native communities and the beginnings of labor organization, throughout the 1920s the Bolivian propertied classes managed to hold on to power and ensure that new participants in the political process generally remained their clients. The situation was forever changed in the 1930s, with the worldwide depression and Bolivia's catastrophic war with Paraguay over a minimally populated zone known as the Chaco Boreal. Chapter 2 looks at the national health crisis created by the Chaco War (1932–35) and the reassessment of Bolivia's social and political system that the humiliating loss to Paraguay forced on the country. After the war many physicians of the Chaco generation espoused a new populist ideology that maintained that health care was a right, not a privilege of the rich or a means of preventing the poor from spreading disease. Yet doctors and other criollos also exhibited a profound ambivalence toward the native soldiers who made up the majority of the nation's frontline troops: on the one hand, they were seen as stoic warriors defending the country under horrible conditions; on the other, they were believed to be spreading disease to the civilian population.

At the same time in which some doctors argued that providing medical care to all Bolivians was a fundamental responsibility of the government, Bolivia received its first international public health assistance in the form of a Rockefeller Foundation campaign against yellow fever. Chapter 3 examines the RF's programs in Bolivia and changing attitudes of doctors and government officials toward the foundation. Early International Health Division representatives in Bolivia displayed, in their approach to fighting disease and in their attitudes toward Bolivians, all the chauvinism and racism associated with imperial doctors. Yet, probably due to Bolivia's indigence and the almost total collapse of the country's health care system during the Chaco War, they were welcomed by most professionals in the country. By the time the RF left the country in the early 1950s, its representatives were considerably more sensitive to local needs, and, in fact, most of its projects were run by Bolivians and connected to the Ministry of Health. Yet, it was in this later period that the RF faced its most severe public criticism in Bolivia.

Chapters 1 through 3 in part tell the story of medicine's role in the breakdown of Bolivia's oligarchic political system and how thinking about public health changed in a more populist political atmosphere. However, the story is not that linear and uncomplicated. First of all, no change toward greater democracy occurred without people fighting for it, and from the beginning of the century the political elite had to contend with demands for land, education, market opportunities, and political rights made by native Bolivians and growing numbers of mestizo or cholo migrants to cities. These protests escalated in the 1930s and '40s and spread to larger sectors of the population. However, even in an exceptional period, such as the aftermath of the Chaco War, when the nation's political center of gravity moved decisively to the left, changes in consciousness can be relative and contradictory. Furthermore, doctors, like other members of the nation's educated elite, were not likely to easily give up the prerogatives of their class, ethnicity, and gender. The pervasiveness of hegemonic ideas and the unevenness of changes in consciousness can be seen most clearly in health policy toward women and the mentally ill.

In chapter 4 I examine women's health between the 1920s and the 1940s, in the context of the social and economic realities of most women's lives, primarily in the city of La Paz. As in other fields of public health, there were ideological changes in emphasis in writings about medicine and women during the period I study. Nonetheless, even the most politically progressive writers tended to connect problems that they believed threatened the future of the country—infant mortality, abortion, prostitution, and venereal disease—to women's failure to fulfill their biological destiny and civic duties as mothers. Furthermore, gender ideologies were integrally connected to stereotypes about ethnicity. Although writers had varying opinions about appropriate roles for non-Indian women and the degree to which they were the cause of some of the nation's most serious health problems, Aymara- and Quechua-speaking peasant women and cholas were considered to deviate the most from the ideal and therefore the most likely to be negligent mothers and to spread disease. In fact, it was in the field of women's and children's health that doctors met some of their most tenacious competition, because most women patients preferred female midwives for gynecological, obstetric, and sometimes even pediatric care. Consequently, part of doctors' critique of women as being unhygienic or not performing their proper social roles has to be understood as related to the contest for medical authority.

In the 1940s the winds of change that were affecting other medical institutions began to be felt at the Manicomio Pacheco, Bolivia's national mental hospital. Some doctors who worked there were influenced by the democratic political trends and believed they should apply even to the nation's most frequently ignored: the mentally ill. All those who treated the alienated were encouraged by various new drugs and techniques that seemed to promise cure or at least improvement for their patients and therefore higher professional status for themselves. In chapter 5 I trace the history of the Manicomio Pacheco and examine articles about psychiatry written by Bolivian physicians between the 1920s and the 1940s. I also look at clinical histories and case records from the hospital for the period. It is most striking that despite more knowledge about mental illness, and the expanded citizenship rights that were being won by women and native Bolivians, doctors' thinking about insanity in women and Indians did not change much. In this last chapter I argue that both were assumed to be psychologically different from, and inferior to, white men (Indian women, as shown in chapter 4, were also considered culturally inferior to white women). Yet for an Indian man or any woman to be too much like a non-Indian man was also a sign of insanity.

This book begins around 1900, when the triumphant liberals consolidated their control in the country and Western biomedicine was beginning to have enough national spread and efficacy to be taken seriously. It ends just before 1952, when the diverse challenges to the old regime came to a head in a multiclass revolution said to represent workers, peasants, and the middle class. By this time medical services were somewhat more broadly available in the country, and Bolivia had had the assistance of a number of international agencies with several health problems. The year 1952 is a logical stopping point for this book even if in public health, as in many other areas, the revolution's achievements fell short of the expectations it raised. If nothing else, the political changes of 1952 definitively established the responsibility of the state for medical care for all citizens (at least until that responsibility was challenged by the privatization imposed by neoliberal reforms at the end of the century). Other struggles went on: the health care system was still inadequate, and epidemic diseases were far from under control. Although doctors were considered more authoritative in health matters than at the beginning of the century, they were still few in number and frequently poorly trained; many Bolivians continued to visit other types of medical practitioners. On the social and political levels, while universal suffrage had been proclaimed, servitude abolished, and an agrarian reform declared to give land to those who worked it, equal rights and opportunities were still far from realities. Nonetheless the 1952 revolution marked a watershed and a new political context for understanding the connections between medicine and social life in Bolivia. There is another story to tell about medicine, race, and gender in the post-1952 world.

A Note on Sources

In this book I have used a variety of primary and secondary materials that are listed in the bibliography. A careful reader may notice that while I have made extensive use of bulletins and other publications of public health agencies, I do not cite the actual records of the Ministerio de Salud Pública (Ministry of Public Health) or any of its variously named predecessors (see chapter 5). This is because the records of the ministry were destroyed in a fire in the 1960s, leaving me and other researchers without access to what undoubtedly would be valuable information. I have tried to compensate for this lack, not only by using official public health publications, city council minutes, and census materials but also by analyzing the original records of the Hospital General and the Cementerio General in La Paz, and the Manicomio Pacheco in Sucre.

1

————•◦⚬⚬◦•————

HYGIENE AND

THE "INDIAN PROBLEM"

Ethnicity and Medicine in the Early Twentieth Century

This chapter examines the proposals of two Bolivian doctors, Jaime Mendoza and Néstor Morales, for improving the health of the native population. These proposals are looked at in the context of a larger debate about ethnicity and citizenship in the first decades of the twentieth century. Intellectuals struggled with what they referred to as the "Indian problem," because the situation of Bolivia's native population was at the core of the elite's contradictory social and economic situation and raised central questions about national identity. On the one hand, the exploitation of Indians as hacienda *colonos* (peons) and workers made possible Bolivia's role in the world market as an exporter of raw materials and financed the lifestyle of the elite. On the other hand, Indians and their culture were considered the main obstacles to Bolivia's entering the world community as a civilized and progressive country. The question of the Indian's role in the nation became a more pressing problem in the early twentieth century, as a growing economy required more labor and as improved communications brought Indians and non-Indians into closer contact. Elite intellectuals began to consider whether Indians might somehow be "improved" enough to be part of a modernizing nation. As pedagogues and politicians proposed and debated means of integrating native Andeans into national life while still limiting their educational, professional, and political roles, indigenous people were taking matters into their own hands.[1] They were seeking better employment opportunities in the cities, demanding education as an important prerequisite for citizenship, and using their political and literacy skills to fight to reclaim lands titled to them that had been illegally seized by hacendados.[2]

The entry of native people into the broader political and social life of the nation, despite efforts to minimize it, became a topic of discussion for doctors and politicians concerned with public health. Elite fears of contagion were awakened by the likelihood that they would have more contact with Indians as the economy expanded and "new elements" entered urban areas. Furthermore, there was recognition that if Indians were to supply the labor power for mining and increased agricultural production, they had to have at least a minimal standard of well-being. Here doctors entered the fray with their own particular professional, humanitarian, and corporate agendas. A central goal for university-trained doctors in the first decades of the twentieth century was proving the efficacy of biomedicine and discrediting other practitioners, particularly Andean herbalists, who were patronized by most people in the country and who arguably had a success rate at least as great as theirs.

The doctors studied in this chapter, Jaime Mendoza and Néstor Morales Villazón, set out to do just that. Of the same generation (Mendoza was born in 1874, Morales in 1878), they both were from families of the provincial elite; they each studied medicine in Bolivia and then pursued advanced training in Europe. Both were influenced by the bacteriological discoveries of the late nineteenth century and early twentieth, and both held important posts in the country's major medical institutions. However, there the similarities between the two men ended. Although Morales was originally

trained as a pediatrician, his main professional focus was bacteriology, and he hoped to make his mark by being the first Bolivian
doctor with a major scientific breakthrough in the field that would
also have a significant impact on the nation's health. Mendoza, in
contrast, practiced and wrote in many medical fields, from psychiatry to pediatrics to infectious diseases. He also was a novelist,
an essayist, and a political activist with a deep nationalist commitment. His approach to elevating the prestige of the medical profession was through the active promotion of public health policies
that would improve the lives of the poorest Bolivians. Some of Mendoza's writings on medicine are discussed in other chapters of this
book. What is striking about a comparison of Morales and Mendoza is that although their political inclinations and medical interests varied widely, in many ways they coincided in their ideas about
the country's Andean majority. They both brought to the discussion
of public health an ambivalence about ethnicity that was typical of
most members of the Bolivian elite.

The Context

In the first two decades of the twentieth century Bolivia enjoyed
something of an economic boom based on exporting tin, which had
replaced silver as the country's most important export around the
turn of the century. Related to the economic ascendancy of the tin
producers was the rise to power of the Liberal Party, which had
seized control of the country from the Conservatives in a military
revolt in 1899, which became a civil war. The nation's most important tin-mining centers were located closer to the city of La Paz than
to the capital in Sucre, the center of silver-mining interests and of
the Conservative Party. Thus 1900 marked a shift in the economic
center of gravity to La Paz that was reflected in the Liberals' decision to move almost all important government offices and functions
to that city.

As mentioned in the introduction, in 1900 Bolivia had a population of 1,633,610 people. About 51 percent of them were Indian,
according to that year's census. About 73 percent of the population
lived in the countryside, and only 16 percent of those over seven
years old had received any schooling.[3] Since literacy was technically

a qualification for voting and there were financial requirements for holding office, political participation was theoretically limited to a small, urban group of educated men. Yet, in fact, suffrage was not as limited as it sounds, because in the first decades of the century mestizos and recent cholo arrivals to cities and towns did participate in elections, often as clients of Liberal or Conservative politicians.[4]

During the two presidencies of Liberal Ismael Montes (1904–9, 1913–17), the government embarked on ambitious programs for improving Bolivia's infrastructure, particularly constructing railroads that would facilitate transporting tin, thus furthering the Liberals' export-oriented plan for development. Encouraging scientific progress and improving public hygiene were also part of the Liberal agenda, and after 1900 a number of initiatives were undertaken: urban electrification projects were begun, smallpox vaccinations were made mandatory in 1902, piped drinking water became available for part of the city of La Paz in 1903, and a modern general hospital was completed in the city in 1920.

The Liberals had come to power by mobilizing Indian communities of the high plateau (*altiplano*) near La Paz to fight for them against the Conservatives, but, when it became clear that if necessary the peasant communities would press their demands for land and self-government against the Liberals as well, the Liberals turned on their native allies, killing the more militant leaders.[5] Andean communities had hoped that in return for their support the Liberals would back them in their efforts to hold on to lands that had been under attack since at least the 1860s, when a series of laws outlawed native communities and proposed various means of privatizing Indian lands.[6] In fact, they were hoping for help that directly conflicted with many Liberals' class interests, especially those in the La Paz area, where creole landowners favored the incorporation of Indians into the haciendas as colonos instead of the theoretical liberal project of small-scale landownership.[7] Despite the serious blow, indigenous communities eventually responded to Liberal betrayal after the civil war by organizing to reclaim usurped lands and to demand the rights (political representation, education, access to markets for their produce) that liberalism theoretically promised all Bolivians.[8]

It was in this atmosphere of struggle that elite intellectuals were revising their assumptions about the roles native Andeans could play in the new liberal nation. Social Darwinism had been the dominant philosophical approach to understanding the "Indian problem" in the last decades of the nineteenth century, with some writers going so far as to hope that in the struggle for survival the Indian would be defeated or even eliminated by the whites.[9] After the turn of the century, and particularly after about 1910, new theoretical constructs were developed that combined biological explanations with environmental ones. Particularly Lamarckian understandings of genetics that emphasized the possibility of inheritance of acquired characteristics now blended with a new ethnographic approach to culture to produce new racial ideologies. These ideologies both explained how the Indian population had become congenitally degenerate as a result of colonial exploitation and also offered some small hope that under very favorable circumstances, Indians might be changed enough to take on a (debated) role in a modern nation. Among those who accepted this more environmental approach were a number of the doctors who wrote on national health problems in the early twentieth century.[10]

Doctors and the Nation's Health

Bolivian physicians were painfully aware of their country's health problems, and medical journals poured out statistics confirming the country's hygienic deficiency. Although they did not use the term, many of the health hazards they pointed to would today be considered the results of underdevelopment. What the doctors themselves said was that the existence of these problems placed Bolivia far behind European, and even some other Latin American, countries on the road to modernity and civilization. For instance, in 1902 Revista Médica stated that out of 3,337 babies born in the city of La Paz in 1900, 1,298 (39 percent) died before reaching their third birthdays, and 19 percent died in the first year of life. Most of these deaths were traced by the author of the article to intestinal infections, which in turn were said to be primarily the result of impure food and water.[11] The poor quality and lack of filtration of the city's drinking water were also said to be the causes of at least a quarter of the identifiable deaths in the city in 1911, and a doctor writing in another medical journal estimated that probably an equal number of undiagnosed deaths were from gastrointestinal illness as well. The same author, on the basis of chemical and bacteriological tests conducted on La Paz's drinking water, classified it as worse than that of any other city for which statistics were available and comparable to water that was commonly used only for industrial purposes.[12]

Epidemic diseases were major killers both in urban and rural areas. A vaccine for smallpox was developed in 1796 in Europe, and Bolivia had first attempted to make the vaccine available after independence in 1826. In 1902 a new law was enacted making vaccination mandatory, but in 1909 it had to be repromulgated in the face of serious epidemics. Even then vaccination was not widespread, and most people remained vulnerable to the disease.[13] Typhoid was always endemic in the country; throughout the first years of the century, there were waves of serious typhoid epidemics that caused high mortality.[14]

Medical institutions—such as laboratories, hospitals, and medical schools—were considered by those who worked in them to be at the best underfunded but diligently run and at the worst to be national disgraces. The library of the medical school in La Paz had only 758 volumes in 1914, and the head of the school indicated that 49 of these had been acquired during his tenure in 1912–1913. He also pointed with pride to the fact that the school would soon have a pathology laboratory for the first time.[15] A report on medical education in Bolivia prepared by a representative of the Rockefeller Foundation twelve years later gives a more somber assessment: "Teaching laboratories, strictly speaking, cannot be said to exist. In a rented building I saw a room 12 ft. square with one ordinary table, a small cabinet, and scattered about on each some miscellaneous pieces of dust-covered glassware. This was called the chemical laboratory. In another, somewhat larger room, containing low public school desks [there] were a few anatomical models. These were referred to in the *regimento interno* as the anatomical museum."[16]

In 1918, before the new Hospital General was completed, a doctor described the city's two main hospitals as the reasons that people preferred to die at home. He also pointed out that the infectious disease sections of the men's hospital were so unhygienic, and the wards so crowded, that a patient could easily come in with one illness and die of another contracted in the hospital.[17] And, as grim as these assessments of the situation in La Paz are, it is important to keep in mind that Western health facilities of any type were entirely lacking in rural areas.

There was considerable variation in how doctors understood these problems, believed they should be ameliorated, and connected them to ethnicity and social issues. However, there were a few key realities that affected public health and the physicians' professional situation. First of all, in the early twentieth century medical science in Bolivia not only lagged behind that in European countries and the United States, but also was backward when compared to other Latin American countries. In the late nineteenth century and early twentieth, European discoveries in bacteriology were very influential; Latin American scientists were inspired to apply this new knowledge to health problems in the region. Carlos Finlay conducted pioneering (although not properly appreciated) research on yellow fever in Cuba; Oswaldo Cruz, Carlos Chagas, and others in Brazil did research on various vector-born diseases, which lead to the discovery of American sleeping sickness, or Chagas disease. Research institutes in some Latin American cities, such as Cruz's Manguinhos Institute, combined bacteriological research with the production of vaccines to fight epidemic diseases, and for many other countries this became a model to emulate. Even Peru, which did not have the resources of Argentina or Brazil, surpassed Bolivia in university research in bacteriology and the development of its public health system in the first years of the twentieth century.[18]

Because of the limited reach of Western medicine in Bolivia (there were only 142 graduated doctors in the country's major cities in 1900),[19] and the lack of medical research institutions, university-trained doctors were generally not accorded the same respect as members of other liberal professions. Indeed, they were not completely differentiated from other medical practitioners in the Western tradition, whom the doctors themselves sometimes referred to as empiricists and often simply as charlatans. Furthermore, despite the advances in bacteriology and other fields of medical science, in all countries in the early twentieth century there were still major gaps in biomedical knowledge: in many instances in Bolivia, herbalists known as Kallawaya or other Andean curers were more effective than academically trained physicians. Consequently, there was a special urgency to Bolivian doctors' writings about social problems and the importance of hygiene, because improving the country's abysmal

public health situation was ultimately linked to the physicians' professional status and credibility. To that end, a good number of doctors began to enter politics at the local and national level and often
used these positions to publicly express their views on medicine and
the public good.

Ethnicity was an especially difficult issue for doctors. There was
an inherent tension in their attitudes toward the Indian population:
on the one hand doctors, like other members of the elite, maintained that native Bolivians were responsible for holding back national progress; yet at the same time the university-trained physicians were struggling to prove they were more effective than Andean
healers. Although the doctors didn't say it, the native population
also posed a problem of identity. There has been a good deal of
scholarship on medicine and ethnicity, or race, that focuses on European colonialism in the nineteenth and twentieth centuries, particularly about the British in Africa and India.[20] While the situation of
Bolivian medical professionals was in some ways comparable to that
of British colonial doctors, it was also more problematic. The fact
that the Bolivian doctors were in their own country, and were for
the most part technically mestizos themselves, meant they could not
achieve the distance of white colonial doctors and view the natives
as purely "other."

Indigenismo and Mestizaje

The doctors' situation was related to the emergence in the early
twentieth century of a particularly Bolivian version of *indigenismo*.
Indigenismo, in the most general terms, can be defined as an interest
by non-Indian people in native culture and historical achievements.
Although there are many variants, indigenismo has not necessarily
meant the defense of native people's rights or a call for the end
of exploitation for contemporary Indians. In Bolivia indigenismo
was somewhat important as a literary movement.[21] There was also a
definite interest in the Andean past among early twentieth-century
sociological and political thinkers, even when they still believed that
present-day native people had lost much of their ancestors' civilization. This type of thinking was clear in the writings of Bautista
Saavedra, who in 1903 published *El ayllu*, a linguistic-historical study

of the development of Andean social organization.[22] In it Saavedra quotes the most important international scholars of the day, including Friedrich Engels, to explain the emergence of Andean family and political structure. Before the publication of *El ayllu*, Saavedra had been called upon by the government to defend a number of Indians accused in a massacre of Liberal troops during the 1899 civil war. Saavedra based his defense on several arguments, including the contention that the defendants had been involved in a political and social cause—the struggle of Indian people to overthrow their white and mestizo oppressors—and therefore couldn't be judged as common criminals. He was unsparing in his attacks on both Spanish colonizers and contemporary white Bolivians for their inhumane, shameless exploitation of Indians. Yet, Saavedra also suggested that the Aymara could require centuries to reach the level of civilization attained by whites or might even be in the last phases of their existence.[23] It is difficult to know whether this was what Saavedra really believed or whether he added it, and other Social Darwinist sentiments, to his defense out of the belief that they would make whites more likely not to find the Indians guilty. Either way, the combination of ethnographic interest, recognition of centuries of abuse, and the conviction that Indians might be beyond redemption apparently rested easily with many educated people who concerned themselves with such matters.

A less scholarly indigenista, Manuel Rigoberto Paredes, wrote a number of studies of the history, geography, and customs of the provinces of the Bolivian altiplano, where he had grown up. Paredes was an early critic of the privatization of Indian lands and their seizure through various means by hacendados. Paredes differed from Saavedra in his specific antimestizo bias: even though the landowners who expropriated Indian lands were primarily whites, Paredes maintained that mestizos and cholos were the main exploiters of the Indians, claiming that those of mixed racial heritage or acculturated Indians had the worst qualities of both cultures.[24]

This antimestizo sentiment distinguished Bolivian indigenismo from the Mexican and Peruvian variants. Indigenismo has been most powerfully articulated as part of an ideology of mestizaje, which has been used as a vehicle for creating a sense of nationhood through the legitimization of the indigenous element in mestizo societies.[25] But, this element of at least theoretical glorification of racial mixture and acculturation was missing from Bolivian discourse on the Indian.[26] Despite miscegenation, well into the twentieth century there were few influential Bolivians who openly identified themselves as mestizos, and certainly none who called themselves cholos. In fact, Alcides Arguedas, one of Bolivia's first indigenista novelists and author of *Pueblo enfermo*, the widely read exegesis of the problems facing the Bolivian nation, became more vituperative in his attacks on cholos-mestizos in later editions of the book. In the 1910 edition his discussion of mestizos is somewhat critical but rather brief, discussing particularly their willingness to follow any demagogic politician who presented himself.[27] In the 1936 edition of *Pueblo enfermo*, however, he devoted more space to discussing mestizos in the most unfavorable light, showing them to have all the defects of both Spaniards and Indians. Perhaps his greater disdain for cholos in 1936 reflects the greater participation of mestizos in national life by the mid-1930s. For instance a section added to the 1936 edition, entitled "Psicología de la raza mestiza," reads: "The cholo politician, military officer, diplomat, legislator, lawyer or priest, never and in no moment bothers his conscience by asking if an act is moral or not . . . because he only thinks of himself and only [wishes] to satisfy his cravings for glory, riches and honors at the expense of any principles."[28]

Rather than view mestizos as the "cosmic race," à la José Vasconcelos, Arguedas could only conceive of them as vulgar rabble who were challenging the creole elite's position of political and economic privilege. Was the cholo for Arguedas and other intellectuals, as Barragán has asked, "a danger they were trying to deny? a mirror too close to their own image?"[29] It was only a few socialist indigenistas, such as Tristan Marof, who condemned Arguedas's racism, and recognized in the accomplishments of the Inca empire and the present-day organization of the Indian community the seeds of the socialist Bolivia of the future.[30]

Because of the hesitancy of Bolivian leaders to embrace mestizaje, indigenismo never became the ideological basis for a major political movement in Bolivia. Although the government began to promote Indian education in the 1920s and declared a "Día del indio" in the 1930s, there was never a party in Bolivia such as Peru's APRA or a leader like APRA's Víctor Raúl Haya de la Torre, whose populism included a notion of "Indoamérica." Not until decades later did a Bolivian nationalism begin to develop around cultural, political, and aesthetic symbols related to a shared mestizo heritage.[31] The absence of an official ideology of mestizaje made the issue of ethnic and national identity ambiguous and difficult for the Bolivian elite. Like other members of their class, doctors were affected by this issue of identity and wanted to disassociate themselves from the backward Indian population, who may have been too close for comfort. But doctors also had a more specific problem with native Bolivians. Indian medical practitioners were consulted by people of all social positions and in many places in the country were the only health professionals available. Many doctors, perhaps unconsciously, mounted a two-pronged effort to discredit indigenous healers: they criticized their curing practices variously as ineffective, barbarous, or simply based on trickery, while they characterized Indian lifestyles as unhygienic and even repulsive.

Kallawaya, and Andean Healing

In the early twentieth century, Bolivia had various types of non-university-trained medical practitioners. Some of these were people who had some experience with biomedicine—nurses, hospital aids, and so on—who were usually from other countries, and who in Bolivia often passed themselves off as doctors with degrees. There were also urban midwives and masseurs and masseuses who were practicing medicine without licenses. These types of practitioners, who generally fell within the western European medical tradition, and were usually referred to as "empirics," are discussed in later chapters. While doctors complained about empirics, or "charlatans" as they sometimes called them, they were far more challenged by indigenous healers, who were patronized by many people when simple home remedies failed.

Andean cosmology understood health as a reflection of balance in nature and the universe. Ill health meant that something was not right in the social, and therefore spiritual, realm. In close-knit communities, where families were very dependent on each other, sickness was believed to result from not living up to one's group responsibilities or from attempting to gain some unfair advantage over one's neighbor. Illness could also be brought on by neglect of the shrines for Pachamama (the earth mother) or those for other spiritual beings. Falling sick was also common after anger, an emotional trauma, or serious fright, and one of the most commonly diagnosed illnesses, especially among women and children, was *susto* (literally Spanish for "fright") in which some profoundly unsettling emotional event caused a person to lose her *ajayu*, or spirit.[32] These health problems were treated in a variety or ways, but the holistic understanding of sickness, and the family and social context in which most healing took place, were congruent with the Andean understanding of the world and the human body's connection to the social body.[33]

Some Andean curers used only spiritual, magical, and psychological methods for alleviating illness. Diviners, or *yatiris*, diagnosed the causes of illness through reading coca leaves and talking to the sick person's relatives. They then prepared elaborate rituals to feed earth shrines (which might be geographical landmarks, rocks and hills, e.g.) with substances such as llama fat, guinea pig blood, and coca. Women diviners especially conducted misfortune ceremonies which symbolically removed bad luck and reestablished social balance.[34]

Historically Bolivia's most famous healers, the Kallawaya, came from an ethnic group in the area of Charazani, in the province now called Bautista Saavedra in the department of La Paz. Kallawaya healers were and are primarily known as herbalists, but they also use divination and some of the spiritual and psychological healing methods of other Andean healers. Many observers since the colonial period have written about the Kallawaya, but the anthropologist Joseph Bastien, who has studied the Kallawaya extensively since the 1960s, gives the most complete description of the understanding of human physiology on which their herbal medicine is based.[35] While Bastien's report is based on fieldwork conducted after the period of this book, there is enough agreement between his accounts of other aspects of Kallawaya healing with what was written earlier in the century to assume that his analysis of Kallawaya ideas of how the human body works is valid for the earlier period as well. According to Bastien, the people of the Charazani area draw analogies between the geographical areas occupied by their *ayllus* (kin-based communities) and the human body, referring to a properly functioning ayllu as similar to a healthy human body. Streams and rivers in particular are believed to flow through the ayllus' territory in a manner paralleling fluids in the human body. The body itself is conceptualized as a hydraulic system through which fluids circulate, are transformed, and are eliminated. Fluids are pumped by the *sonco*, which performs circulatory, respiratory, and digestive functions and keeps centripetal and centrifugal forces in balance. The primary fluids in the body are blood, fat, and air. Air is conceived of as a fluid that cannot be seen but that provides breath. Fat is equated with energy, and blood is the life force circulating through the body. An important belief throughout the Andes, also shared by Kallawaya, is that blood does not reproduce itself, so people frequently are hostile to the idea of drawing blood for medical tests.

Herbalists refer to blood as being hot, cold, wet, and dry. Hot blood may flow too fast and cold too slowly; wet blood is thick and sluggish and dry blood too thin. Different combinations of these qualities are associated with certain ailments. For instance, hot and dry blood has little fat and air and may cause a rapid heartbeat. Cold and wet blood is sluggish, doesn't disperse well to the muscles, and is associated with arthritis. Kallawaya also associate illness with loss of fat, as do many Andean people. Fat is believed to be removed by a *kharisiri*, or cutter, who is often conceptualized as a professional or some type of rich person who preys on peasants. During the colonial period, it was believed that colonists and priests stole people's fat (particularly kidney fat) to make church bells or holy oil.[36] Since a healthy body is one in which centripetal and centrifugal forces balance each other, a body in which too much of any fluid is being dispersed is in danger. And loss of fluids, if not corrected, can cause death.[37]

Although the Kallawaya understanding of illness has many aspects that are Andean, in some respects it is similar to Greek humoral theory that developed in the fifth century B.C. and was brought to the Americas by Spanish colonialists. In this conception of the body, four fluids (blood, phlegm, yellow bile, and black bile) were believed to flow through the more solid tissues. Each of these fluids was associated with temperature and particular qualities: blood was wet and hot, phlegm moist and cold, yellow bile hot and dry, and black bile cold and dry. Health was dependent on a balance of these fluids, and an upset might be caused by an excess of cold or heat.[38] Some anthropologists believe that ideas of hot and cold in Latin American folk medicine are simply adaptations of European humoral theories, while others think they may have originated independently in the New World or that American healing systems may be combinations of indigenous and European principles.[39] In any event, similarities between some aspects of Kallawaya medical theories and ancient European beliefs may have made non-Indians comfortable seeking help from Kallawaya practitioners.

Another reason that people of all types turned to the Kallawaya was because of their knowledge of healing herbs. Even the most skeptical observers agreed that certain herbs in their pharmacopoeia had been proven efficacious. These included quina, the basis of quinine, which Kallawaya had used successfully in Panama during the construction of the canal. Other herbs, which have not been transformed into prescription drugs, were (and are) used in a variety of different forms for different problems. For example, *bilyea* is prescribed by Kallawaya as a maté (or tea) for various types of stomach and liver ailments; it is also used to lower fevers, and its ashes are made into a plaster to heal wounds.[40] The diverse uses for one herb might initially seem unlikely, but pharmaceutical companies also frequently discover that a drug originally developed for one purpose may have side effects that alleviate another complaint. For instance, Rogaine, originally a drug to lower high blood pressure, is now used topically to regrow thinning hair.

According to Bastien, in the late 1980s skilled Kallawaya healers knew how to recognize and use between 180 and 300 different plants, minerals, and animal products. Louis Girault said in the 1970s that most could use between 300 and 350, and he claimed that one Kallawaya he knew had curative knowledge of up to 600 herbs.[41] This knowledge was traditionally acquired through apprenticeships in which young men accompanied master Kallawaya on long trips around Bolivia and to the neighboring countries of Peru and Argentina.[42] Especially in the early twentieth century Kallawaya herbalists seem to have been sought out by many people, including the rich and famous. In the 1910s the Kallawaya Pablo Alvarez became the physician of the former Peruvian president Augusto Leguía, after Alvarez had cured Leguía's daughter of what doctors considered a terminal illness.[43] Because of their travels Kallawaya were quite cosmopolitan, speaking Quechua, Aymara, and Spanish, as well as what has been called a secret professional language that some believe had

its origin in a language spoken by the Inca elite and which others
believe was a form of Puquina, a language that had linguistic links
with Arawak and at one time was spoken from the eastern shores of
Lake Titicaca to the Amazonian lowlands.[44] Kallawaya were also ad-
mired for their dapper dress, which some felt made them resemble
gauchos. The fact that they returned home from their curing ex-
peditions with many European luxury items added to their aura of
sophistication.

In the first decades of the twentieth century, some of the same
indigenista intellectuals who wrote about the customs and conditions of Andean peasants also studied the Kallawaya. Their discussion of the Kallawaya tended to emphasize the potential scientific
benefit that Bolivia might reap from studying the Andean pharmacopoeia while demeaning the magical aspects of Kallawaya healing
and stressing their general backwardness.[45] A case in point is Manuel
Rigoberto Paredes, who in 1920, at what was probably the height
of Kallawaya medical authority, maintained that "[the Kallawaya]
have lost much of their old prestige, both because they have neglected the observations and methods of curing of the ancestors and
because medical training is more advanced in the country and doctors are relatively abundant compared to the colonial period."[46] Although he said Kallawaya did retain enough knowledge of herbs to
make up some prescriptions, Paredes maintained that a good deal
of their diagnosis and treatment was done through trickery. Despite
describing the Kallawaya's fine dress and the luxury goods healers
brought back with them from their professional trips, Paredes describes them—as he tends to describe all the Indians of the altiplano—as exploited by rural mestizos who often tricked them out
of valuable items by giving them alcohol. So, according to Paredes,
on the one hand the Kallawaya were vain tricksters who had lost
their traditional skills and on the other they were exploited and de-
graded by mestizos, who, because of their racial mixture, were without honor.[47] Although perhaps not specifically designed to do so,
Paredes's description of the Kallawaya would have had the effect of
promoting scientifically trained doctors by denigrating their main
competitors.

Although anthropologists through the 1970s and 1980s were still
emphasizing the pharmaceutical competence of the Kallawaya and
the fact that they were patronized by many non-Indians,[48] most

writers between 1900 and 1950 maintained that their knowledge
was greatly diminished. This impression may have been the result
of Kallawaya reticence to discuss their cures with outsiders. When
questioned, the healers frequently were said to divulge information
only about the most commonly known herbs. Also, most intellectuals of the early twentieth century had difficulty comprehending how
the Kallawaya could combine magic (the use of amulets, ritual methods of diagnosis, etc.), which they considered useless, with medicinal
knowledge of plants, which they considered modern.[49]

Néstor Morales Villazón,
Typhoid, and the *Revista de Bacteriología e Higiene*

In the face of Kallawaya competition, one important way that doctors attempted to bolster their reputations was through their professional publications. In 1901 the *Revista Médica* was founded in
La Paz. It ceased publication in 1909, and *Revista de Bacteriología e
Higiene* (RBH) the official journal of the Instituto de Bacteriología,
the city's only bacteriological laboratory, replaced it in 1912 and appeared until 1924. Meanwhile in the city of Sucre, in 1905 the *Revista del Instituto Médico "Sucre"* was founded as the journal of the
institute of the same name, which in its early days was dedicated
primarily to the production of vaccines and serums. The *Revista del
Instituto Médico "Sucre"* is still being published today.
    Medical journals in Bolivia in this period functioned to cre-
ate and maintain a corporate spirit at a time when the profession
was still in the process of formation, and was struggling to prove
that university-trained doctors were more competent than Andean
healers, although very few of the articles dealt specifically with native
curing practices. Occasionally journals were used by researchers to
publish the results of original research. More common were articles
that summarized secondary work published in other countries that
might have been of interest to Bolivian physicians. These pieces allowed Bolivian doctors to keep in touch with scientific research in
other parts of the world. The most common articles, however, were
those on Bolivian public health issues that exhorted the government
to take steps to remedy some problem. In this type of article, doctors
hoped to provide innovative medical solutions to health problems

and enter into national debate with other members of the intellectual elite. This debate often included, in one way or another, analysis
of and recommendations for the future of Bolivia's Indians. Many
articles reflected the doctors' apparent growing confidence in their
ability to influence social policy, even though they were far from
being able to significantly improve the health of the nation. My first
example of the ways doctors viewed health and ethnicity is based on
articles in one of these journals.

Dr. Néstor Morales Villazón, director of the Instituto Nacional
de Bacteriología, was the main force behind the *Revista de Bacteriología e Higiene*. The journal had a number of people on its editorial board, and there were always other contributors, but the RBH
definitely had Morales's stamp on it. Its articles always seemed to
promote his agenda, which combined self-advancement with improving the nation's hygiene. In fact, according to medical historian
Rolando Costa Ardúz, Morales authored 138 of the articles in the
RBH, or 42 percent of those that appeared between 1912 and 1924.[50]
Morales was clearly influenced by the example of other Latin American countries, where research and the production of vaccines and
serums were carried out in laboratories specializing in bacteriology.
He was a pediatrician and had been dean of the Medical School in
La Paz, but it was as head of the Instituto de Bacteriología in La Paz
that he wanted to make his mark, most particularly for his research
on and campaign against typhoid fever.

In its first issue, in April 1912, the *Revista de Bacteriología e Higiene* announced that since the middle of the previous year typhoid
had reached epidemic proportions in the department of La Paz and
had invaded the city itself. The epidemic was particularly severe in
rural estates and communities near the shores of Lake Titicaca; on
some haciendas, the proprietors reported that as many as a quarter
of the indigenous workers had died.

The objective of the April article was to mobilize government support for a campaign against typhoid; it pointed out that the epidemic
was, or should be, of concern to the government for two main reasons. First of all, it raised the specter of food shortages and hunger in
the city of La Paz, since the people most affected were the young of
the "clase indígena" who "thanks to their work maintain the dietary
health of the population."[51] Second, the epidemic presented a direct
danger to people in the city because of the constant traffic between

the provinces and the urban center. The article mentioned the unhygienic conditions of some sectors of the city, "the defective manner in which the lower social classes live," and the horrendous quality of La Paz's drinking water as all conducive to the rapid spread of the disease. The author (who was Néstor Morales himself) went on to spell out the dire consequences of the epidemic: "after the epidemic there will be hunger and the inseparable companion of hunger, poverty, due to the complete paralysis of commerce, the base of economic health."[52]

It is important to point out that in this period typhoid was not the primary infectious disease causing mortality in the city of La Paz. In the first half of 1913, at the peak of the typhoid epidemic, there were 48 deaths in the city from typhoid and 257 from whooping cough (pertussis), the top killer. In the last trimester of 1914 and the first trimester of 1915, there were 753 deaths from measles, 145 from whooping cough, and only 41 from typhoid.[53] Perhaps because measles and whooping cough were primarily diseases of childhood, for Morales they did not represent the economic threat that typhoid did. Furthermore, in this period there were no vaccines for either measles or whooping cough, and so a campaign against them was less realistic than one against typhoid. Finally, Morales may have been so emphatic about the need to attack typhoid because, although it was clearly rampant in the countryside, it was not yet seen as a primary health problem in the city.

To gain support for his efforts Morales, therefore conjured up images in which the urban upper class would be contaminated by disease spread by the lower classes and the Indians. A number of historians and anthropologists have shown how elite fears of contamination can be understood as metaphors for fear of loss of control of society's lower orders.[54] Preventing the spread of disease from a dangerous contaminated sector of the population to other groups is a ritual (and sometimes real) means of preventing disorder and maintaining social hierarchy.[55] Morales's formulation is the "medicalization" of the more general fear on the part of the elite that Indians could leave the countryside and assume new roles in the cities.

However, Morales apparently thought that policy makers still might not be moved to fight a disease that was primarily attacking Indians, because he took great pains to explain that high mortality was serious even if it only affected society's lower orders. Here we see some consciousness that aside from the possibility of contagion and economic decline, there were other reasons that the creole elite could not separate itself from its Andean members. Morales presented a corporatist, organicist argument, but it reflects a connection with the Indians that would probably never have been articulated by a European doctor in an African colony. His sentiments were also in keeping with the opinion of the day that the Indian population needed to be educated and civilized for Bolivia to become a modern nation. He said: "Every person, no matter how humble the sphere of his development, represents a factor in the progressive advancement of a society, which will be that much more prosperous and flourishing when the number of its component elements is greater, more intelligent and more active."[56]

Finally, Morales got down to his proposal for rectifying the situation, saying that there are two ways to address the problem of epidemics: improving the conditions of existence for the "indigenous race" or preventing the disease by means of a vaccine similar to that available for smallpox. He was cognizant of the social causes of the typhoid epidemic, but Morales ultimately rejected the possibility of improving the situation of the Indian population, saying that "it would require, besides too much time—the element par excellence, for this type of social transformations—money in abundance, which, unfortunately, Bolivia lacks even for more urgent necessities."[57] He did not specify what necessities he would consider more urgent.

It is essential, he said, to vaccinate the indigenous population, and he proposed that the government send doctors abroad to learn how to produce a vaccine domestically. He ultimately opted for a limited medical procedure instead of more infrastructural public health measures, such as potable water or rural health care. It should also be noted that when Morales talked about vaccination, he did not mean universal inoculation. Rather, he foresaw the use of the vaccine in epidemic areas to prevent typhoid from spreading. Morales's emphasis on a purely medical approach to typhoid reflects trends in medicine that had begun in the last decades of the nineteenth century. Advances in bacteriology and parasitology raised hopes that it would be feasible to deal with even major problems of public health through vaccines and vector eradication, instead of through the amelioration of unhealthy social conditions.[58]

By 1913 typhoid had spread over wider areas of the republic, and Néstor Morales had developed his vaccine. He now maintained that the vaccine also could be used to cure typhoid, a discovery he claimed to have made several days before the same procedure was proclaimed to be effective in Paris. Actually, a number of physicians in different countries had begun using the vaccine as a therapy at about this time, and it apparently continued to be administered at least as an occasional treatment until 1948, when the antibiotic chloramphenicol was proved effective against the disease.[59]

The articles in the RBH in 1913 by Morales and others involved in combating the epidemic stress that use of the vaccine as therapy was particularly suited to the Indian population.[60] For the native Andean, typhoid was said to be particularly severe and rapidly fatal, "due to the particular conditions in which [the Indian] lived, his customs, etc."[61] Here we have an argument that is not based on presumed biological differences inherent to the Andean population that made typhoid particularly virulent, but on the contention that it had unique clinical characteristics for the Indians due to their lifestyle or culture. But if the doctors pointed to cultural differences, they did not presume to relativism. An ethnographic explanation was more acceptable intellectually (and perhaps psychologically) in 1913 than a purely physiological one, but culture was portrayed as something ponderous and only gradually responsive to change. However, the doctors stopped short of an explicitly Lamarckian explanation that posited that environmental factors had changed that Indians' genetic makeup.

Here is a sample of medical opinion on the subject:

Typhoid is especially malignant among the indigenous because of the extraordinary filth in which they live, because they don't bathe, don't clean their mouths, don't clean their houses which are miserable hovels . . . without light, where the rays of the sun have never penetrated, without ventilation, full of smoke. These dark and cramped quarters serve for every purpose; in them five, six or more people of both sexes cook, eat and sleep in frightful crowding without any care for those who are sick with fever; sick and well alike chew coca day and night.[62]

or

> In Bolivia more than anywhere else it was essential to look for methods to prevent typhoid given . . . the special conditions of the Indian, his unique psychology, his horror of any hygienic measures that oblige him to change his habitual mode of existence.[63]

The cultural explanation may have been particularly satisfying to the doctors because it allowed them to distance themselves from the Andean population. If culture made the indigenous population backward, their own culture made the doctors civilized and more able to fight disease. For Bolivians, who did not embrace the idea of being a mestizo nation, culture was a means of changing racial categories. Culture was what made the doctors (and other members of the elite) white. As Alcides Arguedas said in an attempt to explain the dark skin tone of many Bolivian "whites": "the ethnic quality of an individual is the result of his social position."[64] In this instance Arguedas articulated an understanding of race that has been relatively common in Latin America, in which racial categorization can be altered by economic and social position.[65]

The cure with the vaccine was a kind of shock treatment for patients who, because of their habits, could not be counted on to follow more conventional and less extreme regimens. It involved a series of injections with the vaccine (twice a day or on succeeding days) until the fever was reduced and the patient showed distinct signs of recovery. One problem with this therapy was that it initially made the patient's temperature rise and often provoked an extreme, painful local reaction. After one injection, the sick person and his or her family often begged not to be subjected to any more.[66] Initial testing was done on indigent patients in the charity hospital and the lazareto (lazaretto), who were not given the option of refusing treatment.[67]

Vaccination and vacuno-therapy (as curing with the vaccine was called) were administered by doctors, or more frequently by their assistants, who went to epidemic rural areas when they were requested to do so by local authorities or the federal government. The fact that they ventured into "uncivilized" territory gave their efforts something of the romance of colonial doctors or missionaries bringing enlightenment to previously unexplored territory. They were strangers in their own country. As the RBH reported: "Sr. Orijuela [an assistant in the Instituto de Bacteriología] has had to travel immense extensions of the arid altiplano that are lacking in any resources, searching in the solitary and immense extension of the pampa for the gray stain or the weak puff of smoke, that indicates to the traveler the presence of a human being."[68]

Although there were instances in which people in epidemic zones refused to accept the vaccine, even prophylactically,[69] the RBH waxed eloquent about the great service medical science was providing the indigenous population: "The miserable indigenous, accustomed to carrying only the most difficult part of social obligations, without anyone ever having thought of improving their sad condition, nor alleviating their pain, must have felt happy to see that the Supreme Government has seen fit to make such an effort to improve their humble condition. Perhaps for the first time in the existence of the Republic, the Indians of Curaguara [department of Oruro] have benefited from the attention of the government and the advances of science."[70]

Most of discourse at the time on the typhoid epidemics tended to emphasize "culture" as making the Indians suspicious and resistant to change, "sunk in a state of lethargy" as one writer put it. The Indians' culture made them oppose change; the urban criollos' culture made them welcome it. Today it may sound like some of the more crude formulations of modernization theory. However, there were also a few reports of greater flexibility on the part of the Andean population, which also have the effect of casting the campaign against the disease in a better light. After all, Morales, who wanted government recognition for his efforts, would not have found consistent resistance on the part of his patients the best advertisement. So a report, which points to such flexibility, in the newspaper *El Norte* by Enrique Renjel, an assistant at the Institute of Bacteriology, was probably edifying to Morales and his colleagues. The report also shows that some health workers, based on their experience, had less static views of the Andean population and, in this case, even recognized that the indigenous population had its own medical tradition. Renjel had been sent to the area of Lake Titicaca to treat the victims of typhoid and to vaccinate those who were not yet ill. He wrote:

> At first I encountered a certain resistance on the part of the Indians but the rapid action of the vaccine on two of the ill who were practically

in death's agony immediately attracted all the Indians who arrived in groups asking for the vaccine.

They even brought me nursing infants, and with the naturally sensible criteria of primitive man, who judges the facts by the results, they said to me, "Vaccinate my children too because it's not just that we should be free from the contagion and they should still be exposed to the danger."

From what I have been able to observe, the idea that the Indian is opposed to all progress is false. Here are various photographs of numerous groups of Indians who came to the hacienda house asking for vaccine, accepting without any resistance a curative system completely unknown to them.[71]

Although Morales and his colleagues widely proclaimed the miraculous results achieved with the vaccine, questions about its efficacy gradually surfaced. A few years later Jaime Mendoza, a respected physician and author, called into question how well the inoculations worked, even prophylactically. A clinical study done by a supporter of the vacuno-therapy, comparing the vaccine with more conventional cures (cold water therapy, washing the mouth frequently, enemas), did not produce conclusive evidence that the vaccine was better.[72] It is also debatable whether Indians were particularly adverse to this standard treatment, as doctors claimed in justifying the use of vacuno-therapy: enemas were frequently prescribed by many Andean healers, and the Kallawaya consider them a means of cleansing the body.[73] Eventually there was a long polemic between Morales Villazón and other doctors about the efficacy of the vaccine and whether it represented a true innovation for which Morales should be honored by Congress.[74] One thing is certain about the whole episode, however: the vacuno-therapy was a medical treatment prescribed and used based on doctors' assumptions about cultural and ethnic difference.

Jaime Mendoza: Class and Ethnicity

Morales Villazón attempted to influence government policy through scientific research and active self-promotion in the press and medical journals. Meanwhile, Jaime Mendoza, one of Morales's critics,

Néstor Morales and collaborators at the Instituto de Bacteriología, 1914.
From left: Enrique Renjel, Félix Veintemillas, Néstor Morales Villazón (seated),
Carlos Nieto Navarro, Néstor Orijuela. Credit: Julio Cordero, Foto Cordero,
La Paz, Bolivia.

sought to advance his own medical/social agenda through different
means. In the case discussed here, he did it by writing fiction. In 1911
Mendoza completed one of the best-known Bolivian novels, *En las
tierras del Potosí*. Really the first novel of the mines, it is still widely
read today for its combination of brutal realism and almost poeti-
cally beautiful description. It is also still popular because it is a good
read: a classic tale of a young man leaving home to seek his fortune
and discovering the other in his own society.

Mendoza was born in Sucre in 1874 and graduated from medical
school there in 1901. He did advanced studies in medicine in Chile,
England, and France, and *En las tierras del Potosí* was completed
in Paris. Mendoza held many prominent positions in the Facultad

de Medicina in Sucre, was director of the national mental hospital, worked as a company doctor in several mining centers, and was an army surgeon in the Chaco and Acre wars.[75] In 1930 Mendoza was elected senator from the department of Chuquisaca, and during 1930s he opposed Bolivia's entry into the Chaco War with Paraguay. He died in Sucre in 1939.

Although the protagonist of *En las tierras del Potosí*, Martín Martínez, is a third-year law student in Sucre who leaves school to find employment in the mines, a central figure in the novel is the company doctor and much of the book is about hygiene and disease. The novel discusses the numerous health problems common to mining centers: alcoholism, silicosis, high infant-mortality rates, deaths and injuries due to mine accidents, numerous infectious diseases related to poor hygiene.

If Morales Villazón and his colleagues saw the problem of the Indians as a problem of culture, Mendoza, as a moderate socialist, brought a new analytic category to bear on the issue: class. In fact, his emphasis on class in some cases led him to ignore ethnic difference, as he stressed the workers' common exploitation by the mining companies. He apparently was not blaming indigenous culture for health problems but rather the unjust situations in which people found themselves. Yet, reading a little more carefully, we find that Mendoza too could not get away from the idea that it was "Indianness" that created many of Bolivia's social and health problems and that the native population was somehow complicit in its own suffering.

On the one hand, Mendoza was quite clear that mining accidents were the result of poor maintenance of the mines by the company, poor training of the workers, and lack of rigorous government inspection and regulation. On the other hand, Mendoza was more inclined to blame infant mortality on the mothers, Indian mothers. When Martín (the protagonist) asks if there is an epidemic, because he has seen so many children's funerals, Miguel, an experienced former miner, tells him that an epidemic isn't necessary because the mothers' negligence kills the children. The women, he says, get drunk and carry the children on their backs in their revels. They feed them meat and fruit and *chicha* (an alcoholic beverage brewed from corn) and chili at an early age. They take them out in the elements and hit them cruelly. When they are drunk, they eventually lie down on top of the children and suffocate them.[76] Another example of laying the blame for their situation on the workers themselves is Miguel's explanation for why they tolerate the miserable living conditions. He tells Martín, "Here people are very docile, very submissive, very stupid. We are just poor Indians."[77]

Mendoza was performing some interesting ethnic sleight-of-hand here: the miners, because they were working class, were by definition not Indians and therefore not to blame for accidents and diseases that befell them; the women, because they were women and Indians, had customs that, like those of the Morales' typhoid victims, led to the spread of disease and death. Finally, his last statement was revealing: the workers ultimately were too docile and submissive to organize in their own self-interest because they were Indians. But here he did something interesting: he had the speaker include himself as an Indian, as if to say there was a fatal flaw in Bolivian workers — their Indianness — which kept them from being militant proletarians (something that was later amply disproved in these same mining camps).

The character of the doctor in the book, who has no name but is always referred to as "el médico" or "el doctor," has a number of functions. First, like the doctors of the Instituto de Bacteriología, he is portrayed as having ventured into a miserably cold, desolate, and godforsaken environment in the interest of alleviating human suffering.

Second, through the doctor Mendoza criticizes popular Andean curing methods and home remedies and establishes the efficacy of "scientific" ones. The doctor often visits the homes of the injured or infirm only to find that the family has attempted some useless "indigenous cure." Mendoza is at pains to describe these in the most unpleasant manner possible: A man who has typhoid and is very thirsty is offered a blackish liquid from a dirty bottle that is said to be "an infusion of indigenous herbs."[78] Or, when a character develops typhus, the Indian family does not get the doctor until it is too late to save the person's life, and even then it is a criollo friend who finally brings the physician to the house. When the doctor arrives, he finds the man's female companion "rubbing his stomach with chicken fat and forcing him to drink disgusting potions."[79] Also, there is reference to the bad treatment children receive from their mothers: if they get sick, they rub them with "unimaginable" concoctions, "the least repulsive of which is excrement."[80]

The doctor is usually also shown to be effective where others have failed. When he goes to the home of an injured miner, he is quickly able to stop the blood flowing from the man's arm, whereas someone else had applied a tourniquet that didn't work. In another instance, although everyone else believes a man sick with typhoid is going to die, the doctor prescribes a treatment that saves his life: daily enemas.

When the doctor goes to a patient's home, he usually finds a scene of unrelenting squalor: the ill person lying in rags covered with his own sputum, the children at his side eating and being exposed to the disease, people in various stages of drunkenness looking on. In fact, some of the descriptions in the novel could have appeared in the *Revista de Bacteriología e Hygiene*. In one particularly vivid scene, when the doctor asks for water to wash his hands before examining an injured man, a woman rinses out a chamber pot and fills it with some dirty water. The doctor finally decides to wash his hands with liquor from a bottle a drunk is waving around.[81]

But more than just the representative of Western medicine, the doctor is the modern, rational man. Thus Mendoza set up an equation in which biomedicine equals progress and civilization. However, Mendoza was an unusual person for his era, and some of his ideas were certainly more radical than those of his fellow doctors or other people of his class. In one scene in the novel, for instance, the doctor has a confrontation with the mining company's accountant, who accuses the workers of stealing ore from the company. The doctor agrees that they are stealing but points out that most of them live in caves, that they are undernourished and poorly dressed and are forced to steal if they want to rise above a level of total misery.

The accountant responds: "Savages! I don't accept any of that. Even if you treat the worker well he will keep on stealing because the instinct to rob is in his veins, they rob because of, of, what is it?" He is unable to find the correct word; another person present fills in for him: "atavism."[82] Here the doctor is explaining that the workers steal because they are exploited, that is, giving an environmental explanation, and the accountant is saying it is hereditary, that is, because they are Indian. It is significant that Mendoza made the accountant Chilean, a foreigner from a country with a much smaller indigenous population and who probably considers himself superior to Bolivians in general. He can talk about atavism because he himself does not in any way identify with the Indians. Furthermore, Bolivia had been defeated by, and lost its sea coast to, Chile in 1879 in the War of the Pacific. By making the Social Darwinist a Chilean, Mendoza was appealing to patriotism and nationalism to advance his argument.

Once again we see Mendoza's ambivalence about the "Indian question" when in the same discussion with the accountant, the doctor says: "The situation of the worker is and will continue to be abominable. Which is really not so surprising when you take into account that this is a country of Indians."[83] Although he conveyed the idea that Indians are intrinsically, or by culture, submissive, it is doubtful that Mendoza personally believed in Indian submissiveness; in 1902 his mother was killed by the Indians of Yanani in rural Chuquisaca where the family had its hacienda.[84] It is also interesting that Mendoza talked so much about Indian submissiveness at a time when native people were showing themselves to be combative in reclaiming their lands. One can speculate that Mendoza may have believed that Indians were capable of irrational violence after long years of oppression but that the consistent action necessary to change living conditions could only be achieved through class organization. The struggles of Aymara and Quechua speakers to retain or regain their property might even have seemed backward to Mendoza, since community–land holding might retard proletarianization.

Finally, the doctor is shown, in the best liberal tradition, to reject not only Indian healing beliefs but all types of superstition, including those related to Catholic dogma. When the local priest tells the companion of a dying man that she cannot be in the same room with him because it would be a grave sin since they were not married (and the priest can't marry them because the sick man is unconscious), the doctor tells the young woman and her father not to pay attention to the priest, that the real sin would be not to help the dying man. He then comments to no one in particular: "Always insipid formulas, threats, prohibitions. . . . Marriage, sin, instead of love and charity. How many imbecilities are committed in the name of religion."[85]

Conclusion

Both Jaime Mendoza and Néstor Morales presented the doctor as venturing out into the wilderness to bring modernity to the uncivilized. The doctor, they suggested, was the person best equipped to inform and guide the nation. In Morales's case there was the clearly stated anxiety that if men of science did not, at danger to themselves, go out into the rural areas, disease and social disorder would engulf the civilized city. Mendoza's emphasis was different: in *En las tierras del Potosí*, there is no danger of disease or agitated miners invading the patrician city of Sucre. Rather, in keeping with Mendoza's emphasis on the environment, the doctor in the novel comments on the brutalizing exploitation of the mines that causes even well-brought-up people from the city to lose their culture and become degenerate.

In different ways Morales and Mendoza grappled with the same two issues: how to improve the nation's health and how to advance the professional position of doctors. Both of these goals in turn hinged on the situation of native Bolivians and their roles in the nation. Morales was skeptical of the possibilities for structural change. Although he recognized the connection between economic conditions and the nation's health, he rejected the approach of improving the living conditions of the Indians as too expensive and too time-consuming. Impressed by the scientific-medical advances of the period, he instead proposed that through prophylaxis and therapeutics the spread of disease could be halted. He believed this would allow Bolivia's economy to develop without the dislocations caused by epidemics or by Indians having to leave rural areas for the cities. He understood these medical innovations as being of help to the Indians and something for which they should be grateful, but his interest in their well-being was secondary.

Mendoza, on the contrary, was committed to eliminating the grinding poverty in which so many Bolivians lived and, as a doctor, was not convinced of the bacteriological solutions offered by Morales. He tended to favor social-medical measures that would alleviate some of the root causes of public health problems. (A number of his proposals in this area are discussed in later chapters.) Despite Mendoza's greater recognition of the material causes of Bolivia's medical situation, with respect to Indians his views were not

that different from those of Morales. He saw Indian backwardness
as at least contributing to illness; in some cases Mendoza seemed
to suggest it was the cause. He also linked gender to being Indian
and to indigenous healing. It was the women in the mines who administered home cures or Andean medicine, and their child-raising
practices were depicted as backward and negligent. If Morales saw
Andean culture as creating public health problems, Mendoza saw
women as the main bearers of that culture.[86] Yet, other than midwives, most of the curers that people frequented, from herbalists to
bonesetters to various spiritual curers, were men. Was this then an attempt, perhaps not even conscious, to discredit Andean medicine by
associating it with women? Or were midwives, the most commonly
consulted practitioners by women of all social classes, a particular
challenge to doctors?

Despite the efforts of doctors in the first decades of the twentieth
century to bring health problems to the attention of the government, throughout the 1920s health conditions in Bolivia remained
substantially the same. In 1923 a shocking 51 percent of the deaths
in La Paz were among children under one year of age.[87] In 1928 the
percentage was 38 percent.[88] Throughout the 1920s the most common causes of death in the city were communicable diseases, such
as whooping cough, smallpox, and measles, or gastrointestinal ailments, such as dysentery.[89] In lowland areas malaria was a scourge,
debilitating populations of once prosperous towns, and yellow fever
was endemic.[90] Tuberculosis became a major health problem in the
1920s and was severe in the tropical Yungas valleys, where many
people were already weakened by malaria. Burial records of workers
on agricultural estates in the Yungas list malaria and its complications (anemia), tuberculosis, and respiratory diseases as the most
common causes of death.[91] Grim as this public health picture was,
it was about to get worse as the worldwide economic depression hit
Bolivia and the country became involved in the Chaco War with
Paraguay in 1932. Not only did Bolivia suffer a humiliating defeat in
the war, but the conflict was a medical disaster both in the theater
of operations and on the home front.

During the 1910s and 1920s, as politicians debated the possibilities for "civilizing" the Indian population, and as doctors discussed
the supposed cultural proclivities that made them susceptible to diseases and resistant to treatments, native Bolivians were taking mat-

ters into their own hands. Peasant groups were using the legal system to claim ownership of lands the government was attempting to privatize and also demanding other rights associated with liberal democracy: access to markets to commercialize their products, the establishment of schools, and Indian representation in Congress.[92] They also began to join forces with unionized workers and a few sympathetic middle-class radicals who wanted changes in the country's economic and political system. Tragically, it took a war and enormous loss of life to loosen elite control of the political system. The debacle of the Chaco War eventually discredited the political class that had ruled the country since independence, and it created new political openings and new rhetoric about citizenship and social responsibility. It also forced a change in thinking about health: doctors and politicians had to acknowledge the medical failures of the war years and begin to consider what kind of public health system was appropriate for a nation aspiring to democracy.

2

THE MEDICAL CRISIS

OF THE CHACO WAR

After Bolivia's defeat by Paraguay in the Chaco War, the former director general of military health, Colonel Aurelio Melean, edited a book entitled *La sanidad boliviana en la campaña del Chaco*. In it he and other doctors who were active as physicians during the war outlined the system of health care that was set up in the field, and they contributed essays on some of the most serious medical problems that the army confronted. While acknowledging many of the nutritional and medical deficiencies that existed during the war, much of the book focuses on doctors' innovation in a time of crisis and scientific advance as a result of clinical study under wartime conditions.[1] Other sources, official and otherwise, give a less positive view of war conditions than the doctors, and demonstrate that the health crisis at the front was to be expected given the social conditions that prevailed in the nation as a whole. National racial and class hierarchies were reproduced in the army and were reflected in inequality in medical treatment. Furthermore, as the war drained the national treasury and medical professionals were drafted, the civilian medical services in many parts of Bolivia ceased to function.

In retrospect Bolivia's defeat in the Chaco War has been viewed as a historical watershed, leading to the popular repudiation of the oligarchy that governed the country and contributing to the revolution of 1952.[2] It also contributed to a reevaluation of the nation's public health system. Even doctors who felt they had done their best during the war, began, after the conflict, to conceptualize medical care as a right rather than charity for the poor and to consider the social and political obstacles to its delivery.

In this chapter I examine the medical crisis at the front and in the country in general during the war. Ultimately, Bolivia was just too poor to both fight a war and maintain anything approaching an acceptable standard of health care. During the conflict, some areas of the country had no doctors or medical facilities whatsoever. Of course, in a country as economically and socially unjust as Bolivia, the costs of the war were not borne equally. The prosperous, with their family and social connections, generally managed to get privileged positions and acceptable medical care in the military. Because they could afford private doctors, the elite also did not lack for treatment on the home front. However, as a result of trained medical professionals' being called up by the military, ever larger numbers of unlicensed individuals began to practice medicine. Although they could not provide adequate health care themselves, university-trained doctors attempted to stop the increased activity of these healers because they saw them as a continuing challenge to their professional prestige and were afraid that after the war, patients would continue to rely on the empirics.

If a major preoccupation before the war had been the economic and political roles of Indians in the nation, mobilization rapidly brought native Bolivians to the center of a national project. The nation's leaders had to depend on indigenous men to fight the war even as they continued to treat them as less than citizens. In this chapter I argue that the officers and doctors who organized military hygiene brought a series of racial assumptions to their planning for the war. First was the apparent belief that Indian recruits were so stoic and inured to suffering that they did not need even basic provisions to

be effective soldiers. Along with this conception of Indian temperament and fortitude went a series of stereotypes about natives and
disease: they were considered particularly resistant to some illnesses
and particularly likely to succumb to others. Native Bolivians were
mostly said to be prone to illness because of their dirtiness, yet all
soldiers in the Chaco were forced to endure long periods of horrible filth. Finally, the fact that the country relied heavily on indigenous recruits to fight Paraguay brought to light (if not consciousness) a fundamental contradiction: in the spirit of patriotism the
non-Indian population wanted to support the country's troops, yet
at the same time they associated with disease those who were sacri-
ficing the most in the war. Soldiers did spread yellow fever, typhus,
and other diseases to the general population when they traveled to
and from the front. Soldiers also contracted diseases to which they
had not been previously exposed, such as malaria, from civilians,
yet class and racial bias made the Bolivian upper class focus on the
draftees as propagators of disease. Prosperous Bolivians, especially
women and girls, frequently sent clothing and other donations to
men at the front, but prejudice combined with fear of contagion
to cause them to avoid contact with soldiers in the country's cities
and towns.

The War

War began in July 1932 as a result of Bolivian president Daniel
Salamanca's aggressive policy of pushing Bolivia's territorial claims
against Paraguay in the Gran Chaco, an area that extended from the
southern end of the department of Santa Cruz to northern Andean
Argentina, and from the foothills of the Andes in the west to the
Paraguay River (Río Paraguay) in the east. The Chaco was a generally
inhospitable place, which between the months of November and
April often had temperatures of forty degrees Celsius in the shade.
Because of the climate and ecology the entire region was sparsely
populated, although there were groups of native Guarani-speaking
Chiriguano Indians living there. The Chaco was much closer to the
Paraguayan capital of Asunción than it was to any major Bolivian
settlements; Paraguay had made efforts to colonize the region and
had sold large tracts of land to Argentine developers. Bolivia's foot-

Map 2 Region of conflict in the Chaco War.
Prepared by John Caris.

hold in the Chaco, on the other hand, was only through a series of small forts (*fortines*), which before the war were often only occupied by a few soldiers.

Various explanations have been given for Bolivia's escalation of the conflict from the level of border skirmishes (which had been going on at least since 1927) to full-scale war. One reason given is that the country, still smarting from the loss of its seacoast during the War of the Pacific (1879), hoped that a victory in the Chaco would permit the establishment of a Bolivian port at a strategic point on the Río Paraguay from which the country could reach the Atlantic via an estuary of the Río de la Plata.[3] Another reason often given for the outbreak of war was that international oil interests provoked the conflict in order to control petroleum production in a large area of South America. According to this argument, Standard Oil of New Jersey, which was exploiting oil deposits in Bolivia, saw the possibility of building a pipeline through the Chaco but was prevented from doing this by Royal Dutch Shell, which controlled the commercialization of petroleum in Paraguay.[4] Although Bolivia's desire for an outlet to the sea (however convoluted the route) and the role of big oil in the area cannot be totally discounted, it seems far more plausible that Salamanca forced the countries into war (against the advice of his general staff) as a means of rallying nationalist support at a time when he was failing miserably at dealing with domestic political opposition and the economic crisis of the 1930s depression.[5] The Paraguayan government, on the other hand, while certainly not adverse to territorial gains at Bolivia's expense, was also almost literally fighting for its survival as a nation in the Chaco after it had lost half of its national territory (and possibly half its population) in the War of the Triple Alliance (1865) with Argentina, Brazil, and Uruguay. For Bolivians the Chaco was remote, so remote that the military did not have accurate maps at the beginning of the war. For the Paraguayans the area was perhaps equally inhospitable but much closer to their national center of gravity.

While the first engagements in the conflict did succeed in rallying Bolivian patriotic support, from the beginning the army lost battle after battle. Boquerón, Nanawa, Campo Vía, and other spots on the map that most Bolivians had never heard of before became scenes of retreat and catastrophic loss of life. Over the course of three years the Bolivian military was pushed farther and farther west and south until it was fighting to save Villa Montes, a town in the department of Tarija in the foothills of the Andes, that had previously been safely behind the lines. There were multiple causes for Bolivia's disastrous defeat, including underestimation of Paraguay's military ability, lack of clearly articulated war aims, Argentine support for Paraguay, poor strategic and tactical planning by the Bolivian military high command, and conflict among commanding officers and between the army leaders and President Salamanca.

From the beginning though, communications and supply problems plagued the Bolivian effort and stand out as a major reason for Bolivia's loss. Soldiers traveling to the Chaco from the altiplano generally traveled by train to Villazón, near the Argentine border in the department of Potosí. They then either went by foot or in trucks roughly another 200 miles to Villa Montes; from there they walked to the front which, at the beginning of the war, was about 250 miles beyond Villa Montes. Except for the rare areas where there were watering holes, it was necessary to also bring in water, food, and supplies over this route, often leaving soldiers, who were estimated to need ten liters of water a day in the heat of the Chaco, dying of thirst and starving. In fact the common nickname given to the Bolivian conscripts was *repete*, a reference to the fact that whenever food was distributed, they pathetically begged for more (a repeat). The Paraguayan soldiers at the start of the war had less distance to travel to the lines, covered much of it by train, and therefore arrived relatively rested; they were also better fed and provisioned. This gave the Paraguayan military a distinct initial advantage. Bolivian officers frequently had to retreat from engagements simply because they could not supply their troops, and panic often ran through army divisions that were surrounded by Paraguayan forces, because soldiers realistically had no confidence that their commanding officers would be able to bring in ammunition, water, or food.[6] Yet as the war wore on, and the Paraguayans pressed farther into the Chaco at Bolivian expense, they too did their share of walking. The nickname for a Paraguayan soldier (equivalent of calling the Bolivian repete) was *pila*, a contraction for *patas peladas*, or "bare or peeled feet," because Paraguayan soldiers were often sent into combat without shoes.

If at the beginning of the war there had been general enthusiasm for the patriotic effort, it began to wane as the Bolivian Army lost more ground and suffered more casualties. By 1933 many young

Sapper unit in Chaco. From Juan Lechín Suárez, *La Batalla de Villa Montes* (Barcelona: Técnicos Editoriales Asociados, 1988).

criollos were finding ways to avoid being sent to the front lines and managed to get military desk jobs in Bolivia's cities. More and more of the soldiers were Aymara- and Quechua-speaking peasants, who often were conscripted although there had been agreements made in many areas of the country not to draft hacienda workers (who were overwhelmingly Indians) because it was their labor that supplied the army and the civilian population with food.[7] Once in the army, peasants were either sent directly to the front lines (often without training or weapons), or forced to do the backbreaking labor of opening roads in the area in sapper units. Also as the war wore on, the conscripts were older, as the army called up men who were in the reserves who had done their initial military service longer and longer in the past.

In February of 1934 the much-lauded Hans Kundt, a German general who led the Bolivian military, was forced to resign after the ignominious defeat at Campo Vía, and in November President Salamanca was deposed by a military coup. The situation for Bolivia could hardly have been worse, yet the fighting continued until June 1935, when the Bolivians managed to salvage a degree of national self-esteem by beating the Paraguayans back from Villa Montes. In a peace agreement that was finally signed in 1938, Paraguay relinquished the land it had occupied near Villa Montes, and Bolivia ceded to Paraguay territory in the north-central part of the Chaco area.[8] Bolivia never was granted a port on the Paraguay River.

If Bolivia had won the war, the traditional political groups in the country might have been able to hang onto power and maintain the social status quo. However, the loss in the Chaco forced sectors of the Bolivian population who had previously not done so to confront the class and racial divisions in their society. Members of the middle class grew increasingly critical of elite landowning and mining interests in control of the government since independence. There was outrage at the sacrifices ordinary soldiers (read Indian peasants and workers) had made at the front, while officers, who were often viewed as incompetent, enjoyed relative comfort behind the lines. Surprising sympathy was also expressed for the ordinary Paraguayan soldiers. As will be discussed later, there were protests and even uprisings in the army and on the home front during the war. Given the general staff's inability to craft a successful strategy even after repeated losses, and their continuing sacrifice of soldiers' lives in unwinnable battles, it is remarkable that there was not more of a national convulsion during or after the war. In the end more than 50,000 Bolivian soldiers (out of approximately 250,000) and 40,000 Paraguayans died in the conflict, and in both armies more men died of disease than of wounds. More than 21,000 Bolivians were taken prisoner, and an estimated 10,000 deserted.[9]

The Organization of Medical Care during the War

Before the Chaco conflict no medical section of the Bolivian Army had existed; instead the health of the troops had been overseen directly by the office of the general staff. This meant that when war broke out, there was no system in place to deal with the health of soldiers fighting far from urban areas, where there were no hospitals or medical services. For example, although the war began in 1932 it wasn't until 1934 that some preventive measures, such as an antimalarial program, were beginning to function.[10] The whole system of medical care developed piecemeal as the war was going on and as doctors learned more about the health conditions in the area of the conflict. Intimately related to the health of the army was the problem of supplying the troops in areas that often could only be reached by foot. As mentioned earlier, food and water were in short supply, and malnutrition and dehydration were major causes of illness, evacuation, and death of soldiers.

In the medical organization plan that was gradually put into place, the first line of defense was the first aid post that existed in each regiment. The first aid post was headed by a *sanitario*, who was not a doctor but an army medic who had been trained in the field. Each regiment also had a surgeon, who supervised the sanitarios. Divisions, which were made up of three regiments, had more medical officers, who were supervised by more specialized physicians.

There was also a hierarchy of military hospitals beginning with primitive field hospitals that were designed to be mobile, so they could be packed up and moved when the army retreated from a location. Typical was the Hospital de Campaña de Murgía, made up of six tents and several additional buildings of wood and straw. It had eighty beds and was designed to treat both the wounded and the ill. Patients would often be sent from field hospitals to divisional surgical hospitals, and more serious cases (both the wounded and the sick) were also evacuated to bigger hospitals, such as Hospital Muñoz, on the Pilcomayo River (Río Pilcomayo) south of Villa Montes. Muñoz had five large sheds, each able to accommodate 100 beds for soldiers, and two smaller wards for officers, as well as a building with an operating room, pharmacy, and offices. The wounded and the ill were generally carried either on stretchers or simply in the arms of the porters to the first aid posts; sometimes they were then carried on stretchers or human-drawn carts from there to surgical or field hospitals. If they needed more specialized care, patients could be transported by ambulance or truck to bigger hospitals, such as Muñoz's, and from there they might continue to the central hospital in Villa Montes. From Villa Montes the most serious cases could be flown out to the cities of Tarija or Santa Cruz in small planes.[11] Some even were evacuated to the military hospital in La Paz.

According to the Melean book, by 1934 a prophylactic routine had been established for the majority of soldiers who entered the Chaco via Tarija and passed through the hospital in Villa Montes. Each man was supposed to receive a physical exam, a smallpox vac-

Military Hospital of La Paz with evacuees, 1933. From Juan Lechín Suárez, *La Batalla de Villa Montes* (Barcelona: Técnicos Editoriales Asociados, 1988).

cination, a typhoid vaccination, a delousing procedure to prevent typhus, quinine to prevent malaria, and "social prophylaxis." This last item consisted of information about sexually transmitted diseases and treatment for those who were found to have either syphilis or gonorrhea.[12]

Medical Problems during the War

The statistics on illness and death presented in Melean's book delineate the basic medical conditions that were crippling the army. In 1933 more patients were treated for illness than for wounds at the hospital at Villa Montes (5,231 wounded, 8,731 sick). Furthermore, of the 365 men who died in the hospital in 1933, only 24 died of wounds and related complications; of those evacuated from Villa Montes to hospitals in cities in the interior of the country, 2,549 were wounded and 4,656 were ill. It may not have been much of an exaggeration when one doctor said that overall "for every ten deaths during the war two were produced by the enemy and the other eight by illness."[13]

The single most common disease treated in the Villa Montes hospital in 1933 was avitaminosis (1,999 cases), which was technically the lack of certain vitamins, most commonly vitamin C, but actually was caused by general, extreme malnutrition. Case histories of the ailment record the following symptoms: pains in the legs that eventually became so severe the patient couldn't walk, bleeding gums and loose teeth, sensitivity to light and loss of vision, lack of appetite.[14] Avitaminosis was a result of the inability of the army to provision its troops in the field and was exacerbated by Argentina's (unofficial) support for Paraguay, which meant food could not reach the Bolivian Army through Puerto Yrigoyen, an Argentine port on the Pilcomayo River. Even in the period of greatest supply problems, troops theoretically received each day 250 grams of cereals, 300 grams of meat, 200 grams of wheat flour, 40 grams of sugar, 10 grams of yerba mate, and 20 grams of salt. Those on patrol received less food but were supposed to receive dry rations of meat, *chuño*, and bread.[15] It is clear however from personal accounts of soldiers that, in fact, they often received no food at all.

At least during the first years of the war, malaria was the second most serious health problem to incapacitate the troops, and those who had it often suffered from avitaminosis as well. In 1933, 899 patients were hospitalized in Villa Montes alone due to malaria, and 968 had to be evacuated from the war zone because of the disease.[16] There were many others with malaria who either were not being treated or were treated as outpatients. There were so many ways to get malaria in the Chaco that it was exceptional for soldiers not to have the disease. Many soldiers who came to the Chaco already had malaria (often without knowing it), and the large number of anopheles mosquitoes in the zone rapidly spread it to uninfected troops. Troops also passed through malarial areas on the way to the war, and the disease was endemic to the Chaco itself. In fact, there were large areas where the majority of inhabitants had malaria. The war effectively made malaria more common in a region where the disease was already a serious public health problem.

Nineteen-thirty-three and the first half of 1934 were the worst years for malaria in the army. Dr. Néstor Orihuela wrote that in 1933 the lack of hospital space for patients with malaria forced medical personnel to use the church in Villa Montes to accommodate them. He also referred to "the avalanche of patients evacuated in an endless caravan" who were diagnosed as having both malaria and avitamino-sis.[17] The only small comfort in the situation was that *Plasmodium falciparum*, the parasite that causes the most extreme and deadly form of the disease, was rare in the region. The type of malaria para-site most common in the Chaco (*Plasmodium vivax*) was in general not immediately fatal but tended to wear down its victims' health over a number of years.[18] By the second half of 1934 the distribution of quinine at sanitary posts along the routes most commonly used by the army to enter the Chaco, and the spreading of petroleum on deposits of water that attracted mosquitoes in populated areas, was said to have diminished the spread of the disease to some extent.[19]

Of the patients in the Villa Montes hospital in 1933, 851 had tu-berculosis. The disease was the cause of 27 percent of the cases of soldiers declared to be absolutely unfit to return to active duty once they were evacuated. One doctor remarked that the disease seemed to be the most common among Indians, perhaps because they had been least exposed to the bacillus before and because avitaminosis had so lowered their resistance.[20] His comment was one of many made by doctors during the war about native Bolivians' special sus-ceptibility or resistance to disease.

Few in the army in the Chaco escaped gastrointestinal infections due to impure water and poor food. However, while they were often very serious and even fatal, the statistics on them are hard come by because they were listed as many different diseases and often pre-sented themselves along with other maladies. There also was con-siderable debate among doctors about whether dysentery among sol-diers was primarily amoebic or bacterial. Dysentery enterocolitis was listed as the third most common reason that soldiers were admitted to the San Antonio Military Hospital—which was opened in 1933 to treat the ill so that Villa Montes could concentrate more on surgery. Between July 1933 and July 1934, of 254 patients who died in San Antonio, for 155 some kind of gastrointestinal infection was listed either as the cause of death or a complicating factor.[21]

Venereal diseases, particularly gonorrhea, were common through-out the war. Since penicillin had not yet been developed, if soldiers were treated it was with Neo-Salvarsan, which was generally not very effective. One doctor explained that due to the difficulty of ad-ministering medication systematically—because soldiers were con-stantly on the move—the doctors tended only to try to relieve the most acute symptoms and cautioned men to seek treatment once they were discharged. According to the same doctor, Ricardo Arze Loureiro, many men tried to solicit hospitalization for gonorrhea as a means of avoiding being sent to the front lines and this was another reason that treatment was frequently denied.[22] When hookworm, nephritis, war psychosis, and physical exhaustion are added to the diseases discussed above, it seems amazing that the army managed to function at all, even without taking into account the soldiers who died from or were incapacitated by wounds. Yet these statistics come from official sources. Personal testimonies and nonofficial materials paint an even more disturbing picture of what was going on medically both in the army and on the home front.

Soldiers' Accounts of Health Problems during the War

A good number of soldiers who fought in the war wrote and published memoirs of their experiences; others have told their stories in oral history interviews.[23] In many of these accounts, physical suffering and illness loom large. Undoubtedly the problem most frequently mentioned, and perhaps the most viscerally upsetting to read or hear about, was lack of water. Although the Chaco is bounded by two large rivers and crossed by several small ones, the soil is sandy and the small rivers tend to simply disappear into the sand. Some regions of the Chaco are virtual desert with only low thorny bushes growing; other places are more forestlike, with tall trees, but even there water is scarce. Especially in the dry season, between March and November, water is almost nonexistent except close to the Pilcomayo River in the southwest and the Paraguay River in the east. During the war the army was dependent on finding the rare watering holes, though they often contained stagnant or polluted water.

Carlos Herbas Cabrera gave some of the most horrifying descriptions of thirst in his written account of Bolivian soldiers attempting to escape from Paraguay's siege at Campo Vía in December of 1933. While the troops desperately tried to open a path through forest vegetation to eventually arrive at the Bolivian fort of Saavedra, Herbas Cabrera described leaving behind a trail of unburied soldiers who had died of thirst and starvation. He noted that the water they had been given several days before was completely gone, "even though we only used it to wet our lips" and that the landscape began to seem like a "frightening mansion of thirst." As they made their way out of the Paraguayan encirclement some men begged others to urinate in their mouths, but, as Herbas Cabrera described, the rest of the men were too dehydrated by that point to be able to comply. Finally some soldiers went mad with thirst and shot themselves, committing suicide. The men who managed to survive were finally directed to a watering hole by a Bolivian plane flying overhead that made swooping maneuvers to show them where the water was. For some of the men the water came too late, however: they died almost immediately, falling with swollen bellies by the putrid well.[24]

During the retreat Carlos Herbas Cabrera was reunited with his brother, Julio, who had been evacuated from a hospital at nearby Pozo Negro and had decided to try to escape with the troops who had not surrendered, rather than fall prisoner. Julio had been hospitalized with a serious, often fatal, disease that was also related to thirst. He, like many other soldiers, had eaten a fruit native to the Chaco called *sacha-sandia* (tree watermelon) that hung temptingly low on the branches of trees and was very juicy. The fruit was poisonous and few who ate much, especially of the unripe fruit, survived.[25] Overall in the attack on Campo Vía and in the effort to break out of Paraguayan encirclement, 2,686 Bolivian soldiers died, 4,856, were taken prisoner, and fewer than 1,500 managed to escape.[26]

Although the extremes of dehydration soldiers experienced during the retreat may have been exceptional, almost all enlisted men in the Chaco who gave accounts of their war experiences mentioned lack of water. Quechua-speaking veterans from rural Chuquisaca who were interviewed by Rene Arze talked about commonly going without water for three or four days at a stretch. Several of them also commented on the fact that the officers got better treatment and that professionals generally were not sent to the front lines. One of Arze's peasant informants even contended that Native Bolivians were better able to endure thirst and hunger than the delicate, educated men from the cities, an assumption the military leaders seemed to accept as well.[27] In areas where there were roads, from time to time water trucks would arrive, and one ex-soldier I interviewed talked about how men fought to get a little warm water. He also talked about digging wells thirty meters deep to reach water, only to find that it tasted like saltpeter and could not even be used to wash clothes. Men also urinated in wide-mouthed bottles and then let the urine sit in the sun until they considered that it was purified enough to drink.[28] Many of the soldiers entered the war at the age of 16 or 17, though they were not supposed to be allowed to enlist until they were 19. One veteran attributed the fact that he survived walking kilometers and kilometers without water to being young, saying that the older soldiers often died of dehydration, lack of food, and exhaustion. When asked what he considered "older," he said he was referring to men 25 or 30 years old.[29]

Complaints about lack of water were usually combined with accounts of the heat, long marches, and lack of food. Many of the recruits came from high-altitude areas of Bolivia and were completely unprepared for the heat and lack of elevation in the Chaco. Certainly, even those who were from ecological zones that more resembled the Chaco were pushed to the limits of their endurance by having to walk hundreds of kilometers to get to the front. The veteran Melaneo Sánchez Rodríguez, who was mobilized in Sucre, described walking long distances, sometimes in areas where the army used trucks and the railroad to transport officers. He also described Indian draftees actually carrying upper-class Bolivians on their backs: "From Sucre we went by foot to Potosí. From Potosí to Camargo, by foot. From Camargo we walked to Las Carreras. From there we were given a lift for a stretch. We were transported along with the priests, the lawyers, the best people from Sucre. Then we were walking again and those of us who knew how to travel by foot helped the priests and the lawyers; we carried them."[30] Although after he was mobilized, Daniel Macuaga went a considerable distance in truck or train, he still walked three months from the railhead at Lazareno to arrive in the interior of the Chaco. When questioned, he added that he and other soldiers from the altiplano had done this march without shoes, wearing only rubber-soled sandals (*abarcas*), which they had been provisioned with before they left. Furthermore, they had to get up at 4 A.M. and had only had one meal a day at 6 or 7 P.M.[31] Other soldiers also talked about being given food only once every twenty-four hours. Florencio Vásquez in fact described a mutiny in which a colonel was attacked by mistreated soldiers, one of whose complaints was that they received only one meal a day.[32] Although rations sometimes arrived from behind the lines, there were times when men were left to their own devices and ate whatever they could find that was remotely edible: snakes, iguanas, various thorny plants.

The accounts of both Indian peasant and working-class enlisted soldiers agree on certain points: There were both peasants and workers at the front, and they all were sick; malaria, dysentery, and collapse from thirst and near starvation were the most common illnesses mentioned. They also concurred that their sufferings were the result of poor military leadership and that favoritism allowed the educated and the better off to stay behind the lines, out of danger and living in comparative comfort. Luis Michel, a Quechua-speaking peasant from Zudañez, in Chuquisaca said that the officers were to blame for the lack of water and food at the front, that the Paraguayan officers took better care of their soldiers, and that while the Bolivian officers "were sipping drinks" in Villa Montes, the troops were surrounded by the pilas (earlier-mentioned nickname for Paraguayans).[33] Another peasant from Chuquisaca, Melaneo Sánchez Rodríguez, said, "We were always sent to the front lines. The lawyers, the aspiring lawyers, the doctors stayed in Villa Montes. They gave them jobs there. They separated the professionals."[34]

Although it is not true that there were no better-educated people at the front, the case of Eduardo Arauco, a young man from Sucre, in many ways bears out the accusations. Arauco had gone to high school in England and returned to Bolivia just before the war broke out. Since he was a *bachiller*, or "high school graduate," he was sent to officers' training school and became a second lieutenant. He recalled that the officers also had poor and insufficient food, which he said was only slightly different from that of the enlisted men. However, the meals he mentioned included soups, some meat, and cooked maize. He remembered that when he was on patrol, he had tinned meat and dried corn.[35] Overall, having completed high school at a time when few young men in the country had that much education, speaking Spanish as a first language, and being white were all factors that tended to guarantee better treatment; this background also provided personal networks in the military that helped men to escape some of the war's worst deprivations. This could be true for men with some education even if they were not officers.

What happened to Francisco Iporre Valdez when he got sick was a case in point. A frontline soldier, Iporre became ill after his unit was trapped in a trench in a terrible rainstorm that lasted all night. He developed what he thought was a terrible cold but turned out to be malaria, and he went to the first aid post, where he was given medicine. Shortly after this, his unit was told to prepare for the trip to help the forces of Colonel David Toro retake Picuiba in the north-central Chaco. Fortunately for Iporre, he was traveling in a truck instead of on foot, and several times along the route his command-ing officer tried to leave him in a field hospital but Iporre insisted on continuing. It was not until he climbed down from the truck at Gua-challa that Iporre realized he was too sick to continue. He was also lucky because by not continuing to Picuiba, he managed to escape one of the most painful defeats of the war (to be discussed).

At Guachalla, as luck would have it, he ran into an old acquain-tance from *colegio* (high school) in Oruro, who managed to help him get the approval he needed to be admitted to the small tent hospital there that accepted both the wounded and the sick. His friend was the secretary of the Hospital Guachalla and helped him to bathe, gave him clean clothes, and also made sure that he had sheets (clean) and blankets on his bed (most of the beds had no linens, and the patients were dirty). After he recovered from his bout with ma-laria—because Iporre knew the secretary and because he had been a high school student—instead of being sent back to the front lines, he was able to stay on in the hospital. There he worked first as an as-sistant to his friend, and then, when his friend was evacuated, as sec-retary.[36] His account of his convalescence and work in the Hospital Guachalla, and later as a sanitario in the Hospital de Villa Montes, is a vivid description of the medical problems of the patients and the treatment they received.

As a patient in the hospital, Iporre was in a large tent with about twenty other patients who had a wide variety of illnesses and were thrown together in the most unhygienic conditions. There were ema-ciated soldiers with dysentery who smelled horrible. There were pa-tients with tuberculosis who coughed up blood. Others had yellow skin, and Iporre assumed they suffered from liver ailments. Some had swollen lips and had lost their teeth from avitaminosis. All of the patients had lice, and the tent was full of flies that buzzed around the beds. Iporre commented that he was happy that his bed was near the opening of the tent so he could better bear the torture. The state of the hospital apparently was not exceptional: in the section of his book on field hospitals, Aurelio Melean wrote of the facility at Guachalla: "Provided with a pharmacy and adequate means of transport, it has met its objectives in good conditions."[37] Later in Villa Montes, in a bigger, better-equipped hospital, Iporre worked as a sanitario in the medical section. His job was to give medicine and injections according to the directions of the physician. The doctor in charge also indicated which patients should be evacuated to Tarija, with officers going by plane and enlisted men in trucks.

The most hair-raising part of Iporre's account is his description of being put to work amputating the hands and feet of soldiers with gangrene; this was done because the doctors in surgery were afraid of spreading the gangrene to other wounded patients. The sanitarios from the medical section of the hospital did the surgery in the operating room, while the surgeons stood behind a window and gave them directions. The patient would be sent the next day to Tarija. After each amputation the sanitarios had to bathe in the river using disinfectant soap, change clothes, and wash their dirty clothes, then bring them to the autoclave to be sterilized.[38]

Lieutenant Eduardo Arauco remembered clearly the procedure that was followed after he was wounded. He was initially taken to the first aid post, where his wounds were treated by a sanitario and a medical student who, he said, was called "doctor" even though he was not one. He said all the wounded were immediately given three injections: a tetanus shot, a shot of morphine, and something to prevent gangrene. Then the wound was superficially cleaned and bandaged before the soldier was sent to a hospital. In Arauco's case he was first sent to the field hospital at Muñoz and then eventually went by plane to Villa Montes. There he reported that, as an officer, he received much better treatment than the regular soldiers. According to him, the conscripts were housed in huge sheds that held up to 100 beds, while there were three rooms for officers with 10 beds each. He said the food was good, much better than at the front and that they were well attended by nuns from the Orders of Santa Ana and the Servants of María. He also mentioned that those in the officers' section were bathed in warm water and given clean pajamas and sheets. These were rare comforts that he still remembered fondly more than 60 years later. Before he arrived at Villa Montes, however, he had had to endure the removal of a projectile from one of his feet without anesthesia. According to Arauco, this was probably because the anesthetic had been used up on other patients, since the wounded usually arrived at the hospital in waves. He also said he was lucky that his wounds were not very serious because in the process of triage, as patients were stretched out on the ground to be examined, the most gravely wounded were often left to die.[39]

The Home Front

Even before the war, Bolivia's public health system had lacked human and financial resources and had been far from successful in fulfilling its official obligations. In the 1930s on the national level, public health was administered through the Dirección General de Sanidad Pública, which was part of the Ministerio de Gobierno. The Dirección General was responsible for virtually every aspect of the nation's health, from fighting epidemics, to enforcing the law mandating smallpox vaccination, to inspecting the hygienic conditions of public facilities, to keeping track of health statistics. Yet, on the national level in 1931, its entire staff consisted of five people: a director, a secretary-general, an inspector of pharmacies, a health inspector, and an office assistant/secretary. Each department (equivalent to a U.S. state) had a departmental director (*director departamental*) of health, and each province (similar to a county) was supposed to have a *médico de sanidad* (sometimes called a *médico titular*; titular doctor). Each department was responsible for maintaining offices of Asistencia Pública in its cities, which were supposed to provide first aid in cases of accident or severe illness, organize vaccination campaigns, run clinics for venereal diseases, and carry out the directives of the Dirección Nacional in the case of epidemics or infectious diseases.[40]

If the national office was understaffed, on the departmental level the situation was more precarious because each Dirección Departamental received part of its budget from the national government and the rest from the department or municipality. Funds from any of these sources could be cut or eliminated, and frequently they were. Even before the war, the national government spent less than 2 percent of its budget on public health.[41] Yet despite the limited resources, people relied heavily on the Asistencias Públicas. In Cochabamba in 1935, the office saw 6,594 patients who came for smallpox vaccinations, to have wounds treated, to receive injections, and for a variety of other causes.[42] Outside of the cities, on the provincial level, in many areas health care simply did not exist. Although a 1906 law mandated that there be a médico de sanidad in each province, some departments had no budget to pay these practitioners, and the positions were either filled by local doctors, who received no payment, or were vacant. Yet these doctors were supposed to be the first line of defense in the event of epidemics and were responsible for treating the poor and recording medical statistics.[43]

Once the country was on a full war footing, the military was given priority for doctors, medical equipment, supplies, vaccines, and so on. The public health system, extremely thinly spread already, reached even fewer people. Those in charge of military hygiene could finally announce in 1934 that preventive health care had become more systematized and effective, but improvements in the field of operations were at the expense of the general population. In the central office of the Dirección General de Sanidad Pública, the administration changed frequently because doctors and other functionaries were mobilized to serve in the army. The same happened in the departments, with the *directores departamentales* replaced by other doctors who had not yet been mobilized or who had returned from the Chaco. Although there was lack of continuity, at least most of the public health positions in cities were filled. This was not the case in the provinces, where many médicos titulares had gone off to war. By 1933 most provinces had no public health doctors; many had no doctors at all, and the local officials constantly requested medical personnel from the central office.[44] By the beginning of 1934, it was agreed that doctors evacuated from the war would be assigned as médicos titulares in the provinces. The general director of public health, Enrique Lara Quiróz, expressed satisfaction that this would be mandated by a military order which the doctors could not disobey.[45] The fact that doctors might refuse to serve if not ordered to do so by the health division of the military indicates how unsatisfying they found these positions. The jobs offered little or no pay, few medical supplies, and no office furniture, but the doctors were expected to treat any patients who presented themselves.[46]

In the absence of licensed physicians, many empirics and foreign doctors without Bolivian licenses provided medical treatment. These practitioners had always existed along with Andean health specialists as alternatives to the medical establishment, but during the war more people patronized them, and in some regions the government was forced to give them recognition because they were the only health care providers available. Also, the Dirección General de Sanidad Pública was so overextended that they could not prosecute all those practicing medicine without licenses: empirics advertised in newspapers, and licensed pharmacists filled the prescriptions they wrote. Many of the unlicensed healers who were eventually barred from practicing were foreigners, and Bolivian physicians maintained that the public had a preference for anything foreign. Since the non-Bolivians seemed to attract the most prosperous clientele, the local doctors may have especially wanted to put them out of business. Señorita Southwell, who called herself a *naturalista*, was said to attract the most "select clientele," as did Señor Ramón Carné Cort, who could count among his patients the minister of education and the Spanish ambassador. It was particularly galling to doctors with proper credentials that the minister of education patronized Carné Cort, since it was his ministry that was responsible for licensing doctors. Upon investigation Carné Cort turned out to only have been a nurse in his native Spain. Somewhat less select, but still serving an urban population, was the *masajista* (masseur) Walter Lanz, who was convicted of practicing medicine without a license when one of his patients lost the movement in his arms as a result of a series of injections Lanz had given him. Then there were James Price and Frank Beck, doctors from the United States who had never regularized their licenses in Bolivia. Beck had come to Bolivia as a Methodist missionary doctor in the 1930s and eventually set up a Methodist hospital in La Paz, which was sometimes referred to as the Clínica Americana. Both he and Price took advantage of a special law promulgated during the Chaco War that said that foreign doctors who served in the army for six continuous months, or a year with interruptions, could legally practice their professions. The law seems to have been drafted especially for Beck and Price, and there were Bolivian physicians who were concerned that the law might be applied to other unlicensed healers who did some service in the Chaco. Some doctors also expressed the opinion that Beck and Price had never really been properly licensed in the United States.[47]

All of these empirics treated people in cities, a market in which they were directly competing with Bolivian doctors, even if many of the latter were temporarily serving in the military. Probably it was because they were at least potential competitors, that the public health authorities investigated some of the most successful empirics and began proceedings against them. There were other unlicensed professionals whom the authorities either ignored or gave special permission to practice: these were mostly in rural areas where there was an absolute lack of health care. In fact, some of the *titularías*, the positions held by provincial doctors, were filled by men who had never completed their medical studies.[48] The entire department of Beni had only four licensed doctors and, despite the contention of the departmental health director that many of the deaths in the department were due to incorrect diagnosis and treatment by empirics, the government had to turn a blind eye to the activities of various heterodox healers. The departmental director also commented that under the circumstances, local women considered themselves medical specialists and did not hesitate to prescribe remedies.[49] In fact government representatives had proposed at one point that foreign doctors who lacked Bolivian certification be allowed to practice legally in the Beni and other remote areas. Apparently these practitioners' skills were considered good enough for poor rural people but not for city dwellers, who had access to licensed Bolivian doctors.[50] Nonetheless, it would seem that even foreign doctors without licenses did not find professional prospects in the Beni promising, because there are no records of any working there.

Not only did doctors leave their practices to go to war but pharmacists did as well, and there were few licensed professionals to replace them. Under these circumstances, the Dirección General de Sanidad Pública was forced to accept pharmacies run by empirics.[51] Also, as a result of necessity, during the Chaco War many soldiers had been trained as sanitarios to provide first aid and to assist doctors. By the end of the conflict, many of these men were quite competent and had been promoted for their skills. There was concern in the medical corps that when these soldiers were discharged, they would form a large contingent of curanderos, competing with university-trained doctors.[52] Also, Kallawaya and other Andean healers who were in the army often continued to provide cures. They were enlisted to be sanitarios, and sometimes were relied on especially to cure malaria using quina (the natural form of quinine). Some were sought out by the army physicians because of their medicinal skill. For instance, when Antonio Alvarez Mamani, a well-known Kallawaya and peasant leader, enlisted in the army he was assigned to work as a sanitario in several hospitals. Toward the end of the war, he worked in the hospital in Tarija with a number of distinguished doctors who encouraged him to use herbal remedies because of the shortage of other medicines.[53]

For all medical practitioners, licensed and unlicensed alike, the main medical challenges in Bolivia in the 1930s were a wide variety of infectious diseases; these all became graver dangers in wartime, when large numbers of people were traveling across the country to get to the front. Smallpox, for which vaccination was theoretically mandatory, was a serious scourge because municipalities, chronically short of funds and personnel, did not consistently vaccinate their populations, although the vaccine was produced in labs in Sucre and La Paz. Even high health officials themselves were not vaccinated; in 1933 the departmental director of health for La Paz came down with smallpox.[54] Initially the military had neglected to vaccinate soldiers before they were sent to the Chaco, and it only began doing so when civilian health authorities intervened.[55] Although smallpox vaccination was theoretically universal in the army by the later years of the war, there were still outbreaks among troops that spread to the unprotected civilian population. In 1935 there was an epidemic of smallpox in the department of Santa Cruz that began among Indian soldiers of a sapper unit stationed in the town of Montero.[56]

If smallpox was far from under control in the 1930s, other diseases for which vaccines did not exist, or for which there was no effective treatment, were greater public health threats during the war. Tuberculosis, had long been a serious disease in Bolivia but had not been addressed directly by the Dirección General de Sanidad Pública. Rather, in the 1920s the National League against Tuberculosis had been founded; it was run by prominent citizens who had no particular scientific expertise and no budget, and could only make recommendations to the government and appeal to the public for support. Although initially full of ambitious plans, by 1933 the only project of the league that was partially effective was the creation of a school for "weak children" in a suburb of La Paz.[57] Other than a few public lazaretos (lazarettos) that were designed to isolate people with various contagious diseases, the country had no facilities to treat people with tuberculosis. The situation was made more dangerous because it was impossible to get reliable statistics on tuberculosis in the country: the stigma attached to the disease caused many people, especially those with some economic resources, to deny that they or their family members were ill.[58]

The state just described was before the war. As a result of the war, according to the director of public health, the problem had increased geometrically. Tuberculosis was one of the illnesses for which soldiers were evacuated from the front and for which they were often declared absolutely unfit for service. In military hospitals they were most often simply treated for malnutrition, and once they showed some signs of improvement they were discharged to make room for other wounded or ill soldiers. Consequently, they returned to their homes to spread tuberculosis to their families and others with whom they came into contact.[59]

One of the most widespread diseases in the country during the 1930s was epidemic typhus, or *tifus exantemático* as it was called because of the exanthem, or skin rash that was characteristic of the disease. As with tuberculosis, there was stigma attached to having typhus, which was spread by lice, because of its association with lack of hygiene and poverty. For this reason it often was not reported to public health officials or was incorrectly reported as typhoid, which sometimes had similar symptoms.[60] Especially during winter months, typhus took on epidemic proportions in many areas of the country and was estimated to kill at least 10 percent of those infected.[61] The director of public health in Potosí reported that in the winter of 1934 there were days when as many as sixty people came to the Hospital de San Juan de Dios with typhus. Health workers there were unprepared to deal with the patients who flooded the small, antiquated hospital. A new, modern hospital had been built in the city before the war, that *potosinos* claimed was the best in the country, but it had been taken over by the military.[62]

Typhus created near panic among the population in La Paz in 1933 and 1934, and its proliferation was associated with the large number of troops who were always in the city. A survivor of the disease, Elsa Echalar, believed she had gotten the lice that spread typhus while traveling to school on a streetcar surrounded by soldiers. During the war, the epidemic was so serious in La Paz that the Hospital Municipal (municipal hospital) had a special green van (*carro verde*) that was used to pick up typhus victims to take them to the hospital. Once in the hospital patients often died due to lack of attention from the overworked staff. Seeing the carro verde in a neighborhood caused fear among residents and brought shame to the household of the sick person, because the disease was associated with filth. Echalar believed she survived typhus because her godfather was a doctor at the newly opened, private Clínica Alemana (German Clinic) and she was admitted there rather than being sent to the municipal hospital.[63]

While it was probably true that the upswing in typhus cases was related to the movement of troops throughout the country, there was definite class and racial bias in the association of the illness with the army. The vast majority of soldiers were workers or Indian peasants, whom the elite never tired of accusing of being ignorant of the most basic rules of hygiene, though the army often provided filthy, overcrowded barracks with no bathing facilities for the soldiers. Dr. Trifón Quiróz, departmental director of health for Potosí, expressed a commonly held belief when he said that typhus was spread to the city of Potosí by Indian recruits who were "unwashed because of idiosyncrasy."[64] If people in Bolivia were eager to disassociate themselves from the Indians, from the poor, and from the dirty who carried the typhus-spreading louse, they also wanted to defend themselves from the critiques of their neighbors, the Argentines, who were expressing alarm about the epidemic. The director of public health, Juan Manuel Balcázar, maintained that the typhus epidemic had been overblown in the press and that it had been relatively mild. He believed that the press's sensationalism had only fed the anxiety in Argentina, where authorities had questioned Bolivia's "ability to assure a satisfactory sanitary condition."[65] Balcázar's concern about country's image and criticism in the press was more than a defense of himself and the public health system he led; it was also an attempt to show that Bolivia was not simply a nation of unhygienic Indians. This defense was particularly important in the case of Argentina, whose population was far less indigenous and more European than Bolivia's.[66]

Sexually transmitted diseases also spread to more of the population due to the Chaco War, and this fueled discussion among health professionals about the reasons for the increase and the best ways to combat it. Doctors often traced the general increase in the diseases to the military authorities' tolerance for commercial sex in the cities where troops were mobilized.[67] Others looked for more sociological explanations: the director of departmental health in Oruro hypothesized that without male authority in the family (because men had been conscripted) there had been a general weakening of moral ties, and, that this, combined with poverty and the tolerance of the authorities, caused young women and girls to prostitute themselves.[68] The issue of prostitution, in a broader context of women's health, will be discussed in chapter 4.

Truly effective drugs to fight venereal disease did not exist in the 1930s, and the facilities that could dispense the ones that were available were inadequate. Public clinics to treat patients with venereal diseases operated in Sucre, La Paz, and Santa Cruz. All three were said to be inadequate in meeting the needs of the large numbers of people who sought out their services. In La Paz the office was only open from 7 to 9 P.M., lacked most drugs, and was run by an unpaid intern. The plumbing and electricity in the clinic were in need of repair, as were the autoclave and other sterilization equipment.[69] In Tarija, one of the cities closest to the front and with a high rate of venereal disease, the military health service ran a clinic that was open to the public. However, with the cessation of hostilities in 1935 it was about to close; the departmental director of public health asked for aid from the national Dirección General de Sanidad Pública to set up a dispensary to replace it.[70]

The inability of the government to carry out the types of infrastructural programs that could eliminate many diseases—and the lack of drugs, personnel, and facilities to treat the ill—often led to frustrated denunciations by health officials, but strangely also could cause them to minimize or deny the existence of grave problems. In general, even those physicians who were outraged about the lack of government attention to health were apparently so inured to certain serious illnesses that they often described as *leve* (unimportant, light) outbreaks of typhoid, flu, typhus, whooping cough, and so forth that caused considerable numbers of deaths and much suffering. Of course, they were caught on the horns of a dilemma: admitting the gravity of certain health problems did not reflect well on them, despite their lack of government support and resources to combat them.

Public health officials also sometimes minimized the seriousness

of outbreaks for political or ideological reasons as Juan Manuel Balcázar had probably done with typhus. Another example of this occurred at the end of March 1932, when Balcázar, then interim director of national health, and Dr. Luis Prado Barrientos, a military
bacteriologist, went to the city of Santa Cruz de la Sierra to investigate reports of a possible epidemic of yellow fever. Balcázar's and
Prado Barrientos's first day of visits to the sick, perusal of health
records, and meetings with doctors ended with statements to the
local press that the epidemic was mild, and probably not yellow
fever. Balcázar acknowledged later that his first desire had been to
calm the populace, which was on the verge of panic.[71]

The disease in question seemed to have originated in the barracks
of the Colorados regiment in Santa Cruz, and the most severe cases
were among the soldiers stationed there while waiting to be sent to
the Chaco. Part of Balcázar's anxiety to reassure the city's inhabitants was due to the impending war and the fact that the civilian
population, instead of patriotically supporting the troops, was almost literally fleeing from them. Here again fear of disease and disdain for poor Indian and working-class soldiers combined. Yellow
fever was probably most severe among highland Indian conscripts
because the disease tends to be most serious among young adults
who have not developed any immunity from having had the disease as children, when it often is relatively mild. Coming from highland areas, where there were no *Aedes aegypti* mosquitoes, allowed
the Native Bolivian conscripts to avoid yellow fever altogether until
they found themselves at lower altitudes. On the other hand, people
native to lowland Santa Cruz often had some immunity from bouts
with the illness early in life, so if they got yellow fever again as adults
it was not generally life threatening. This apparent coincidence of
sickness and ethnicity allowed *cruceños* to view Indian recruits as the
cause and focus of a dread disease.[72] In fact it was the living conditions of the recruits in Santa Cruz, not the soldiers themselves, that
should have been cause for alarm. The 150 soldiers housed in the
building where the first cases of yellow fever occurred were lodged
in the most crowded and dirty area of the city. There was no running water anywhere in the building they occupied, and there were
no toilet facilities. Fifteen to twenty soldiers were lodged in each of
the house's small rooms.[73] There were no screens to protect the soldiers from mosquitoes or to prevent mosquitoes from biting yellow

fever patients and spreading the disease. One wonders if the army justified the accommodations they provided these draftees by saying that Indians and the poor customarily lived in crowded, unhygienic situations and that therefore they did not have to provide anything better.

At the same time Balcázar was telling the press that the epidemic was "leve," and trying to convince the people of Santa Cruz to be patriotic and accept the military presence, the governments of Argentina and Brazil were both concerned enough by a possible outbreak of yellow fever near their borders to send medical teams to the area to investigate. Although some Bolivian public health doctors resented this action, they were forced to rethink the situation when in April 1932 five out of six blood samples sent to the Instituto Oswaldo Cruz in Brazil were diagnosed as positive for yellow fever.[74] Several positive autopsies were also done, and the Argentines threatened to close their border with Bolivia. Shortly after this, just as the war with Paraguay had begun, the International Health Division of the Rockefeller Foundation signed a contract with the Bolivian government to combat yellow fever in the country. As Dr. Fred Soper of the foundation commented at the time, "the Bolivians are sincerely glad we came along and so are the Argentines."[75] In fact, the joint Rockefeller-Bolivian Yellow Fever Service was to be one of the only civilian health services that consistently functioned during the conflict, and yellow fever did not present a major danger during the war years.

Whereas yellow fever in urban areas was quite rapidly brought under control, this was not the case with malaria, which was endemic before the war in many areas of the country and became a graver problem during the conflict. Before the war broke out, the departmental director of health for Tarija estimated that 80 percent of the population had some form of the disease,[76] and the main route to the front for soldiers who came from nonmalarial areas was through Tarija. These soldiers commonly became ill and could then spread the disease to the civilian population in areas where there were appropriate vectors as they traveled to the front or were demobilized or evacuated (as many of those ill with malaria were).[77]

Because at least three-fourths of the nation's territory was malarial, Bolivian public health officials considered malaria the country's number one health problem. Although a variety of attempts were made to address it before the Chaco War, the only program that got under way was a test project against the disease in the town of Mizque in the department of Cochabamba.[78] Mizque was chosen as a test site for fighting malaria for two primary reasons. First, the disease was so widespread in the area that Mizque was seriously depopulated, and a number of other previously prosperous towns in what was once a rich agricultural zone were totally uninhabited. It was hoped that a concerted campaign against malaria could help restore the region's former prosperity. Second, Mizque was on the road between the cities of Cochabamba and Santa Cruz, and the railroad that was being built between these two capitals would pass through or near the town. Fighting malaria in Mizque was seen as a means of stopping the spread of the disease to regional commercial and political centers.[79]

According to the director nacional de sanidad pública, Dr. Adolfo Flores, who wrote a 1929 study of Mizque, the town had a population of about 800 people. This was in sharp contrast to the 22,000–30,000 inhabitants the town was said to have had in the eighteenth century, before the presumed first outbreak of a disease. In 1929 everyone in Mizque suffered from malaria, including the elementary school teachers and their 101 students. In the region the most common type of malaria parasite was not the extremely malignant *Plasmodium falciparum*, but the somewhat milder *Plasmodium vivax*. Nonetheless since people generally were not treated effectively and developed only limited immunity, they had recurring bouts of the disease; as the parasite devoured their red blood cells, they developed chronic, debilitating anemia. According to Flores, the effects of malarial anemia were evident in the lethargy of people too weakened to improve their own hygiene and living conditions. He described a town in ruins, houses in the process of falling down, and streets crossed by irrigation ditches that were full of weeds and stagnant water, ideal breeding grounds for *Anopheles* mosquitoes. There was no potable drinking water, and the back patios of houses were used as toilets. Most of the town's occupants were poor; Flores described a family of six who lived in three rooms as among those few who had "economic resources." Given the description of sanitary conditions, it seems likely that the people of Mizque suffered from other diseases in addition to malaria, but the town had no doctor, and, according to Flores, the people were inured to being ill. One local citizen, Don Pablo Morales, had taken it upon himself to distribute quinine at his own expense to those who asked for it.[80]

Six years later, Dr. Demetrio Frontaura, director of the Zona Sanitaria Mizque, which was established to fight malaria, reported that some things had improved in the area but that others remained depressingly the same. The population had further declined and in 1935 was down to only 600 people. Dr. Frontaura commented that this was because people with malaria who had some money left the area to seek treatment and then never returned, while the poor stayed and died of complications of the disease.[81]

A special presidential decree allowed the Zona Sanitaria to conscript laborers for public works that would eliminate or reduce the areas where mosquitoes bred. It seems that most of what was achieved in the zone was the result of these brigades of forced workers. With the "brazos de la prestación sanitaria" (compulsory sanitary work) the project had been able to clean and weed areas that attracted mosquitoes, including swamps, irrigation ditches, and the town's streets and plazas.[82] By the end of 1935 Frontaura reported that only 39 percent of the people in Mizque were suffering from malaria, while at the beginning of the trial project 95 percent had been, although he does not say whether these figures were based on clinical observation, tests for parasites, or the percentage of people with enlarged spleens.[83]

Although in the three years he had been head of the project, Dr. Frontaura could point to some achievements, much of his report reads like a rant against the people of Mizque whose personal habits he had been unable to change. His first effort upon arriving in the town had been to reopen the hospital with the hopes of isolating those suffering from malaria from the healthy. This apparently was a failure; he said that the locals did not have the habit of isolating the sick; that the hospital was in detestable conditions, without screens or mosquito nets; and that the municipal council claimed it had no money to make improvements.[84] He went on to explain that Mizque had few white people—most of the inhabitants were mestizos and Indians. To Frontaura's surprise and indignation, the white people lived in the same squalor as everyone else. He said the total lack of sanitation was excusable in "los del pueblo," since no one had taught them about hygiene but he couldn't understand what was wrong with the whites, some of whom he said were of "regular cultura." He said rooms in people's houses, especially bedrooms, were full of insects and that people lived in complete harmony with chickens, ducks, dogs, pigs, sheep, lice, and fleas. Furthermore, according to Frontaura, almost all the inhabitants of Mizque were alcoholics. He concluded his report by saying that he thought the antimalarial efforts should be concentrated on other areas, those where the population was greater and there was more economic activity. The train line between Cochabamba and Santa Cruz had bypassed the town and was three kilometers away, and, since Mizque was surrounded by five rivers, the area flooded during rainy season and wàs inaccessible to vehicles for six months of the year.[85]

Although Frontaura obviously left Mizque demoralized, it is remarkable—given the war and the absolute lack of resources—that the pilot project accomplished anything at all. An analysis of the Rockefeller Foundation's projects in Bolivia in the next chapter illustrates how the foundation's strategic use of resources for limited objectives permitted them to be successful while the overburdened public health system floundered.

Conclusion

Instead of rallying the nation behind the government, Salamanca's adventure in the Chaco created mutinous conditions in the army and nearly resulted in civil war in the country. Despite the belief that Indian soldiers would endure any hardship, throughout the conflict there was open protest by frontline soldiers against their officers in the Chaco. That these were more than isolated incidents is proved by the fact that officers frequently had to simply acquiesce, apparently uncertain about whether they could prevail against large numbers of rebellious soldiers. As early as 1932, after Bolivia's defeat at Boquerón, approximately 3,000 out of 4,000 men simply refused to fight the advancing Paraguayans and abandoned the *fortín* at Alihuata.[86] At many other points during the war, exhausted soldiers wandered off to look for water, ignoring their officers' orders. The callous disregard some officers had for their men's well-being in the horrible Chaco conditions almost guaranteed that military discipline would not hold. In December of 1934 Colonel David Toro wrote to Lieutenant Colonel Félix Tabera—whose men were in rags, barefoot, and crazed with thirst—that they must defend Picuiba-Yrendague, though he (Toro) could not send water trucks. He wrote, "One must not have the least consideration for the fatigue of the troops of whom it is vital to demand the maximum effort."[87] More than fifty years later, indigenous veterans still remembered with anger and disdain their officers' incompetence and the favoritism shown in the military toward the country's upper class.

It was not just military discipline that broke down. All over the countryside, alarmed hacendados reported protests and even uprisings by their colonos and by members of nearby Indian communities. The reasons were multiple: Communities that had gladly contributed food to the war effort at the beginning of the war, later saw themselves virtually expropriated of animals and provisions by the authorities. Abusive military conscription of rural workers who often were supposed to be exempt, and the usurping of lands by haciendas while community members were off at war, provoked a wave of resistance that some political authorities attempted to blame on communist agitation or on efforts of the Paraguayan government to create civil war in Bolivia.[88]

In the post-Chaco era new radical working-class parties were formed, including the Partido Obrero Revolucionario of Tristán Marof and José Aguirre Gainsborg. A revitalized, militant labor movement protested postwar inflation. The political center moved to the Left in the face of the general repudiation of the governing elite, who had pushed for the war and then been unable to win it. In 1936 two former military officers, David Toro and Germán Busch, seized power from José Luis Tejado Sorzano, who had become president after Salamanca was overthrown. The Toro and Busch administrations (1936–39) were reformist affairs that attempted to both accommodate and contain the demands of radicals and not totally alienate the national elite.

In some ways the war and its calamitous results forced health care onto the government's agenda, something doctors such as Jaime Mendoza and Néstor Morales had been advocating for years. The alarming incidence of illness in the army, which contributed to Bolivia's loss of the war; the public spectacle of sick and malnourished soldiers in urban areas; and the spread of new diseases to large sectors of the civilian population were problems so grave they could only be tackled through government initiatives. In 1938 a new

Constitution was drafted that, similar to the Mexican Constitution of 1917, made the government responsible for citizens' health and well-being. This step was a recognition by the nation's leaders that the piecemeal, charitable approach to medicine—typified by private citizens' leagues against tuberculosis, charity hospitals run by nuns, and hospices organized by beneficence societies—simply was inadequate for the country's needs. One result of this shift toward health care as a government service was the gradual increase in doctors' prestige and political clout. Doctors were the ones who could propose solutions to the nation's pressing medical problems; increasingly medical men were elected or appointed to political positions that gave them the opportunity to introduce policy. So unlike the situation in some other countries, it was a populist, democratic discourse about health and medicine that helped cement doctors' professional authority. Of course Bolivia's resources did not begin to match its needs in the field of public health. Many people, through preference or because of lack of medical facilities, continued to patronize various Andean healers or empirics. Yet through government backing—which included making the practice of herbal medicine illegal in some places—and improvements in medical knowledge, by the late 1930s and 1940s the doctors were in ascendancy despite many medical challenges they could not meet.[89]

Many doctors were also radicalized by their experiences during the war and the socialist ideas that became popular in its aftermath. The spirit of the 1938 Constitution and a new class consciousness were very much evident in doctors' writings about public health in the 1930s and '40s. For instance, at the First National Medical Congress in 1939, Dr. José Antezana Estrada, while presenting a project for a new national sanitary code, characterized Bolivia as a "semi-colonial" country with the lowest economic level in the world.[90] A summary of another medical conference held in the same year reported that at the meeting, two political tendencies emerged: one that "defended established interests" and another that "supported the rights of the proletarian classes."[91] Yet, despite the radical rhetoric about class exploitation, there was often a serious blind spot with respect to ethnicity in doctors' writings. Doctors might be influenced by socialist and populist ideas—which, after all, had acquired prestige in Europe and the United States during this period —yet still consider indigenous people to be culturally backward and unhygienic. Class organization was one thing; that native Bolivians should unite around ethnic issues was either viewed as inconceivable, preposterous, or dangerous. Doctors and other privileged Bolivians had been forced by the social upheaval during the war to reevaluate some of the racial and class premises on which their society was founded. Still, there is evidence from medical writings and practice that some of the new democratic approach was only rhetorical and that older ideas about Indians, cholos, women, and health had not vanished.

Significantly, at the same time that doctors were integrating reformist conceptions into their thinking and trying to figure out what they would mean for public health, another medical model was being welcomed by public health officials in the country. This was the top-down, highly authoritarian approach of the Rockefeller Foundation. In their efforts to take more responsibility for public health, the government was only too happy to welcome the RF's International Health Division as a collaborator. The next chapter examines the Rockefeller Foundation's projects in Bolivia, how they changed over time, and how Bolivian doctors' attitudes toward the programs evolved.

3

THE ROCKEFELLER FOUNDATION

IN BOLIVIA, 1932–1952

It has generally been assumed that the mission of the Rockefeller Foundation's International Health Division (IHD) in Latin America was to promote U.S. economic and political interests through the eradication of epidemic diseases and the development of U.S.-style medical institutions. Yet as historians have examined the foundation's activities in different Latin American countries, it has turned out that while these may have been the overall goals, they were not always easy to implement in a linear way. Representatives of the RF arrived in Latin America with specific agendas they hoped to follow, but they often found that what they accomplished was also shaped by the social and political situations in the host countries. The priorities of national political leaders, reactions of targeted populations to RF health campaigns, and even the personal qualities of Rockefeller representatives and local public health authorities were important in determining the types of programs implemented. In some cases, the RF was welcomed by national governments that saw it as a strong ally in consolidating public health services; in others, the government could use criticism of the foundation as a representative of United States as a means of proving its nationalism.[1]

This chapter examines the Rockefeller Foundation's roles in Bolivia and the changing receptions the organization and its representatives received from health officials and the public at large. I argue that when the IHD first began a yellow fever eradication project in 1932, the country's dire financial situation and public health crisis caused by the world economic depression and the Chaco War led most government officials and doctors to welcome the foundation. Although there was some resistance on the part of the public to RF representatives' authoritarian, condescending approach to disease control, the success of the campaign against yellow fever in urban areas won the organization praise in official quarters and from many city residents. Furthermore, although the RF staff was initially relatively small, many doctors hoped to be hired by the IHD. Not only was the prospect of full-time, comparatively well-paid public health work attractive, but for many doctors the association with the U.S. experts promised prestige. Good relations between doctors, policy makers, and the RF also may have prevailed because foundation representatives and members of the Bolivian elite were in fundamental agreement about the nature of Bolivian society and its social problems. International Health Division representatives frequently repeated racial stereotypes about Indians and cholos that they culled from Bolivian sociological classics or heard from Bolivian colleagues. Although the North American doctors also sometimes looked down on Bolivian physicians as being poorly trained and even irresponsible, the two groups could concur on the ignorance of the Indian population and the obstacles it presented for the promotion of public health.

By the late 1940s and 1950s, there had been a number of changes in Bolivia that made doctors and policy makers less inclined to uncritically accept Rockefeller leadership in public health. First of all there were other international health organizations operating in the country, and this allowed the government to choose the groups it believed would offer the best programs. Rockefeller was no longer the only option when the country needed outside medical aid. Second, by the 1940s for a variety of reasons, the RF had acquiesced to Bolivian requests that it expand its services to other problems besides yellow fever. As it tackled more diseases—including malaria, yaws, typhus, and hookworm—the RF found itself overextended and unable to achieve the type of success it had had with eradicating urban yellow fever. The more limited achievements of later RF-sponsored programs began to erode the foundation's prestige among some professionals, who now felt other international groups, or even Bolivians, might be more effective.

Finally, the changing political climate between the end of the Chaco War and the eve of the 1952 national revolution affected thinking about almost every aspect of social life, including public health. The democratic-populist atmosphere, while particular to Bolivia, was integrally related to the principal international ideological currents that characterized the period between the depression and the beginning of the cold war. These trends also affected Rockefeller policy and initiatives in Bolivia and contributed to a more holistic public health approach by the foundation. The IHD now emphasized that it was important for Bolivian doctors to run all RF programs and that the government public health service should take over projects when the RF left the country. Yet, at least partially because of the changes in philosophy that created these efforts, they were met with more resistance than early campaigns that blatantly championed American know-how and assumed Bolivian incompetence. In other words, the same democratic rhetoric that was evident in RF postwar programs also made Bolivians less likely to unquestioningly accept RF help and authority. Ironically, however, despite the new democratic impulses on the part of the RF and the more critical stance of Bolivian doctors and government officials, both groups remained in substantial agreement about the negative effects of Bolivia's racial composition.

Why Bolivia?

The Rockefeller Foundation's decision to begin an anti-yellow-fever campaign in Bolivia after the disease was diagnosed in Santa Cruz in 1932 was almost certainly a result of the foundation's involvement in Brazil. Brazil was the largest country in Latin America, and RF officers had been impressed by the work done there against plague and yellow fever between 1903 and 1909 by director of public health, Oswaldo Cruz. Brazil was also seen by foundation representatives as having a federal system of government and state universities somewhat similar to those in the United States. Therefore the country was considered to be appropriate for RF programs for scientific research, training of doctors, and public health administration. By 1923 the foundation had begun a campaign against yellow fever in Brazil, and in 1924 it made an initial grant to the country of US$400,000 to establish research laboratories.[2] An epidemic in Bolivia, which was in the geographical center of South America and shared a border with Brazil, not only threatened control efforts in the foundation's Brazilian showcase but presented a danger to all of the continent. Furthermore, in 1932 RF officers realized that Bolivia's impending war with Paraguay, and the large number of nonimmune people moving throughout the country as a result of mobilization, would certainly spread yellow fever. It was largely as a result of the war that the foundation also set up a yellow fever service in Paraguay in 1932.[3]

In fact, for many years Bolivia had not been of interest to the foundation, and no representative visited the country until 1926. In 1916 an American businessman named J. C. Luitwieler had tried to interest the foundation in funding a private academic high school for prosperous Bolivians and an agricultural school for Indians. The RF never became involved in the school projects, but did take advantage of Luitwieler's overture to collect information from him on Bolivian society and on education in the country.[4] Ten years later, R. A. Lambert, an RF employee, made a site visit and produced a report on medical education.[5]

Visits to countries to determine their appropriateness for Rockefeller intervention were common in the first decades of the twentieth century. Between 1916 and 1929 the International Health Board/Division did country studies[6]—with an emphasis on the state of medical education—in sixteen Latin American nations, visiting some of them more than once. As Marcos Cueto has pointed out, for the RF the surveys served several purposes. They permitted the foundation to claim that their philanthropic programs were rational ("scientific"), because they were based on presumably in-depth knowledge of a country's culture, politics, and demographics. Also in this period the RF was changing its approach to improving health in Latin America, placing more emphasis on the education of local physicians rather than on campaigns against epidemic diseases. The surveys of medical education allowed the foundation to decide which countries had sufficient infrastructure and human capital to make worthwhile RF investments in training doctors and in improving medical and research facilities.[7]

In 1928, perhaps because of information taken from the country surveys, the foundation decided that it would discontinue, or not initiate, programs in extremely impoverished ("backward") countries because it was felt that they did not have strong enough economies to develop and maintain medical excellence.[8] Bolivia was almost certainly one of the countries eliminated in this philanthropic triage, and had it not been for the yellow fever outbreak of 1932, and the threat it posed to RF work in Brazil and other neighboring countries, the foundation might never have set up shop in the country at all. It was only in the 1940s that the RF broadened its efforts beyond yellow fever in Bolivia to include other areas of public health. Still, Bolivia never received the type of investment or numbers of scholarships for its physicians that more medically advanced countries like Mexico, Brazil, or even Colombia or Chile did.

Rockefeller Surveys Bolivia

Although Luitwieler's assessment in 1916 and the 1926 survey did not lead to an immediate commitment by the RF in Bolivia, the studies provide some information on the social and health conditions in the country in the period. More important, they tell us a good deal about the values and assumptions of the Rockefeller personnel and the type of information on which they based their interventions. They also suggest the approach the foundation would take when it did begin projects in Bolivia some years later.

Considered essential for assessing the possibility of success in a country was not just a report on health conditions, hospitals, and medical schools but also an overview of customs, political culture, and socioeconomic conditions. Thus in 1916, when Luitwieler was interviewed by a committee of RF officers, he was asked to "characterize" the population of Bolivia. He explained that the *gente decente*, descendents of the colonial Spanish ruling class, formed about

10 percent of the population and only engaged in the professions and "[would] not take any commercial positions." Cholos, who did engage in commerce, were a "mixed class of the upper and Indian class—mostly by illegitimate intercourse" and were "not as good a type as the Indian type, though that is a matter of opinion." The Indians made up about 80 percent of the population. Of the Indian, Luitwieler commented: "He is most morose, never smiles except when he is drunk."[9] Whether these observations were based on Luitwieler's own experience or on works such as Alcides Arguedas's *Pueblo Enfermo*, which was popular at the time, can be debated. In any event, these brief generalizations were considered useful for understanding national character and deciding how to proceed in the country.

Luitwieler went on to explain that only about 500 boys and girls attended high school in the country; that perhaps 15 percent of the population had access to Western medical care; that the nation's hospitals were "awful" and "entirely in the hands of the sisters of mercy," who had no training; and that there was no medical care whatsoever in the countryside.[10]

Dr. Robert Lambert went to Bolivia in 1926, and having done surveys for the foundation before, he knew how to focus in on what the RF was interested in at the time: facilities of medical schools, number of full-time faculty, faculty-student ratios, relationships between the schools and hospitals, and in general how closely the system of training doctors resembled that in the United States. He also knew how to complete his studies quickly and defended a rapid, superficial overview of a situation by saying "Hastily acquired impressions may be faulty but they are more vivid and . . . often more accurate and just than the ideas of old residents."[11] His diary of his visit to Bolivia begins with the complaint that due to transportation difficulties, he would have to stay in La Paz (and the country) five days instead of three.[12]

Lambert found little to praise about the medical school in La Paz, its personnel, or curriculum. Teaching laboratories, according to Lambert could hardly be said to exist, the library had only 500 or 600 volumes compared with 48,000 in the medical school library in Buenos Aires or 11,000 in Montevideo, and the school's budget barely covered the professors' salaries. He was somewhat more impressed by the new Hospital de Miraflores (also called the Hospital

General), where clinical teaching was done. Lambert reported that it was cleaner and better run than most of the charity hospitals in Brazil and much better than the Asunción hospital. But he noted that in the infectious disease unit, patients with various ailments were all together in the same overcrowded pavilion and that people with tuberculosis were scattered throughout the hospital. According to his report, the venereal disease wards of the hospital were full, but there were few patients in the children's and maternity wards. Like Luitwieler, Lambert was disturbed by the use of nuns in the hospital instead of professional nurses, saying that it was difficult to attract educated young women to the field because "[n]ursing in the local mind is low class work." He did mention, without comment, that of 125 medical students, 4 were women and that there were also four women among the forty students of pharmacy.[13]

Yellow Fever

Yellow fever inspired great fear because of its high mortality rate and the rapidity with which it could spread in communities, though malaria was unquestionably a more serious public health problem in Bolivia.[14] It was in part this public fear that had caused Dr. Juan Manuel Balcázar, the director of public health in 1932, to deny that there was an outbreak in the city of Santa Cruz (see chapter 2). The RF campaign against yellow fever was carefully targeted to stop a fearful disease before it became widespread, rather than to eliminate one that affected some two-thirds of the national population, as public health officials estimated malaria did. Earlier campaigns against yellow fever led by the foundation had shown that relatively limited resources, such as the RF was willing to spend in the country, could bring yellow fever under control in urban areas in a short period of time. Unlike the Bolivian government, which by one means or another had to attempt to deal with a depressingly large number of public health problems, the Rockefeller Foundation could select battles that were at least potentially winnable and in which success might bring the organization international prestige.

    The initial contract between the foundation and the Bolivian government called for each party to contribute $18,000 to cover an

Hospital General (Hospital de Miraflores), shortly after construction in 1920. Credit: Julio Cordero, Foto Cordero, La Paz, Bolivia.

A men's ward in the Hospital General with nun in attendance. Credit: Julio Cordero, Foto Cordero, La Paz, Bolivia.

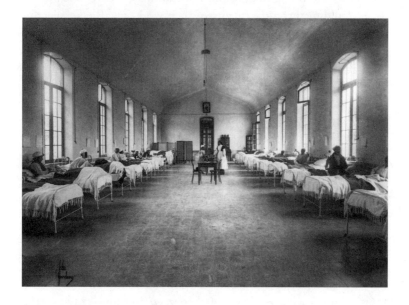

eighteen-month period. The contract was to be evaluated for re-
newal annually. While $24,000 a year might seem a modest budget,
in the Bolivian context it was substantial: the annual budget for the
Mizque antimalaria project was only bs. 13,000, or approximately
$2,600. In June 1932, just as the Chaco War was beginning, Dr. Allen
Moore Walcott—an RF representative who had run the foundation's
yellow fever program in Recife, Brazil, in the 1920s—began operations in the city of Santa Cruz. Within days of arriving in Santa Cruz,
Walcott met with local officials, found an office, and began inter-
viewing men to work as inspectors for the Servicio Fiebre Amarilla
(Yellow Fever Service). His diary does not indicate how applicants
for the inspectors' positions were located, but they had to pass exams
in reading and math as well as a vision test. Within a few days twenty
inspectors had been hired at salaries of bs. 60 a month. Two Bolivian
doctors, René Valda, who had studied at Oswaldo Cruz's Manguinhos Institute in Rio, and Angel Claros Escobar, were also hired to
work for the service. Altogether—including office staff, a porter, a
chauffeur, and five fishermen—the Rockefeller Foundation project
in the city of Santa Cruz had thirty-eight employees.[15]

Walcott arbitrarily divided the city of 20,000 people into four
zones and assigned five inspectors and a chief inspector to each. The
inspectors had broad responsibilities, and the success of the project
depended directly on the quality of their work. The Rockefeller approach to yellow fever control was antilarval: the focus was on destroying *Aedes aegypti* (also known as *Stegomyia*) larvae, which commonly bred in water containers in or near homes. Storing water in
large jars or cisterns was common in Santa Cruz because few residents had water piped into their homes. The inspectors were responsible for going door to door, identifying larvae and mosquitoes, and
either placing larva-eating fish in water tanks, covering water supplies with a thin layer of petroleum, or disposing of water containers
all together. In their house-by-house inspections, they were also supposed to take note of any people who might be ill with yellow fever
and report them to the service's doctors.[16]

By the time the RF began operations in Bolivia, medical researchers were realizing that yellow fever had a more complicated etiology than had previously been believed. Campaigns early in the
twentieth century in Cuba, Panama, and elsewhere had operated on
four assumptions: (1) only the *Aedes aegypti* mosquito could spread

the disease; (2) only humans were susceptible to it; (3) surviving the disease conferred lifelong immunity; and (4) if the *A. aegypti* were eliminated in large cities (where there would always be non-immune people), the disease would die out elsewhere as well. According to this theory, yellow fever was always introduced into small communities or the countryside from urban centers. By the late 1920s scientists were discovering that only one of these assumptions was true: surviving yellow fever did confer immunity. In fact, mosquitoes other than the *A. aegypti* could and did spread yellow fever, monkeys as well as humans were infected by the disease, and it could spread from monkeys to humans through a variety of vectors. This meant that yellow fever could be endemic in rural areas and spread to cities from there. These new understandings dampened the optimistic view that the disease could be eliminated worldwide and caused the Rockefeller Foundation to rethink its strategies for controlling it.[17]

Although in 1932, when Rockefeller began work in Bolivia, the exact nature of transmission of yellow fever in rural areas was still being debated, the foundation modified its policy of only focusing on cities and initiated control efforts in small communities as well. A doctor, a chief inspector, and an inspector were located in Villa Montes, a town of about 300 houses that was a main stopping point for troops on the way to the Chaco, and site of an army hospital. Fourteen other inspectors were assigned to communities with 300 people or more, some of which were only accessible by horse or mule. Although the RF did not take on the task of fighting yellow fever in the war zone, doctors from the service made a tour of the Pilcomayo River area, where Bolivia had forts and other areas where troops passed in large numbers or were stationed. Military doctors were supplied with instructions on the identification of mosquitoes, destruction of larvae, treatment of water containers, and diagnosis of yellow fever. Dr. Walcott commented tartly in his diary, "If after these [instructions] are out the Army doctors allow yellow fever to spread it will be their own fault."[18]

In the 1930s the Rockefeller Foundation did not encounter in Bolivia the organized resistance of the medical community it met in some other Latin American countries. This seems to have been primarily because there was no established yellow fever service in Bolivia, whose leaders might have resented Rockefeller representatives taking over control efforts. Even Dr. Juan Manuel Balcázar, who had denied the existence of the yellow fever epidemic that first brought the RF to Bolivia, seemingly welcomed them cordially; as director of public health later, he asked them to establish an anti-malaria program as well. The government apparently realized the vulnerability of its public health system and accepted any help it could get. In fact, although they were initially unsuccessful in getting Rockefeller to help establish a malaria control program, health officials frequently commented that the antilarval campaign of the foundation indirectly reduced the incidence of malaria as well: despite targeting *A. aegypti* larva, the efforts frequently killed malaria vectors too. By September of 1932 residents of Santa Cruz were commenting on the reduction in mosquitoes, and Dr. Walcott himself mentioned that he didn't need a mosquito net at night.[19] Even the fact that in September 1932 the foundation signed a contract to establish a yellow fever control program in Paraguay, with whom Bolivia was at war, did not provoke protest from the government or in the press. Nor apparently did the fact that the Yellow Fever Service got its oil free of charge from the representatives of Standard Oil of Bolivia.

This does not mean that there were no objections to the program. Many residents of Santa Cruz and other towns did whatever they could to keep the inspectors out of their homes and to prevent them from pouring fuel oil on their water supplies. Inspectors were physically assaulted fairly regularly, though a law had been passed requiring citizens' cooperation with the Yellow Fever Service.[20] Nor did the service always use diplomacy in trying to gain entry to homes where people had denied inspectors access. Dr. Walcott would tolerate no resistance and was determined to set an example for residents who might consider turning away the service's representatives. In one case, Walcott, another doctor working for the service, and two inspectors all forced their way into a woman's home. She responded by hitting Walcott with a club, slapping him in the face, and throwing a brick at him. Walcott in turn hit her in the jaw, after which she acquiesced and allowed her water containers to be oiled.[21] In another case Walcott personally oiled a water tank of a man who refused to put fish in it. The incident ended with a tussle in which both Walcott and the resident were splashed with a good deal of petroleum.[22] Eventually most people in the city chose to get fish from the service

Dr. A. M. Walcott, 1923. Courtesy of the Rockefeller Archive Center.

for their tanks, judging that fish feces were less noxious than fuel oil.[23]

While Walcott's heavy-handed approach may have alienated residents in the neighborhoods inspected, the medical community, at least in the press and its official publications, had nothing but praise for his energy and vision and gratitude for the virtual elimination of yellow fever in the city of Santa Cruz.[24] Perhaps because he was a foreigner, Walcott could take an authoritarian approach, whereas few Bolivian health workers would have dared. Certainly Dr. Angel Claros, who later became head of the service, used a lighter touch in dealing with citizens who were skeptical about RF techniques, spending lots of time convincing people of the importance of anti-larval work and trying to persuade them that giving blood for yellow fever protection tests would not harm or kill them. These blood tests were important to the RF because they indicated if people had had the disease in the past—perhaps mild cases that were not even diagnosed—and therefore provided important epidemiological information. There was the belief in some villages that drawing blood had caused children's deaths a few days later. Others held the popular conviction that blood did not reproduce itself and that losing blood was the cause of the weakness (anemia) from which most residents of the area suffered. In the face of these fears, health workers often could not get samples even by offering to pay for them.[25] Dr. Angel Claros also reported that "the indigenous, the mestizo and even the white" resisted having their deceased relatives subjected to viscerotomy puncture (removal of a piece of the liver from a corpse for histologic examination) and that municipal authorities didn't cooperate with the RF but rather allowed secret burial in unguarded cemeteries so that people could avoid the test.[26] Despite this general suspicion of many RF procedures, several years later an IHD officer reported that Andean healers often were good at performing viscerotomies, because they had the authority to convince families to permit them to take samples, and that they were paid for the tissue they obtained from each puncture.[27]

Walcott himself was not only intolerant of residents who didn't immediately accept RF procedures; his diary reveals an impatience verging on disdain for the Bolivian inspectors and even the doctors who worked for the Yellow Fever Service. While Dr. Claros remarked that the inspectors had been trained with remarkable quickness to do their jobs,[28] almost from the first days of operations in Santa Cruz Walcott was criticizing their performance. They didn't use the daily work sheet properly, didn't find foci of larvae, didn't destroy small water vessels, skipped houses they were supposed to inspect, and frequently when words seemed to fail him, Walcott just said their work was "very rotten."[29] His diary is also full of scorn for the two Bolivian doctors he had hired: they took too long out in the field, didn't turn in their diaries or set up an office file system as quickly as Walcott wanted, didn't push the inspectors hard enough, mislabeled tanks of petroleum, and so on.[30] Although there is occasional praise from Walcott for an inspector or a local physician, overall one gets the impression from his diary of a man who feels that only his constant vigilance will prevent the whole project from falling apart.

By the end of the Chaco War the Servicio Fiebre Amarilla had been successful in eliminating yellow fever from the city of Santa Cruz, where the index of *A. aegypti* became zero. It also could be credited with bringing public health workers to areas of the countryside that had never had medical care of any kind and with making rural people more conscious of yellow fever and how to combat it. However, for a variety of reasons, controlling the disease in the countryside was more problematic than in the city of Santa Cruz. Dr. Angel Claros, head of the service in 1935, had discovered cases of yellow fever in rural regions where there were no *A. aegypti* mosquitoes. He realized that he was dealing with jungle yellow fever, which he believed was spread by *Aedes scapularis*, or perhaps some other vector, from monkeys to humans. Under these conditions Claros believed, correctly as it turned out, that it would require the development of an effective vaccine to really bring the disease under control.[31] By the late 1930s, a vaccine based on a mutated, attenuated yellow fever virus was developed for just this reason.[32] Dr. Claros also pointed to a number of other problems in the small communities where the service was operating, among them, the inspectors' fear of antagonizing important local citizens by destroying their water containers or oiling their water, and the lack of support for the inspectors from those local doctors and political authorities who didn't make an effort to explain to the inhabitants why it was important to cooperate with the service.[33]

The Rockefeller Foundation and
Bolivia in the 1940s

The decade of the 1940s—from World War II to the cold war— saw vast changes in the role of the United States in the world. The struggle against fascism gave rise to a temporary, and at best tentative, alliance between the United States and the Soviet Union, as well as international rhetoric emphasizing democracy and the "brotherhood of man." With the end of World War II, the United States abandoned its strategic cooperation with the USSR and began a many-fronted effort to undermine, isolate, and destroy noncapitalist countries. Part of this worldwide plan included offering reformist alternatives to socialism, including public health and social welfare programs in other countries. In the 1940s new U.S.-government sponsored health, educational, and agricultural agencies began operating in Bolivia and other Latin American countries.[34] At the same time UNICEF (United Nations International Children's Emergency Fund) and the WHO (World Health Organization) were establishing public health programs in the area. In the 1940s the Rockefeller

Foundation was also reevaluating its roles on the home front and in the rest of the world.

Changes in RF policy during the war are evident in the review written by RF's president, Raymond W. Fosdick, in the foundation's 1942 *Annual Report*. One concrete impact the war had on RF policy was that it forced the philanthropy to suspend projects in many areas of the world that were now war zones and concentrate more of its efforts in the Western Hemisphere. There were ideological changes evident in Fosdick's review as well. He pondered the detrimental effects on democracy and free intellectual inquiry that the very struggle to protect democracy might produce, and he provided a definition of freedom that included collective human rights. He wrote of "the threat to freedom which comes from poverty and insecurity, from sickness and the slum, from social and economic conditions in which human beings cannot be free."[35] In other words, he articulated a broad definition of human rights that was in keeping with wartime democratic commitment. His understanding of the structural problems facing many of the world's people was remarkably similar to that of those Bolivian doctors who in the post-Chaco period were acknowledging the social causes of illness. Furthermore, Fosdick's analysis would seem to suggest that the foundation had adopted a more comprehensive understanding of what would be required to improve the health of people in poor countries such as Bolivia, that campaigns against specific diseases or the development of vaccines might not be enough.

In part reflecting recognition of the broader causes of illness was the trend away from focusing on only one health problem in Latin American countries. As Lewis W. Hackett, assistant director of the IHD, commented in 1941, all recent Pan-American health congresses had been against one-disease campaigns and for a generalized health service with a "polyvalent" director supported by specialists.[36] In keeping with this trend, Rockefeller increasingly understood its role to be the establishment of more general public health programs based on the countries' expressed needs; its role included training full-time professionals who would continue to run the national system when the RF left. This was to remain the foundation's fundamental approach as long as it was operating in Bolivia.

This type of help was what doctors and policy makers in Bolivia had been asking for almost since the RF arrived in the country in

1932. The financial contribution that Rockefeller made to Bolivia's public health budget, while small, was certainly one motive for seeking more help from the foundation, especially in the 1930s, when the country was dealing with the depression and the Chaco War. Yet, impoverished as the country was, money was probably not the primary reason some doctors and politicians wanted the RF to play a larger role in the country—especially since a standard feature of the agreement with Bolivia was that each year the government assumed more of the expense of running the yellow fever program while the RF contributed less. Rather, doctors involved in public health tended to see an RF contract with the government for the alleviation of various health problems as a means of cutting through the overlapping jurisdictions of the national and departmental health officials (and arguments about appropriations) and preventing the interference of deputies and other political actors who frequently tried to dictate health policy.[37] Of course the instability of the health system, the lack of full-time public health doctors, and the general poverty of the country were exactly the reasons the foundation had been reluctant for many years to take on any more responsibilities in Bolivia. Now ideological changes, new models for public health interventions, and the inability to launch or maintain major projects in Europe and other parts of the world all finally brought the RF around to the Bolivians' point of view. It is striking that the foundation decided to make a more significant commitment to Bolivia around 1940 despite the fact that, only two years before, the government had confiscated the holdings of Rockefeller's Standard Oil and no plan for compensation had as yet been worked out between the government and the company.

The year 1940 in fact marked a turning point in RF policy in a number of Latin American countries. After 1940 the philanthropy gradually turned away from the disease eradication model; it instead concentrated on education abroad for individual scientists and aid to research institutions deemed competent to carry out basic medical-scientific research.[38] However, the foundation still did not consider Bolivia to have sufficient infrastructure and trained scientists to warrant the type of investment the organization was making in Argentina, Brazil, Mexico, or even Peru. The few fellowships awarded to Bolivians were limited to fields specifically related to public health, not for training researchers.[39] In some ways the RF program in Bolivia after 1940 can be seen as a combination of the older disease control model with a more holistic approach to public health, which supported the creation of multipurpose health projects that were eventually to be run by the government.

One of the program's goals in Bolivia remained the elimination of all *Stegomyia* (*A. aegypti*) mosquitoes from Bolivian territory, which the RF wanted to be able to announce at the Pan-American Sanitary Conference in 1942. In 1941 Assistant Director Hackett made a deal with the government and with Dr. Nemesio Torres Muñoz, then the head of the Yellow Fever Service. If Torres Muñoz could rid the country of *A. aegypti* within a year, he would be transferred to La Paz and become head of a new division of endemic diseases.[40] In fact by late 1941 "Stegs" were increasingly difficult to find in Bolivia, and the new rural endemic disease service was being designed. Put into effect in 1942 it initially focused on two problems in addition to yellow fever, which continued to exist in its sylvan form though *A. aegypti* were no longer a problem. The other efforts were against malaria and hookworm. The malaria project was to include prophylactic work in the areas surrounding the city of Cochabamba; in the town of Mizque, where it had long been a scourge; in the Yungas valleys of La Paz; and in the Cinti valley in the department of Chuquisaca. With respect to hookworm (uncinariasis), the service would undertake epidemiological studies and prophylactic measures directed principally toward the installation of latrines, treating the ill, and educating the public about preventive measures.[41] The entire program began with a budget of bs. 3,000,000 (about US$60,000), with the Bolivian government contributing about three-fourths of the funds. Although the total budget increased somewhat in subsequent years, in each year the government assumed a greater percentage of the cost of the service. In addition to the sums allocated for the three programs, the contract stipulated that the Rockefeller Foundation would provide fellowships for doctors to study abroad.[42]

Dr. Torres Muñoz became the chief of the new rural endemic disease service, which was part of the Ministry of Labor, Health, and Social Welfare (Ministerio de Trabajo, Salubridad y Previsión Social). From the beginning the RF saw this new service as the potential core of a new national public health system. Assistant Director Hackett was afraid that a Bolivian doctor alone would not be able to maintain control in the face of "departmental ignorance

Dr. L. W. Hackett, 1950. Photo by Erich Hartman, 538 5th, NY 19, NY. Courtesy of the Rockefeller Archive Center.

and inertia," rivalries among doctors, the agendas of different politicians, and the fierce competition that would inevitably develop over limited money,[43] With those concerns in mind, the International Health Division regional officers decided that a representative of the RF would be the inspector general of the service and would select the other professional personnel.[44]

For the first years of the contract, in fact, the representative of the IHD in Bolivia was Dr. Hackett, whose office in Buenos Aires was responsible for Argentina, Chile, Ecuador, Paraguay, Uruguay, and Peru as well as Bolivia.[45]

Despite having a more integrated plan for public health than that of his predecessor, Allen Walcott, Hackett's understanding of Bolivia seemed hardly different than that expressed by Walcott or by Robert Lambert in his 1926 survey. In his 1941 overview of the health situation in the country, he listed what he called "demographic difficulties," including "lack of communications, Indians, enormous areas with sparse population, diversity of languages and cultures, poverty, food deficiencies, toxico-manias, VD, illiteracy." He also mentioned all the country's serious illnesses and that 90 percent of the population suffered from malnutrition. His summation of the situation was "This is a discouraging picture and yet is common to all primitive populations no longer protected by isolation from any of the diseases of human kind."[46] In addition to listing "Indians" as a demographic difficulty, Hackett also repeated many of the same racist stereotypes about the population that earlier Rockefeller observers had, finding satisfaction in attributing them to an unidentified Bolivian author. For instance: "The Indians make up 75% of the population, the Mestizos almost all the rest, the Whites a very small proportion indeed. The Indians think only of themselves, the Whites of the nation."[47] He also found it pertinent to describe to his superiors how "amusing" it was to watch three Indians trying to negotiate a revolving door in La Paz and wrote that Indians were cautious about crossing streets in the capital, which Hackett thought was "a great contrast to Albanians."[48] Hackett wasn't only scornful of backward Indians; he was also critical of the medical populism that many doctors espoused in this period. In his diary, he derisively dismissed Dr. Abelardo Ibáñez Benaventa, minister of Labor, Health, and Social Welfare, for stating in a report that "Public health cannot be fundamentally improved by drugs or hospital," but requires basic changes in living and working conditions.[49] Despite his appalling ignorance, chauvinism, and racism—and the differences in approach between Hackett and some members of Bolivia's medical corps—there were apparently no major protests against RF programs or serious objections to the philanthropy's initiatives while Hackett was the foundation's representative in Bolivia, perhaps because he was only in the country occasionally and Dr. Torres Muñoz was actually in charge.

In 1946 Dr. George Bevier was sent to Bolivia as a full-time representative. Bevier's reports and diaries reveal him to be more thoughtful and more inclined to spend some time learning about Bolivia than other RF officers who had worked there or passed through the country. By the time Bevier arrived, the work of the foundation was more extensive and the public health situation complicated by the presence of other international organizations. The Division of Rural Endemic Diseases (sponsored by the RF and headed by Torres Muñoz) had taken on typhus and yaws (in addition to yellow fever, malaria, and hookworm). Also, a general health service, the Unidad Sanitaria, had been established in the Yungas with financial support of the Society of Yungas Landowners in addition to that of the government and the RF.

In terms of international groups, the U.S. government through

Dr. George Bevier.
No date. Courtesy
of the Rockefeller
Archive Center.

the Office of Inter-American Affairs (OIAA) had created Institutes
of Inter-American Affairs in various countries. In Bolivia since 1942,
these had undertaken rural educational reform through the Servicio Cooperativo Inter-Americano de Educación (SCIDE) and health
programs through the Servicio Cooperativo Inter-Americano de
Salud Pública (SCISP). The stated mission of SCIDE was to "greatly
influence political thinking in favor of U.S. political and economic
models and the American way of life."[50] Its educational programs
had been consciously established as alternatives to radical indigenista schools, such as Warisata, which had been developed to promote literacy, political participation, and defense of community-
held lands.[51] The SCISP's ambitious programs of health centers,
health education (coordinated with SCIDE), and some sanitary engi-
neering plans clearly had the same overall goals in mind. Since
SCISP's goals were explicitly propagandistic, the organization chose
to focus on administering direct health care (vaccinations, opening clinics) that would make SCISP visible and hopefully give local
people a favorable view of U.S. medicine.[52] The Rockefeller Foundation had always avoided this type of approach, concentrating in-

stead on public health measures and research aimed at eliminating endemic illness—leaving "doctoring" to national physicians. Also operating in Bolivia in the 1940s was the Pan-American Sanitary Bureau (PASB), which was affiliated with the World Health Organization. The PASB was primarily involved in antimalaria work, and it collaborated with the RF-sponsored endemic disease service.[53] The United Nations also was collaborating with the government on health projects in the 1940s, including efforts against tuberculosis; through UNICEF, it was proposing to help the government develop children's hospitals and child welfare organizations.

Bevier of the RF managed to navigate the increasingly complicated world of international health aid in Bolivia, apparently cooperating with the other agencies in the country to bolster programs and prevent unnecessary overlap in their efforts. Interestingly, although he never said anything negative about SCISP and the Americans, both he and the IHD's director, George K. Strode, specifically agreed that it would be better for the Pan-American Sanitary Bureau (of the WHO), rather than SCISP, to take over any RF projects not directly run by the government when the foundation left the country.[54]

Of the projects undertaken besides yellow fever control, the Division of Rural Endemic Diseases (and the RF) probably had the most success with malaria. The budget for the Mizque program alone was increased to bs. 216,000 (it had been bs. 13,000 in the 1930s); beginning in 1947, DDT was used extensively there and in the nearby communities of Aiquile, Tintin, and Quiroga. Although they managed to reduce the average rate of enlarged spleens associated with the disease in these towns from 52 percent to 16 percent, by 1948, malaria control stalled at that point in the area, probably because the *Anopheles pseudopunctipennis* mosquito did not remain in sprayed homes after feeding. This meant that spraying needed to be combined with more antilarval work and possibly new drugs in order to reach near eradication.[55] Malaria was also reduced in the Yungas valleys of the department of La Paz, where the RF, the government, and the Society of Yungas Landowners all contributed to fund multipurpose health centers in the towns of Chulumani and Coroico. In the Yungas, malaria was said to be reduced enough so that residents of the highlands no longer avoided coming to the agricultural zone to work.[56] And when Torres Muñoz answered a WHO questionnaire in 1951 about health conditions in the country, he was able to say that rural areas of Tarija had also benefited from malaria control efforts, as had Guayaramerin, a town in the Beni on the Brazilian border that had previously been losing population because of the disease.[57] Ultimately, though, the type of resources necessary for an all-out campaign against malaria didn't exist in Bolivia. A full-scale effort by the Italian government to eliminate malaria in Sardinia, in which the Rockefeller Foundation participated, cost more than $US 12 million between 1946 and 1950, and at the peak of spraying and antilarval work employed more than 32,000 people.[58]

Efforts against the other diseases the Division of Rural Endemic Diseases was responsible for were less successful than the campaigns against malaria. A combined project with UNICEF to spray people and their clothes with DDT to kill lice did not prevent an epidemic of typhus in 1948, although by 1951 Torres Muñoz claimed that with spraying the disease was less likely to become epidemic.[59] With respect to hookworm, a 1943 report indicated that virtually 100 percent of children in the Amazonian basin region of Bolivia had the disease. In his 1951 overview Torres Muñoz admitted that little progress had been made against it, saying that all campaigns based primarily on education were very slow.[60]

The Rockefeller Foundation and the Political Crises of the 1940s

George Bevier's diaries give the impression that he had a good grip on the day-to-day operations of the various sections of the Division of Rural Endemic Diseases and had cooperative relationships with the Bolivian doctors who worked for the division. His reports are full of details about the number of inspectors and the amount of equipment necessary to carry out various projects. He took account of the difficulties of communication in many areas of Bolivia, figuring out, for instance, how many mules it would take to carry medical teams to remote areas. But if Bevier had a good hands-on approach and worked well with Torres Muñoz and the other doctors, he does not seem to have been very conscious of the social and political changes that were occurring in Bolivia in the volatile 1940s. This lack of awareness certainly was at least in part responsible for why the RF was caught off guard when it came under the most severe and generalized attack it ever experienced in Bolivia.

As the United States was developing its health and education programs to forestall radical alternatives and to win support (and access to crucial raw materials) during the 1940s, the Bolivian elite was trying to put its ruling coalition back together after the social upheaval of the Chaco War and the experience with military socialism of presidents Toro and Busch. Although in the 1940 elections the candidate of the ruling class, Enrique Peñaranda, became president, a return to the pre–Chaco War status quo turned out to be elusive. The organization of native Andean communities and hacienda colonos to demand land, political rights, and education; militant union organization among the nation's tin miners; and the appearance of three influential Left-of-Center political parties willing to make alliances with these groups—all guaranteed that the pre-Chaco political class was going to find it difficult to retain power. As Herbert Klein pointed out, even though Peñaranda won the presidency, the socialist José Antonio Arze managed to get 10,000 votes out of 58,000 cast in 1940.[61]

In the 1940s the alliance of traditional parties, known as the Concordancia, was challenged by the pro-Soviet Partido de la Izquierda Revolucionaria, founded by Arze and Ricardo Anaya; the Trotskyist, Partido Obrero Revolucionario, which had been formed in the 1930s by Tristan Marof and José Aguirre Gainsborg; and the populist, and initially Fascist-influenced, Movimiento Nacionalista Revolucionario (MNR) of Carlos Montenegro and Víctor Paz Estenssoro. In 1943 the MNR joined with a group of dissident army officers and overthrew President Peñaranda and put army major Gualberto Villarroel in office. Although Villarroel was eventually overthrown himself, and lynched by a mob outside the presidential palace, it was during his term in office that a National Indigenous Congress was held in La Paz. The outcome of the conference was controlled by the government, and fell far short of meeting the demands for agrarian reform raised by hacienda colonos and community members, but it nonetheless set important precedents. Its final document outlawed *pongueaje* (unpaid labor demanded of hacienda colonos) and mandated the establishment of schools on all haciendas. Native groups from many parts of the country militantly insisted that these decrees be carried out, and in 1947 there was a series of Indian uprisings against the hacienda system, often with support of radical workers' groups or of the MNR.[62] Finally in 1949 the MNR, no longer in alliance with the military, organized a civilian armed revolt that had strong support from the miners; the revolt managed to hold out against the army in several areas of the country for two months.

Not totally oblivious to the changing social and economic situation, Rockefeller representative Bevier was sensitive to the rising cost of living in the 1940s and tried to arrange raises for Rockefeller employees.[63] He also expressed a certain guarded approval of the "socialization" of basic goods and services, although he was more skeptical of "socialized" medicine.[64] Yet, he did not seem to recognize the profound discontent of large sectors of the population or how rapidly the political scene was changing. During the rebellion of 1949 Bevier was primarily concerned with spraying against malaria in areas where troops were traveling and making sure that they were vaccinated against yellow fever. After the uprising he reported in his diary what he had been told by RF staff doctors César Moscoso and Heriberto Torres: "Indian miners from Potosí did most of the damage and that these Indians were drunk most of the time" and "rebel leaders on the radio urged Indians in Quechua and Aymara to loot and rape, but didn't get much response." He concluded that now that the war was over and the menace of an MNR rebellion had been eliminated, the government should be in a strong position.[65]

Bevier's willingness to accept these facile, racist explanations—and his failure to comprehend the magnitude of the events that were unfolding—also prevented him from realizing that the volatile political climate could have repercussions for Rockefeller projects in Bolivia. Nationalism and anti-imperialism were important elements of the programs of all opposition parties; and the nationalization of Bolivia's resources, especially the tin mines, was a popular demand. Rockefeller's Standard Oil had been expropriated in 1938, but resentment against the corporation lingered, as did the belief that the Chaco War essentially had been a contest between oil companies at the cost of many Bolivian and Paraguayan lives. Perhaps, it was only a matter of time before an event would provoke nationalist attacks against the Rockefeller Foundation. The occasion turned out to be a yellow fever epidemic in 1950.

The attacks on the RF were varied, as different constituencies interpreted the situation differently and attempted to use it to their advantage. Bolivian doctors not affiliated with the foundation, or who had had some conflict with the organization, saw an outbreak of yellow fever as an opportunity to criticize an organization they believed had ignored their skills or treated them unfairly.[66] The epidemic also allowed regions of the country that felt neglected by the federal government, particularly the departments of Chuquisaca and Santa Cruz, to make a case for more funding and attention. President Mamerto Urriolagoitia and his ministers, facing bankruptcy and challenged by the MNR, hoped to deflect public criticism and to appeal to nationalist sentiment by creating panic about yellow fever and outrage at the U.S. foundation about how control of the disease was handled. Most important, opponents of the government used the epidemic, and RF involvement in the Yellow Fever Service, to discredit the conservative Republican president's administration.[67]

The issue of health and the apparent failure of the foundation to provide proper care joined land, education, and political rights as a point on which to attack President Urriolagoitia. The fact that public health was now seen as a responsibility of the nation, and that the government was perceived to be reneging on its mandate by trusting the RF to carry out such an important function, was actually a triumph for the medical community. In earlier years epidemics, such as that of 1950, were considered unavoidable. Now with greater medical weapons to fight disease (including many of the programs put in place by the RF), sectors of the public assumed they were entitled to protection against certain diseases and were outraged when it was not provided.

Yellow fever first came to the attention of the authorities in January of 1950 in an isolated triangle formed by the cities of Sucre, Santa Cruz, and Camiri, when two employees of a company working on a petroleum pipeline died of the disease and at least six others became ill. Ominously, one of those who died had been vaccinated against yellow fever.[68] In early February several people became ill in the small hamlet of San Pablo de Huacareta and several people died of what local residents believed was *colerín*, a fever induced by bad humors following anger or emotional crises. The deaths were later confirmed to be due to yellow fever. Next, also in the beginning of February, at least thirty-four cases of yellow fever and six deaths were reported in the town of Monteagudo in the department of Chuquisaca. By 11 February Dr. Doria Medina, of the Yellow Fever

Service of the Division of Rural Endemic Diseases, had vaccinated 1,500 people in Monteagudo. Then he and an assistant vaccinator, Alfredo Augsten, began to make their way from Monteagudo to Huacareta, vaccinating people along the way.[69]

By the beginning of March, 21,000 people had been vaccinated in the area between Monteagudo and Camiri and along the Río Azero and the Río Parapetí, an area where RF doctors thought the epidemic might have originated in October of 1949 but went unreported. Augsten, who had worked for the division as a viscerotomy organizer before the epidemic, left a hair-raising account in his diary of their travels through the affected area in the rainy season. In its description of the sacrifices he and Doria Medina made to fight the disease, and the gratitude of the vaccinated, his report is reminiscent of those written by doctors vaccinating against typhoid on the altiplano in the early 1900s (see chapter 1). They traveled day and night on horseback in pouring rain. Their clothes were completely destroyed, and both Augsten and Doria Medina fell ill with fever (fortunately not yellow). The workers who were with them, and who helped to carry the vaccine, at several points collapsed and refused to continue (it is unclear from Augsten's account if they were also on horseback, but it seems likely that they were walking). In most places the team was welcomed by local inhabitants, who obligingly rounded up people for vaccination. Augsten reported only three instances in which people refused vaccination. One who did was the *corregidor* (local political official) of Huacareta, who refused to send his colonos to be vaccinated, saying it was not necessary. He later repented and asked Doria Medina and Augsten to come back and vaccinate his workers and his family after some people on his property died. Everywhere Doria Medina and Augsten went, people begged them for medical attention, for yellow fever and other illnesses. They gave away all the malaria medication and other drugs they had but could not stay to treat people, because their top priority was to vaccinate as many people as possible.[70] By 3 March the situation was considered to be under control; Doria Medina, along with the provincial médico de sanidad and the local authorities, read a statement saying as much. On 4 March Torres Muñoz and Bevier prepared a statement, which was read on the radio, detailing the work of the Yellow Fever Service and saying that the team had traveled as fast and far as they could given the weather and the nature of the terrain.[71] Bevier was ready to heave a sigh of relief, but he and Torres Muñoz soon discovered they might have worse problems than the difficult campaign against the epidemic.

Early in February Bevier had commented in his diary that there was no panic in the area of the epidemic but that there was considerable panic in Sucre.[72] At the beginning of March he noted that although the outbreak seemed to be about under control, there was still agitation and alarm in the cities (which were never threatened by the disease). He attributed it, rather cavalierly, to the efforts of regional authorities to "get some attention and pry some money out of the La Paz government."[73] He also mentioned that people in the zone of the epidemic felt abandoned, because drugs and doctors had not been sent to the area to treat people. Although there was no specific treatment for yellow fever, Bevier encouraged Bolivian public health officials in Sucre to get doctors to volunteer to go door to door in the area of the epidemic to reassure people, tell them to keep patients quiet, and advise about a proper diet. According to Bevier, the response was that there were no doctors available and that yellow fever was not their responsibility.[74] This insinuation that treating patients with yellow fever was solely the responsibility of the Rockefeller Foundation (the Yellow Fever Service) should have been a warning of the attack that would begin on 18 March 1950, with an article in the La Paz newspaper *La Razón*.

The article's headline reads, "Minister of Health accuses Rockefeller Foundation of punishable neglect for not maintaining prophylaxis in the country," and the text goes on to quote the recently appointed minister of health, Félix Veintemillas, as saying that despite repeated entreaties by political authorities and health officials, the RF had arrived late to the area of the epidemic. He accused the foundation doctors of being "comfortably installed in Cochabamba" and claimed that he had had to demand that they go to the area of the epidemic. As a result of the Yellow Fever Division's inaction, Veintemillas said, he was forced to ask the PASB to send vaccine to Bolivia.[75]

Félix Veintemillas had graduated from medical school in 1913 and was a disciple of the bacteriologist Néstor Morales Villazón. He is pictured as a young man with Morales Villazón in a photograph in chapter 1. At one point Veintemillas had been director of the Instituto Nacional de Bacteriología founded by Morales. Like his mentor, Veintemillas had hoped to make a name for himself through bacteriological discoveries and became involved in several public polemics about his research on bubonic plague and bacterial dysentery.[76] He was not disposed to be conciliatory when he believed he was in the right, and the apparent failure of the Yellow Fever Service in 1950 was not an issue he was prepared to let go of. In addition to defending an increasingly unpopular government, Veintemillas — as a man who had not successfully proven his scientific originality or received the international attention he believed he deserved — may have found personal satisfaction in pointing out the failures of foreign philanthropy.

On 23 March, *La Razón* published a response to Veintemillas written by Dr. Nemesio Torres Muñoz, head of the Division of Rural Endemic Diseases. Torres Muñoz said that Veintemillas knew perfectly well that it was rains that had destroyed the roads and prevented the landing of airplanes that delayed doctors from the Yellow Fever Service in arriving, but that Veintemillas had not admitted as much in his attack. Nor, according to Torres Muñoz, did the minister mention that 21,000 vaccinations had been given in the area of the epidemic. Stressing that all the service's employees were Bolivian, Torres Muñoz defended the professional dedication of the personnel, saying "Any conscientious public servant (or even one with an average sense of responsibility) does not have to be ordered to do his job." He then went on the attack: the actual problem was that the epidemic had probably started long before January of 1950 but was only reported when it was already widespread. And if there had been any public health officials in the area, as there were supposed to be, the illness would have been discovered far earlier. Some people might conclude, he wrote, that the lack of any medical authority in the whole area was the fault of the Ministry of Health, but he understood that the smallness of the budget did not allow the ministry to hire enough personnel. Nonetheless, he pointed out that the doctors of the departmental and provincial public health services did not help out at all during the epidemic with vaccination or epidemiological studies, but instead limited their activity to sending telegrams complaining about the inaction of the Yellow Fever Service.[77]

The controversy seemed to die down a little after Torres Muñoz's letter, especially since the representative of the Pan-American Sanitary Bureau (of the WHO) personally defended the actions of the Yel-

low Fever Service in a meeting with the minister of health. However
in August in an article in *Los Tiempos*, a Cochabamba newspaper, a
former Rockefeller employee claimed that the RF was maintaining
a vast and expensive bureaucracy and spending little on materials.
Its author said the fight against rural endemic diseases in Bolivia
"run by the Rockefeller Foundation had become a source of parasit-
ism."[78] Bevier and the head of the malaria section, Dr. César Moscoso, wrote a letter defending the RF that was published in *Los Tiempos* two days later. They said that for all the endemic diseases the
division dealt with (yellow fever, malaria, typhus, yaws, hookworm,
relapsing fever), they had only 112 employees and that few of these
worked in the office: most were inspectors, vaccinators, those who
did viscerotomies, and doctors who agreed to travel constantly. They
pointed out that the "delousers" who worked in the typhus program
worked on a fixed annual schedule and only returned to their homes
once a year. Moscoso and Bevier said that the costs of material were
low but that application was expensive because all division employees worked full time. This was a dig at the Bolivian medical system,
in which public health doctors received a minimal payment from the
government, essentially a small supplement to what they earned in
private practice. Under these circumstances, public health functions
frequently were neglected. Finally Moscoso and Bevier stressed that
the objective of the RF in Bolivia was to "develop in the country a
technical organization that was exclusively national for the control
of some rural diseases."[79]

It was not long after the yellow fever crisis that the International
Health Division of the foundation began to make plans to leave
Bolivia (although some scientific research programs of the RF continued). In 1951 George Bevier made clear that its contract with the
Bolivian government, which was due to expire at the end of 1952,
would be the last. It is not entirely clear from RF records why the philanthropy chose to leave at this point. After the yellow fever crisis of
1950, bridges were mended with the government and better relations
were established with Veintemillas's successor as minister of health.
In 1951 Bevier wrote to IHD Director, A. J. Warren that "the situation in this country particularly in regard to our activities, is now
highly satisfactory."[80] Rockefeller Foundation documents suggest a
series of reasons for the IHD's departure, however. First, there were
various other international medical aid groups working in Bolivia by

the 1950s, and the RF was less sought after as successive governments attempted to see what services they could get from different organizations. Second, Bevier seems to have felt that they had largely accomplished their objects of institutionalizing their programs and having them taken over by Bolivian doctors as part of the public health system. However, the decision could also have been influenced by the growing instability in the country. Despite Bevier's comment that the situation was "highly satisfactory," he still expressed anxiety about political unrest, commenting in his diary that eventually "Moscow communists" would come to power in Bolivia and other countries in South America.[81]

Finally, the International Health Division probably left Bolivia because by the 1950s the foundation no longer considered endemic disease control the most effective way to spend its money and promote U.S. interests abroad. While heroic efforts against disease had been successful in some places, in others they had fallen far short of their objectives and actually highlighted the difficulties of the eradication model. By the 1950s the RF was more interested in training scientists, promoting American-style medical and research centers, and introducing scientific agriculture in Latin America. The foundation also ended its public health programs in Mexico in 1951.[82] Just as this philanthropy had come late to Bolivia—out of the feeling that the country was too poor to benefit from its programs until the 1930s—in the 1940s and early '50s Bolivia was also considered too backward scientifically to receive much support from RF's new programs that aimed to develop the human resources and institutions necessary to pursue basic science or modern agricultural techniques.

Conclusion

Sorting out the truth of the various accusations and counterclaims that swirled around the 1950 yellow fever epidemic is not simple. Perhaps the Division of Rural Endemic Diseases was negligent and could have prevented the outbreak by vaccinating in the area sooner. But leaving the issue of the epidemic aside, one can still find plenty of grounds for opposition to the Rockefeller Foundation by different sectors of Bolivian society. The RF had a long history of high-handedness and authoritarianism in the country, including a patronizing attitude toward Bolivian doctors and their professional abilities. The Bolivians, even without reading the RF representatives' diaries, must have been aware of this condescension. Furthermore, foundation representatives never wavered in their certainty that the U.S. system of full-time public health experts and medical school professors was essential, even in a country where this type of work was clearly not an option for most doctors. And in the highly polarized political climate of the 1950s, the RF with its association with John D. Rockefeller and Standard Oil, was certainly a symbol of U.S. imperialism.[83]

From another perspective, there were many actors in Bolivia who saw the 1950 yellow fever epidemic as an opportunity to attack the RF for their own political ends, whether the Division of Rural Endemic Diseases had handled the situation correctly or not. In an economic and political crisis, Health Minister Félix Veintemillas and the government of Mamerto Urriolagoitia were able to accomplish two objectives at once by attacking the RF: they could drape themselves in the banner of nationalism at a time when their opponents were accusing them of being tied to the oligarchy and foreign interests, and they could divert attention from the political situation by creating panic about the epidemic. Those sympathetic to the MNR or other opposition parties could use the apparent failure of the Rockefeller Foundation as an opportunity to embarrass the government because of its association with the U.S. philanthropy, while local officials believed that creating widespread alarm about the yellow fever outbreak might get them larger public health appropriations from the government. Finally, doctors shunned by the foundation, and those who had once worked for the RF but had been removed from their positions, could use the events to criticize an organization that had rejected them and to recoup some professional self-esteem.

In all fairness, the Rockefeller Foundation must be credited with helping Bolivia deal with some of its serious health problems, most significantly eliminating yellow fever in urban areas, and beginning a systematic attack on malaria. By the time the IHD left the country in 1952, it had totally reversed its original policy in Bolivia: having begun with the limited objective of controlling yellow fever, it ended up attempting to deal with almost all endemic diseases. In an attempt to assume responsibility for all the health problems the government requested that it tackle, and in its effort to develop a generalized health service, it was spread too thin. Torres Muñoz and Bevier finally admitted that they had accepted broad responsibilities without adequate funds, and that in the last years there were areas where it had only been possible to vaccinate on an emergency basis.

Changes in the attitudes of doctors and politicians toward the Rockefeller Foundation's management of endemic diseases, from embrace to rejection, were also related to evolving thinking about health care in general. The nationalism that was expressed in the form of dissatisfaction with the RF was part of a populist discourse that also maintained that health care was a right for all Bolivians, not a commodity available to those who could afford it. This more democratic rhetoric logically should have included changes in fundamental assumptions about Indians as patients and as citizens. However, in the history of the Rockefeller Foundation in Bolivia, one thing that is striking is the high degree of agreement between RF representatives and Bolivian doctors about native Bolivians. As late as 1949, doctors who worked for the foundation offered stereotypes about drunken Indians as explanations for a complex political situation, and George Bevier accepted and repeated them.

The next two chapters look more closely at the question of how growing sympathy among doctors for a more democratic political system and a more just society affected their attitudes toward Indians and women as patients and as citizens. Chapter 4 examines medical policy toward women between the 1920s and the 1940s. There were some changes in attitudes during the period, including some doctors who recognized the important roles women played in the national workforce. Yet most of the writings about women and public health focused on prostitution, venereal disease, and the need to educate women about their "natural" reproductive functions so they could raise healthy children for the nation. Chapter 5 looks at the mentally ill and the new treatments for psychiatric disease that began to be used in the 1940s. It also examines how the new populism common in doctors' writing influenced psychiatric theory and mental-health care for women and indigenous people.

4

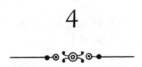

WOMEN AND PUBLIC HEALTH,

1920S–1940S

In 1996 the La Paz daily, *La Razón*, ran a story with the headline: "Abortion, a big headache for public health." The article cites estimates from several recently published studies that indicated that approximately 115 illegal abortions were performed a day in Bolivia and that of every 1,000 Bolivian women, 600 would have at least one abortion. According to official statistics, 43 percent of all maternal deaths in the country were due to botched abortions, a percentage the author indicated was probably low because of underreporting. The article also states that in the Hospital de la Mujer in La Paz, more than five women were treated each day because of complications of clandestine abortions. Doctors at the hospital said that generally these women only came to the hospital when they were in critical condition due to hemorrhages.[1] Another article published in 2000 confirms the same general picture and says that every sixty minutes, five women in Bolivia had abortions.[2]

These recent conditions are certainly not novel for Bolivia. Since the early 1900s, politicians and doctors have frequently discussed what they have considered to be the high rate of illegal abortions, generally in a broader public health context which has included other issues viewed as women's problems: infant mortality, prostitution, and venereal disease. In this chapter I examine attitudes of physicians and policy makers toward women's and children's health in the context of the social and economic realities of most women's lives between the 1920s and 1940s, focusing primarily on the city of La Paz. I argue that there were changes in thinking about women and medicine during these thirty years, with a shift after the Chaco War toward holding the state responsible for the health of all Bolivians. I also maintain that although there was a range of opinion, doctors and policy makers generally did not understand medical care for women to be the same as for men, but instead almost exclusively considered women's reproductive health and eugenic functions in the nation.

Perhaps there is no other issue that more clearly demonstrates the connection between medicine and politics than the debate about women's health, because it was at base a debate about citizenship and women's roles in the nation. Up to the 1950s women did not have full political rights, and in the 1940s even the most progressive doctors could not conceive of women as separate from their reproductive and nurturing functions. Many writers throughout the period continued to link certain problems they believed threatened the future of their country—infant mortality, abortion, prostitution, and venereal disease—to women who were not fulfilling their biological destiny and civic duty as mothers.

This question also was inseparable from ethnicity, since indigenous women were often singled out as being unhygienic and most likely to spread disease. This was sometimes linked to the fact that Indian women and cholas were often seen as deviating the most from women's motherly, domestic roles.[3] In this chapter I also argue that doctors' criticism of women, and particularly indigenous women, was a matter of biomedical authority. The attempts of physicians to regulate women's actions and hold them accountable for health problems reflect the fact that it was in areas related to women's and children's health that doctors met some of their stiffest competition or experienced their greatest failures. Midwives, both indigenous and not, were the main providers of obstetric services; throughout the period of this study, women continued to overwhelmingly prefer midwives to university-trained doctors for attention in childbirth. Also, while doctors never tired of pointing out that uneducated women were responsible for infant and child mortality, pediatrics was an underdeveloped medical specialty in Bolivia and doctors were apparently helpless to reduce the massive mortality caused by "childhood" diseases.

La Paz and Its Women

In 1928 the city of La Paz had 142,549 inhabitants.[4] The population had almost tripled since 1900, when 52,697 people were counted in the city; it would more than double again between 1928 and 1950.[5] Since infant mortality was extremely high in the first decades of the century, much of the growth between 1900 and 1928 was due to immigration to La Paz—the city became the commercial and political capital of the country after the turn of the century, when tin mining became Bolivia's most important economic activity.

The statistics given on professions in the 1928 city census provide a picture of the employment, and general economic situation, of women in the city in that year. Excluding 14,178 unemployed female children, 46,491 women (87 percent of the adult female population) were employed outside of their homes. Among these, a tiny minority held professional positions: there was one female lawyer, one doctor, two dentists, nine pharmacists, and one cartographer. The largest single occupational group (8,095) was made up of merchants, probably overwhelmingly small ones who worked in public markets. They were followed by 5,946 agriculturalists, whose large number indicates that there were still rural areas near or within the city limits. Considerable numbers of women were also employed as cooks (3,522), domestic servants (4,275), laundresses (2,150), porters (1,943), and weavers (1,355). There were 378 teachers, 40 typists, 1,051 public employees, and 91 midwives.[6]

In a society where doctors and politicians were fond of proclaim-

ing that a "woman's ultimate goal was to be an affectionate and respected mother"[7] and that it was the "woman's first responsibility
to protect the health of [her] children,"[8] women were clearly busy
doing many other things. Necessity forced most women to work, but
illiteracy or minimal education guaranteed that the vast majority of
them would be concentrated in menial, low-paying jobs. In 1928, of
the women and girls of school age or above in La Paz, 36 percent had
received no instruction.[9] In 1900 only 17 percent of the population
of the country was literate; by 1950 the literacy rate had only risen to
31 percent.[10] There was no normal school in the country until 1909,
and until the second decade of the twentieth century there were
no primary schools financed by the federal government; those that
existed were either private or the responsibility of municipalities. It
was also only in the 1910s that the first postprimary schools for girls
were opened.[11] If educational opportunities were absolutely scarce,
they were virtually nonexistent for most of the approximately 50 percent of the population that spoke Quechua, Aymara, or other native
languages: all education was in Spanish, and only a tiny minority of
the Indian population could function in that language.[12]

   According to the 1928 census, women had many pregnancies but
high infant mortality reduced family size. In 1928 in La Paz, 4,816
children were born,[13] but in that same year out of 3,330 deaths, 39
percent were children under one year of age (1,297) and 64 percent of
those who died were ten years old or less (2,143). The mortality rate
for infants one year and under was 270 per 1,000 births. Most of the
people who died in La Paz in 1928 succumbed to contagious diseases
such as whooping cough and tuberculosis, or respiratory illnesses
such as bronchitis and pneumonia, or diarrhea and intestinal infections.[14] But according to the municipal council, epidemics in 1928
had not been severe; in some years diseases such as typhoid fever or
typhus took on epidemic proportions, causing higher mortality and
morbidity.

   Something of the conditions in which most people lived can be
gleaned from the census's summary of housing in different neighborhoods. Excluding the population of rural sections of the city,
127,084 people lived in 5,724 houses. Even allowing for large extended families, this made for exceptionally crowded conditions,
especially in older and more popular sections of the city. Poorer dis-
tricts, such as Alonso de Mendoza and El Tejar, had averages of more

than 30 people per house; while recently settled areas, such as Sopo-cachi Central and Miraflores, had household averages of 9.8 and 7.1 residents respectively. Luis Isaac Landa, an ophthalmologist who concerned himself with social issues, described most La Paz urban dwellings as *conventillos* (tenements) with several internal patios. Generally, the rooms off the first, or principal, patio would be occu-pied by the members of a comparatively prosperous family, often the owners of the building. Internal patios (those farther from the street) frequently served as toilets and places to wash laundry, and each room opening on these spaces was commonly rented to a large family. In these second or third patios, or sometimes in rooms facing the street, artisans had small shops that also served as living quar-ters for their families. Women who ran small stores on the ground floors of buildings frequently had one room that was used both for business and home.[15]

Although some areas of La Paz had piped drinking water as early as 1903, in the late 1920s many less prosperous areas, far from having residential plumbing, did not even have public spigots available in the streets. While a few sections of the city had electric streetlights at the turn of the century, in the 1920s most homes were still lighted with fuel-burning lamps and with candles.

If women's lives in general were hard in the 1920s, it was also a decade that saw important changes for women and the begin-nings of organization that would become more pronounced in the 1930s and '40s. Upper-class women in Bolivia had more access to education; they began publishing the first women's magazines and forming cultural and artistic groups.[16] Also in the 1920s, the first unions of women workers were organized as part of a larger anarcho-syndicalist movement predominantly made up of artisans. By the mid-1930s there were separate organizations for cooks, flower sellers, market women, and female traveling merchants. Organized into the Federación Obrera Femenina (FOF, Federation of Female Workers), these groups raised issues related to their professions, but also made gender-based demands that later governments would be pleased to take credit for implementing, such as child care facilities for work-ing mothers. Such was the appeal of the FOF in La Paz that it was capable of rallying thousands of women to participate in demonstra-tions. More than simply raising labor union demands, the anarcho-syndicalist movement in Bolivia called for a just society without private ownership of the means of production, and it promoted human relationships that were more in keeping with equality and true democracy. Many women active in the FOF reported having more equal relationships with their male companions than other women did in the period. This was probably in part because of the conscious efforts of anarchist women and men to change patriarchal family structures, and in part because of the women's economic independence.[17]

Infant Mortality

Infant mortality was probably the number one public health problem in Bolivia in the first half of the twentieth century. It was an inevitable consequence of poverty, malnutrition, a lack of potable drinking water, thinly spread and inadequate medical facilities, and a generally low level of education. Accurate statistics for the nation as a whole are not available, because many infant deaths in the countryside went unreported, but most cities had rates similar to those of La Paz in 1928, which were cited earlier. In 1933, a year in which typhus was ravaging much of the country, Potosí had one of the highest rates in the world, with 347 infant deaths for every 1,000 births. La Paz was not far behind with 318 per 1,000, while Sucre had 248. By comparison, the rate in 1933 for Santiago de Chile was 244 per 1,000, for Rio de Janeiro 175, Mexico City 139, Paris 76, London 67, and New York 52.[18]

In the late nineteenth century and early twentieth, doctors and politicians in Europe became concerned with a decline in the number of children born and the high infant mortality rate. Particularly in France the specter of a depopulated country, and the physical and moral degeneracy of an unhealthy population, contributed to the fear that the nation would lose its political and cultural preeminence. The recognition of children as national resources, coupled with advances in bacteriology and vigorous public health programs, allowed European countries and the United States to reduce their infant mortality in this period.[19]

The infant mortality rate is often seen as the most sensitive indicator of the overall health of a population.[20] While many of the conditions in Bolivia that contributed to the situation were entirely beyond the control of the nation's doctors, the alarming incidence of infant mortality and what it meant for public health in general did not reflect well on their profession. Doctors in Bolivia were aware of some of the infrastructural causes of child death; early in the century, they had pointed to gastrointestinal infections as the main killers of children and singled out La Paz's contaminated water supply as a cause of infantile diarrhea.[21] They also knew about successful European and U.S. strategies for reducing infant mortality (promotion of breast-feeding, visiting nurses who worked with mothers and babies), but the country lacked the resources to establish programs on the scale necessary to ameliorate the situation.

In discussing the problem and proposing solutions, Bolivian experts, like their colleagues in Europe and the United States, generally saw women as both the cause and the potential cure for the high number of infant deaths.[22] Infant mortality could be linked to ethnicity, immorality, ignorance, economic hardship, selfishness, lack of government initiative, and so forth, but the solution was generally to change women so they could better perform their maternal functions. Since the overriding concern of politicians and doctors was population growth, many of those who wrote on infant mortality associated it with what they believed was Bolivia's low birth rate, combining an analysis of the causes of babies' deaths with abortion and other factors that prevented women from reproducing.

In 1920 Jaime Mendoza, a novelist and essayist as well as a physician, wrote an article about infant mortality among the working class. Having served as a company doctor in several tin-mining centers, Mendoza was most interested in the children of miners who lived in some of the highest altitudes and under the most extreme weather conditions in the country. While emphasizing the physical hardships infants and children faced in these conditions, Mendoza was more concerned about focusing on what he referred to as "the human factor" in infant and child mortality. When he talked about the human factor Mendoza did not mean the mining companies or the government that supported them; rather, he meant the children's parents: "The cholo and the chola, the indio and the india, dispossessed of any intellectual or moral culture, or at the most retaining through simple imitation certain barbarous practices of their ancestors, cannot offer their children anything except misery, unawareness, vice and filth."[23]

Mendoza stressed not only the poor diet of the female workers as affecting the quality of their milk when they breast-fed their children; he also emphasized high maternal alcohol consumption as detrimental to the mothers' health and that of their babies. Even worse off, according to Mendoza, were the children who were not nursed by their mothers, who often received impure milk or canned condensed milk as soon as they were born.[24]

At points in the article Mendoza showed a certain understanding of the horrible working conditions most women faced and how those conditions could affect their children. He wrote: "In the mines it is a daily spectacle to see women, carrying their children, walking sometimes up to four or five kilometers in the mountains to arrive at the places they work. . . . There, near the entrance to the mine, at four or five thousand meters above sea level, suffering the most extreme weather, from six in the morning until six at night, one sees the poor women — the *palliris*, the washers, the peons — working with their children on their backs or at their sides.[25]

In the next paragraph, though, Mendoza described a horrific scene of drunken mothers abandoning their hungry, ragged children "in the middle of their orgies" or falling down with them on their backs while dancing.[26]

Mendoza was an acute observer, and this type of neglect and degradation probably existed in the mining camps. How he understood its causes and the solutions he proposed to rectify them are what is significant. While he indicated that working conditions and environmental factors had a role in creating the situation, he also believed the backwardness of the Indian workers (specifically the women) made a major contribution to their children's misery. In outlining his general recommendations for ameliorating the situation, Mendoza mentioned a number of efforts that would aid working-class people, including "raising the cultural level of the worker, struggling against the universal scourges of poverty, alcoholism, prostitution, drafting laws that protect children and pregnant women, etc."[27] He stopped short of specifically attacking the exploitation of the mining companies, although he himself reported that many miners worked twenty-four-hour shifts and that mining families frequently lived in caves.[28]

More specifically, he focused on one recommendation: he called on the "good will and patriotism" of Bolivia's industrialists to set

up day care centers where mothers could leave their children while they went to work. He believed that the government could help in this effort by drafting appropriate laws and persistently pursuing the effort. In the end, he did not insist that the companies pay for these nurseries, though he pointed out that the companies would get more work out of their female employees if the centers were established. Rather, he advocated using the 1 or 2 percent of the salaries the workers already paid into a welfare fund to finance the day care centers. Then he worried that the "very people" who would "benefit [from the centers] are mostly unconscious and bestial" and therefore it would be difficult to convince them that their children would be better off under other people's care, rather than their own, which he describes as "blind and torpid."[29] Despite Mendoza's contention that workers would refuse to use child-care facilities, it was the demonstrations of organized working women ten years later that forced the government to begin to establish centers. Although Mendoza often played the role of social critic, there was a quality of noblesse oblige in many of his writings that advocated programs that would civilize the Bolivian proletarians/Indians and improve their offspring.

In 1926 the *Revista del Instituto Médico "Sucre,"* an important Bolivian medical journal, published another article on how to reduce infant mortality among the working class, by the respected Uru-

Palliris: female
mine workers
who separate ores
according to grade.
Ricardo Alarcón A.,
director, *Bolivia
en el primer
centenario de su
independencia*
(Sucre, Bolivia:
1925).

guayan pediatrician Dr. Luis Morquio.[30] There were a number of
aspects of Morquio's analysis that made it strikingly different from
Mendoza's or from those of other Bolivians who wrote on the subject. First of all, he did not say a word about race or ethnicity,
categories that Bolivians almost always included in their recommendations. Furthermore, rather than only emphasizing mothers'
responsibility for infant mortality, he also faulted doctors. He accused doctors of misdiagnosing children's illnesses and being inade-
quately trained in pediatrics. He questioned why it wasn't just as
important for a physician to correctly identify a condition in a child
as it was in an adult, and he asked: "Could it be because the death of
a child does not so clearly indicate the ineptitude of the doctor?"[31]
The fact that a child's death would not reflect as badly on a doctor as
an adult's, was, of course, a tacit acknowledgement of the frequency
of infant mortality.

Morquio contended that while instruction in pediatrics for future
doctors was improving, that the same was not the case for midwives. He pointed our that the midwife was the primary caregiver
for women before, during, and after birth and that the midwife was
the person mothers turned to for advice on their children's health.
Rather than favor the elimination of midwives, or their stricter polic-
ing by doctors, as some physicians did, Morquio advocated better
training for them. He proposed a course in obstetrics for midwives

that would include both theoretical training and practical experience in a hospital nursery.[32]

Morquio's third proposal was a more traditional one and was based on the commonly held conviction that modern women were becoming too liberated, were escaping the confines of the family, and didn't know how to take care of children. He quoted an Italian expert who said that young women were prepared for everything except " 'the life that awaits them as women and as mothers.' "[33] Nonetheless, his suggestion was an academically serious one, even if it excluded boys. He recommended that in secondary and normal schools, girls should have a course in "infant hygiene" taught by a doctor and then complement this theoretical training with a practicum in a nursery or a clinic for newborns.

The fact that the *Revista del Instituto Médico "Sucre"* published Morquio's paper, which had been given at a major medical conference in Argentina, showed that doctors in Bolivia were entertaining new approaches to infant mortality, though the country was far from being able to widely implement Morquio's proposals. Bolivian doctors also began to publish new proposals for dealing with the problem, stressing government assistance rather than private charity as the appropriate means for dealing with public health problems. This more democratic attitude, which emphasized state responsibility for personal well-being, was part of the post–Chaco War radicalization of medical professionals that caused them to reconceptualize medical care as a right, not a privilege.

This new thinking was reflected in an article published in 1933 during the Chaco War by Doctor Enrique Lara Quiróz in the *Boletín de la Dirección General de Sanidad Pública*, an official government journal. Lara's approach still stressed women's culpability for children's deaths and other health problems, but his solutions emphasized state intervention to help women be better mothers. Lara pointed out that although many people were concerned about the depopulation of the country because of the war, Bolivia's "horrifying infant mortality was an important factor that also contributed to the decline of the population."[34] He went on to mention practically all the factors that doctors generally pointed to as causing either low birth rates or early infant death. He said the problem was "partly due to people's ignorance with respect to puericulture, and at the same time to the lack of moral principles among certain elements of the population . . . who did not have any compunction about dumping the fruit of their wombs in public places."[35] He also mentioned maternal syphilis as a major cause of spontaneous abortions (miscarriages) and early death of infants, along with alcoholism, tuberculosis, cancer, and gynecological diseases. However, Lara differed from some earlier writers in his recognition of social and economic factors that prevented women from being ideal mothers, mentioning the poverty that affected large sectors of the population and the overwork of mothers who had to raise families and work outside their homes.

Except for intentional abortion, which surprisingly he did not list, Lara touched on almost all of the main public health issues that doctors saw as related to fetal and infant mortality. Although he did not mention prostitution, it is implicit among his causes because it was generally believed that prostitutes were the main propagators of venereal diseases.[36] For the purposes of his article, numerous serious illnesses or social problems were highlighted, not because they in and of themselves caused terrible suffering but because they would lead to the depopulation of the country.

Although Lara viewed reducing infant mortality as a woman's responsibility, his recommendations to ameliorate it were in keeping with the progressive, populist policies more in favor in Bolivia in the 1930s and '40s. His proposals essentially were designed to give governmental support to women so they could be better mothers. They included visiting nurses who would both educate future mothers and provide basic prenatal care; special homes for unmarried pregnant women; free public maternity clinics, including mobile units for rural areas; child and infant care facilities for working mothers; and so on. Since Lara's article was published in the bulletin of the government's public health office, his proposals can be viewed as reflecting official policy, even if Bolivia was far from having the resources to make them realities.

In 1937, Dr. Juan Manuel Balcázar, at the time a professor at the medical school in La Paz, wrote a book entitled *Protección y crianza del niño (El libro consejero de la madre)* (The Protection and Upbringing of Children: The Advice Book for Mothers). Despite the fact that the book was addressed to mothers, Balcázar admitted that his objective was also to "awaken uneasiness and interest in the state and the population in the interest of children."[37] Here, once again

was the clear articulation of women's responsibility for a major social problem. But a mother picking up the book for some practical
advice on teething, or toilet training, or perhaps common childhood diseases—in order to better do her job—would be sadly dis-
appointed. This was not a how-to book. Rather, it was a mixture
of stereotypes about Indians, self-righteous attacks on people who
wanted to shirk their social duty, and some analysis of the economic
causes of infant mortality and morbidity.

The indigenous child, wrote Balcázar, "comes into the world in
the worst filth; his mother feeds him unconsciously, like a beast,
and, very soon, abandons him to his free will, among the animals,
without any defense but his instincts."[38] Here Balcázar was expressing the opinion commonly held by the urban upper class that the
rural Indian population lived in "promiscuity." What promiscuity
generally meant was not only that whole families might live in one
or two rooms, but also that there frequently was not a clear division
between the inside and the outside of indigenous homes. Furthermore, in the countryside rooms might be used for various functions (sleeping, cooking), there were often people other than the
immediate family in the house, and family animals were not re-
stricted to barns or pens. Marcia Stephenson has argued that rural
Bolivian homes, where the boundary between interior and exterior
was fluid, were functionally well suited to a household economy in
which women's work was essential to family survival. Women could
watch their children and cook, tend family animals, spin and weave
in an environment that was both domestic and public.[39] Note that
in his description of Indian child-rearing practices, Balcázar not only
has the child living with animals but the mother herself has been
turned into a "beast."

Balcázar mentioned the various causes of infant mortality, particularly gastrointestinal infections, but directed much of his attention toward women who by one means or another avoided having
babies. He wrote of women who had illegal abortions, left their infants at the door of an orphanage, or tossed them in rivers. Dr. Lara
had also spoken with alarm of women who abandoned infants in
public places, and in fact during the 1920s and 1930s the press frequently reported that the bodies of babies had been found in the
city's rivers. Most were said to be only days old and "of the white

race." Analysis of the causes of the infanticide varied somewhat according to the editorial policy of the newspaper. On 28 March 1930 the conservative *La Razón* said that newborns were thrown in rivers by "unnatural mothers who wanted to hide the fruit of their illicit loves."[40] In 1936 the socialist daily, *La Calle*, reported that the bodies of fourteen children had been found in rivers during the year and commented: "these occurrences are the sign of the depravity to which the people have descended for multiple causes," including "the stupid respect for morality that has converted the single mother into a victim of social repudiation."[41] With respect to the most recent child discovered, the reporter for the *La Calle* article asked, "Is this child the daughter of a wretched, poor woman who killed because of hunger? Or is it a comfortable girl who, in order to hide her sin, dropped from her lap the fruit of her clandestine loves?"[42] Either way, the situation was conceived of as a woman's problem: men apparently had nothing to do with it, although *La Calle* made some effort to put infanticide in a larger context.

Juan Balcázar believed that abortions were mostly resorted to by poor women who were afraid they would lose their jobs if they had children. He also maintained that it was poverty that drove women to steal or to prostitute themselves.[43] Yet, if he seemed to have some sympathy for the indigent, he had none for wealthier women who limited the size of their families, through what he and others referred to as "artificial sterility." In the first pages of the book Balcázar criticized the lack of equality between men and women, saying women were paid less for the same work, received less education, and had their personal freedom limited.[44] Yet he proceeded to speak scathingly of women who did not want to have children because they felt they would be " 'trapped in the house' " and cut off from their friends. Balcázar bemoaned the fact that modern refinements and pleasures had "erased from the human mind the obligations that must be met," and that hard work and sobriety were things of the past. He added puritanically that now what people thought they should do was "attend nightclubs, stay up all night, sleep until advanced hours, eat and drink copiously." With this lifestyle, according to Balcázar, children were only an inconvenience to be avoided.[45] While his Nick and Nora Charles description of fun-loving, childless couples might confuse a reader who thought the book was about Bolivia,[46] his message was clear: Indian women endangered their children because of their ignorance and neglect, while more prosperous, creole women were too independent and couldn't be bothered.

A less judgmental, more populist position was advanced in 1949 by Dr. Emilio Fernández, a former director of Bolivia's public mental hospital, in an article titled "Protección a la madre y al hijo" (Protection of Mother and Child). Although still conceptualizing children's health as the mother's responsibility, Fernández rejected the idea that private charity could or should attempt to alleviate poor women's situations. Instead he maintained that the welfare of women and children was a primary obligation of the nation to its people. He proposed paid maternity leave for female workers, child care centers staffed by well-educated teachers, and economic assistance for single mothers. He also recognized and approved of social roles for women beyond motherhood, stressing women's importance in commerce and industry.[47]

It appeared that with Fernández a new, more egalitarian ideology was gaining acceptance. And it was, but for one exception: the Indian woman. While Fernández stressed the importance of being sure that social welfare legislation covered rural indigenous women, his attitude toward them and their methods of raising their children was not very different from Balcázar's or Mendoza's. Indigenous midwives were unhygienic hags who made women give birth in the "praying position," which caused hemorrhages and uterine inversions. Indian babies were covered with dirty rags and wrapped in tight girdles that made them into human "cigars." Indigenous children were destined to lives of oppression and suffering because of their mothers' backwardness.[48]

While doctors wrote about infant mortality, little was done by the local or national government to promote preventive medicine or changes in infrastructure that would cause it to decline. One of the La Paz Municipal Council's pet projects was the construction of a *posta de maternidad*, or maternity clinic, to supplement the service available at the new Hospital General, which had opened in 1920 (see photo in chapter 3). The hospital only had thirty beds in the maternity section, and it was located in an area far from what was then the center of the city. In 1923 the council acknowledged the difficulties the poor had reaching the hospital, partly because they could not afford to pay for public transportation. According to the councillors, the distance women had to travel to the hospital led to an increased number of babies born in the *vía pública*. Since at this time most women preferred to give birth at home with the assistance of a midwife and only called a doctor in emergencies, it was either women with serious medical complications or the poor, who could not afford to pay midwives, who made their way to the hospital.[49]

To help these needy women, a space in the center of La Paz was donated for the posta de maternidad, and tax funds were earmarked to pay for the construction of the building. In 1924, the city council said in an official ordinance that infant mortality was higher in La Paz than in other more populous cities, and consequently the council would assume direct responsibility for protecting the city's children. To this end they proposed that additional offices with preventive functions be included in the posta, which until then had only delivered babies. These new services included a pediatric clinic and a gynecology office that would "examine and cure honest women."[50] The stress on honesty was to distinguish this office's clients from those of the gynecology division of the Department of Health, which treated prostitutes (see the section "Prostitution and Venereal Disease"). Pediatric services were to be provided completely free of charge for all, while gynecological care would be free for the poor and offered at a reasonable rate for those deemed able to pay. The council proposed a variety of ways of publicizing the existence of these new offices: notices in daily newspapers, distribution of flyers in "neighborhoods inhabited by proletarian people," announcements at Sunday masses, and posters displayed in churches.[51]

Ultimately, though, much of the council's plan depended on coercion, directed primarily at the city's working-class women. Those who wanted to work as wet nurses, nursemaids, and servants would have to go to the gynecology office and receive certificates verifying their good health every three months. Failure to be examined and obtain the proof of good health would result in a fine for the first infraction and a bar from the profession for a subsequent one. These regulations were never put into effect on a wide scale, and efforts in the 1930s to impose similar rules on professional cooks resulted in militant protests (discussed in the section "Prostitution and Venereal Disease").

The ordinance on child health also included clauses that placed the blame for children's deaths on their parents, rather than on poverty, poor sanitation, and lack of health facilities. To force parents to seek medical attention for sick children, the council required that they present a "certificate of medical assistance" to the police in order to receive permission to bury any child under twelve years of age. If the parents could not prove that they had sought medical care for a child who had died, they could be sentenced to work for a specified period of time in a charitable institution. They would also be publicly humiliated by having their names published in the daily press.[52] The council apparently believed that the establishment of one free public pediatric clinic (with one doctor) was sufficient to meet the city's needs and that any family that did not take advantage of it warranted punishment. The regulation probably also was designed to prevent parents from taking their children to Kallawaya (Andean herbalists) or other healers, who were the doctors of choice for many people in La Paz and challenged the medical monopoly of scientific doctors (see chapter 1).

In 1924 the posta de maternidad was said to functioning well under the direction of Dr. Natalio Aramayo. It had a ward for ten patients, an examining room, and an operating room; the waiting room was said to be elegant and comfortable. The city council heard reports that it was offering invaluable service in emergency cases and that important surgery had been successfully completed at the posta. Yet it apparently did not have running water, because the lack of a water faucet in the patio of the building was said to cause many inconveniences.[53]

Despite the creation of the posta and the coercive measures put into place to get people to go there, there is no indication that infant mortality went down in the city. Deaths of children one year of age and under represented between 35 percent and 40 percent of the recorded deaths at least until 1944.[54] In 1931 even Natalio Aramayo, the doctor originally in charge of the posta, wrote an article in the *Boletín de la Dirección General de Sanidad Pública* that detailed the lack of resources available in the city for children and pregnant women. He stressed that if more women received prenatal care, doctors would be able to treat many undetected cases of syphilis, help women avoid miscarriages and premature births, and particularly aid in the prevention of eclampsia, which was said to be very common in La Paz.[55] He called for maternity leave for working women. Recognizing that most women preferred to give birth at home, he suggested the creation of a visiting midwives' service with follow-up care for mother and child. He emphasized the fact that there were currently very limited facilities for sick children. While conscious of the glaring deficiencies in Bolivia's health system, Aramayo still maintained that a major part of the problem was the mother who was ignorant of "the obligations inherent to the principal function that nature has given her."[56]

A report based on an inspection made in 1937 and published in the *Boletín del Ministerio del Trabajo, Previsión Social y Salubridad* painted an even grimmer picture than did Aramayo. However, its critical tone is evidence of greater consciousness of the types of health and welfare services the population ought to receive from the government. The report's author said inspections of the city's hospices and orphanages, as well as the Hospital General and the posta de maternidad, had demonstrated the abandonment of mothers and the "incipient and weak help" that was given to children. According to the report, the maternity section of the Hospital General still had only thirty beds for a city with a population of 200,000 people, and the posta de maternidad in its fifteen years of existence "ha[d] not given any efficient service to the unfortunate mothers who have knocked on its doors in search of relief." The *Boletín* recommended the construction of a model maternity hospital with 200 beds in the most populated part of the city.[57]

The report's author went on to say that the only center for the protection of infants in La Paz, the Asilo Carlos de Villegas, did not meet its goals, because of lack of professionally trained staff and shortage of funds. The Asilo de Huérfanos San José (orphans' asylum) was "a perfectly medieval institution that did not have the least idea of its important role in the education of preschool and school-age children." According to the author, the Patronato de Huérfanos de Guerra (Foundation for War Orphans), had because it was under state direction "a more modern organization, but still was not a model institution." The article concluded by saying that infant mortality was so high that it was fair to estimate that "the vegetative growth of the country has been nil in the last 50 years."[58]

Midwives and Abortion

In the eighteenth and nineteenth centuries in Europe and the United States, the consolidation of a largely male medical profession included making obstetrics and gynecology specialties practiced by university-trained physicians and surgeons rather than by female midwives. Part of the process of making these fields the domain of university-trained doctors included accusing midwives of endangering women's and infants' health because of lack of hygiene and knowledge of medicine; they also accused them of providing abortions, which, perhaps not coincidentally, were made illegal in many countries around 1800.[59] In fact, until relatively recently in many places in the world, midwives and perhaps other women as well did have knowledge of herbal abortifacients, which they could prescribe for their patients.[60]

In the United States (until a revival of medical midwifery in the late twentieth century) doctors had almost total success in abolishing the midwife, while in England and some European countries the approach was to bring midwives under medical supervision and increase their professional training.[61] This was also the approach taken in a number of Latin American countries, with varying degrees of success. In many Latin American countries there were often at least three types of midwives: (1) a relatively select group, often from Europe, who were presumably trained in obstetrics and were patronized by the urban elite, (2) a large group of midwives who had no biomedical training but were part of the native, African, or European folk medical traditions, and (3) a smaller number of young women who usually had no experience in the field but took advantage of programs offered by some medical schools beginning in the nineteenth century to become professional midwives. It was this last group that medical educators and some governments attempted to promote and enlarge. These women were given varying degrees of classroom and clinical training and were supposed to attend only in normal births. At the first sign of an emergency, they were supposed to bring in a doctor.

In Mexico the School of Medicine began training and certifying midwives in a special obstetrics program in the 1830s. While a reasonable number of midwives attended the school throughout the nineteenth century, many empirical midwives continued to exist; in some rural areas indigenous midwives were the primary birth attendants through out the twentieth century.[62] In Costa Rica a school of obstetrics began functioning in 1900. Open only to women between the ages of eighteen and thirty, it was apparently designed to train women who had not previously practiced midwifery. Women of relatively humble circumstances eager for professional opportunities attended the program. According to Steven Palmer's estimate, by 1927 perhaps a quarter of the births in the country were attended by midwives trained in the school.[63]

In Buenos Aires by the late nineteenth century, midwives were licensed by the state and often even ran clinics where they delivered babies and cared for women and their infants after birth. These licensed midwives had to report all their cases to the Office of Public Assistance and were often called on as expert witnesses in court cases. According to Kristin Ruggiero these urban, trained midwives were so closely connected to the government and to male doctors that they were relied on as a sort of "gyneco-police" especially in cases of suspected infanticide.[64]

In contrast to these efforts to have medically trained midwives act as adjuncts to doctors, in Salvador de Bahia in the nineteenth century, the pioneering group of doctors known as the Tropicalistas attempted to convince women that physicians themselves were more capable in obstetrics than traditional midwives. They met with quite limited success in this effort, partly because obstetrics and gynecology were weak specialties in the local medical school, and also because folk medicine, which drew on European, Native American, and African healing techniques, was generally accepted. Perhaps it was the strength and popularity of this folk medical tradition that also retarded the establishment of official schools of midwifery; most of the medically trained midwives in Brazil during the nineteenth century were French women in Rio de Janeiro.[65]

In Bolivia the assertion of preeminence by academically trained doctors came later than in other Latin American countries. Most women not only were assisted at birth by midwives but also saw them as their most trusted advisers in matters related to child care and gynecology. In Bolivia, as elsewhere, wealthier women in cities preferred to patronize educated European midwives or practitioners who had the superficial trappings of European training. In the countryside childbirth was attended by women trained in Andean healing traditions. But by the 1920s obstetrics, gynecology, and pediatrics had become more important medical specializations in Bolivia, and midwives were increasingly criticized by doctors for being responsible for puerperal infections due to their lack of knowledge of antisepsis. A few physicians argued for greater obstetrical training for the midwives, as Dr. Morquio did; there had been inconsistent programs to train midwives in the medical school since at least 1916.[66] In 1930, as part of a renewed government effort to protect infants and children, a more rigorous program in obstetrics was opened at the university in La Paz in order to give midwives "the broadest medical knowledge possible." In order to enroll in the program, women had to have at least six years of education and be able to pass an entrance exam.[67] Since many midwives certainly lacked formal education, the course was probably designed to attract students without previous experience in midwifery who might have been more inclined to accept physicians' authority. Programs in obstetrics for women did not attract many students in Bolivia: there was a small urban market for their services, and in many areas of the country Andean birth attendants were the practitioners of choice. The strong Andean medical tradition made Bolivia more like Bahia than like Costa Rica in this respect.

Nonetheless, there was an attempt to bring midwives more closely under doctors' supervision and to strictly limit their professional activities. For instance, in 1929 Dr. Adolfo Flores, general director of public health, sent out a circular to the director of the Division of Departmental Health and Public Assistance specifying the tasks midwives should be permitted to perform. These included helping in normal births, washing the child, cutting the umbilical cord, pre- and postpartum care for mothers when there were no complications. Midwives were prohibited from prescribing medications. All complications, infections, or abnormal births were the exclusive province of the medical doctor. However, at the end of the circular it was noted that in areas where there were no doctors, these prohibitions did not apply.[68] Since well into the 1940s there were many rural provinces that had no resident doctors, it appears that university-trained physicians were far from being able to provide all the obstetrical services necessary in Bolivia. In fact, women's health may have been the area in which doctors had the most difficulty triumphing over nonprofessionals, both of the European and Andean varieties.

Part of doctors' argument for limiting midwives' professional independence was that they were performing illegal abortions. In 1923 the La Paz Municipal Council discussed an instance of illegal abortion that was unusual because the woman who had had the abortion identified the person who had performed it.[69] The event became publicly known when Julia Chumacera was hospitalized for "a generalized infection of the blood" and admitted to the intern in the lazareto (communicable-disease hospital) that the midwife, Lola de Brandt (note the European-sounding name), had caused her to abort. The *Memoria* (report) of the municipal council indicated that of all the women who ended up in the hospital because of incomplete abortions, this was the only one who would name the abortionist since women who sought out abortions were also liable to criminal prosecution. In general, women who had abortions and needed medical attention afterward maintained that they had miscarried unintentionally. The fact that the same word, *aborto*, is used in Spanish for both "abortion" and "miscarriage" added ambiguity to the situation.

There was a notable lack of sympathy on the part of the councillors for the woman who almost died as a result of the abortion; they wanted her to be given an exemplary punishment along with the midwife. The case would probably never have come to light if the woman who had the abortion had been the daughter of an elite family. In this instance, however, there was good reason to believe that Julia Chumacera was a prostitute. The fact that she was hospitalized in the lazareto is the giveaway. The lazareto was where prostitutes who had venereal diseases were confined, despite the fact that while they were there they often contracted tuberculosis or other serious illnesses. Also, Chumacera was referred to in the council's records as "la *mujer* Julia Chumacera" (emphasis mine). She is not dignified by being called Señorita or Señora.

The summary of the council's deliberations stated sanctimoniously that "the municipality should ensure the growth of the population";[70] it went on to specify that midwives were only authorized to help in normal births, not difficult ones, "much less to establish offices for internal exams and treatments, because these are part of the gynecological specialty, which belongs exclusively to the medical profession."[71] Nonetheless, it seems that many midwives did have offices, advertised in city newspapers, and one council member claimed they performed "infinite abortions." He also maintained that they were even patronized by girls "of good families" who wanted to hide from their families and society the fact that they were pregnant.[72] The municipal council proposed the closing of all clinics run by midwives, and demanded the immediate prohibition of Lola de Brandt from practicing the profession; they specified that these steps were not substitutes for criminal prosecution of both Brandt and Chumacera, which they maintained should be undertaken by the proper authorities. One councillor pointed out that many of the midwives whose offices would be closed had received their professional titles from the university and asked whether the municipal council had the right to interfere with the free exercise of a licensed profession. His qualms were quickly brushed aside, and the motion passed unanimously.[73] Still, the draconian measures appear not to have had lasting effect: in 1937 midwives were still advertising their clinics in La Paz dailies.[74]

Actions against midwives clearly did not stem the tide of abortions in the city, which probably were more numerous because of official and church opposition to birth control, or what Juan Manuel Balcázar called "artificial sterility." A sampling of the records of the gynecology department of the Hospital General from 1942 to 1949 indicates that the single most common cause for admission to the department was incomplete abortion.[75] Out of 224 records sampled, 30 percent (65 women) were there due to postabortion complications. Sixty-six percent of those who were treated for incomplete abortions were between twenty and thirty years of age, and 60 percent were married. All but ten of the women who had had abortions had been pregnant before, although the records do not indicate how many children were currently alive; 85 percent of the women had had two or more pregnancies, and 60 percent had had four or more.[76] Clearly, then, most of the patients with postabortion complications were not single women trying to avoid a pregnancy outside of marriage (as assumed by the city councillors) but married women who already had children.

Since the Hospital General was the city's only public hospital at the time, the people treated there were socially heterogeneous. They probably did not include the most prosperous residents of La Paz, though, because by the 1940s they were frequenting private clinics. Of the sampling of the women in the gynecology section in the 1940s, the vast majority (77 percent) were listed as mestizas, 21 percent were white (47 women), and slightly under 2 percent were Indians. The most common professions listed for those admitted to the section were housewife (27 percent), seamstress (20 percent), cook (12.6 percent), servant (9.5 percent), merchant (8 percent), and laundress (5.5 percent). In other words, with respect to employment they were fairly representative of the female population of the city.

Many of the women in the gynecology section, regardless of the cause of the present admission, had had previous abortions. In the intake interview, all patients were asked about abortions/miscarriages and their causes. Fifty-three percent of the women said they had had at least one abortion, and 19 percent two or more. For the women who had *not* had abortions, the intake form did not simply say "none" or "0"; rather, *niega abortos* (denies abortions) was written in, suggesting that the person conducting the interview did not entirely trust the women's statements.

There was less information given about the causes of abortions or miscarriages, since induced abortion was illegal. In most instances there was simply no answer to the question. Sometimes they were recorded as spontaneous or were attributed either to physical injury (blows, a fall, overexertion, being caught in a crowd), or to emotional upset (fright, psychic trauma), but there were a few cases in which the women admitted having directly induced abortions, usually by taking laxatives. The fact that women were questioned closely on the issue implies that many miscarriages were not believed to be spontaneous.

Prostitution and Venereal Disease

Policy makers and doctors saw prostitution as a grave medical and social problem that through the spread of sexually transmitted diseases prevented Bolivia's population from growing. Furthermore, doctors, who experienced firsthand the physical and mental degeneracy caused by venereal disease, considered it one of the main obstacles to Bolivian eugenic improvement. With greater professionalization of medicine and increased government responsibility for health care, doctors were able to persuade public officials that new forms of social regulation were necessary. In the case of venereal disease, as with abortion and infant mortality, that control was specifically gendered. In this instance, one group of women—the prostitutes—were blamed for spreading disease, and other women—the madams who ran brothels—were accused of exploiting the prostitutes. The government set out to control them both. As more progressive politics became the order of the day in the 1930s and '40s, opinions changed about the reasons women became involved in sexual commerce, but authorities continued to maintain that women were responsible for the country's lack of population growth and for its ill health.

This was in contrast to postrevolutionary Mexico where, in roughly the same period, social reformers at least attempted to alter male sexual behavior and the law penalized not just prostitutes but also male procurers.[77] Also in Bolivia no effort was made by the government or women's groups to offer educational or career alternatives to women who worked as prostitutes, nor did unionized working-class women or middle-class feminists defend the rights of women involved in sexual commerce. Despite the post–Chaco War radicalization of political discourse, attitudes toward prostitution and the women who practiced it in Bolivia changed little. From the 1920s through the 1940s, government policy focused on isolating "public women" in licensed brothels and, should they fall ill, imprisoning them in the lazareto. Any official deviation from this practice was viewed as scandalous and criminal, as a much publicized 1922 case demonstrates.

In that year the surgeon general of hospitals sent an official note to the La Paz municipal council denouncing a "grave event whose repercussions for the health of our youth are enormous."[78] It seemed that two prostitutes from licensed brothels had been sent to the lazareto because they were suffering from syphilis, but shortly after their arrival the director of municipal hygiene had ordered their release, saying that they could be treated at home. The surgeon general protested that only the physician in charge of the lazareto had the authority to discharge patients, that these women had secondary syphilis—the stage considered to be the most contagious—and that they had continued to practice "their immoral commerce from the very day they left the lazareto."[79] A motion was passed by the municipal council that the director of the Office of Hygiene should be suspended from his position.

The main function of the Office of Hygiene was to police La Paz's prostitutes and to force them to have gynecological exams twice a week. Since the early 1900s the city had officially regulated prostitution and attempted to isolate women who practiced the trade in specifically registered houses. Significantly, women who worked in the official brothels were referred to as *asiladas*, indicating the authorities' desire to prevent them from being part of the general population of the city. The La Paz Reglamento de Prostitución was very similar to the statutes regulating prostitution that were established in Italy in 1860, Argentina in 1875, and in Mexico at various times in the nineteenth century.[80] The theory behind regulation was that prostitution was a necessary evil because of men's uncontrollable sexual desires, and therefore that it was best to recognize and police the commercialization of sex in order to maintain some level of hygiene and decorum.

Regulation was adopted in France, Italy, and in some places in England during the nineteenth century. In France the objective of control and the sexual attraction of apparently willing but captive women was summed up in the term used for women confined to brothels: *filles soumises*, literally submissive girls (*fille* if not preceded by *jeune* could also mean prostitute). However, in these countries where prostitution was legal and regulated, movements to abolish the regulation system also developed by the 1870s and '80s. The anti-regulationist forces were mixtures of those opposed to the exploitation and dehumanization of women (socialists, anarchists, some feminists) and others, who in addition to rejecting government controlled prostitution, were moral crusaders opposing all extramarital sex and preaching the gospel of male sexual self-control.[81] In Argentina opposition to prostitution initially focused on the so-called white slave trade that presumably brought young European women to Argentina under false pretenses and then forced them to work in brothels. It wasn't until after World War I in Argentina that a movement which included feminists, public health doctors, and socialists mounted a campaign against regulation in general.[82] In Mexico, by the 1930s, various groups including public health professionals, middle class feminists, women from the Communist Party and other radical organizations, and eugenicists were demanding the end of licensed prostitution.[83]

In La Paz some things happened later and some not all. Although the first generally recognized brothel in La Paz, the Casa de las Limeñas (because the women were supposed to be from Lima, Peru), is said to have opened in 1875, the first statute to confine prostitutes to *casas de tolerancias* was not drafted until 1906. This law remained fundamentally unchanged throughout the first half of the twentieth century; it was not until the 1930s that some doctors and policy makers began to oppose regulation. Even today prostitution in Bolivia is controlled by local ordinances that attempt to restrict it to certain geographical areas, control sexually transmitted diseases by requiring that each worker have a health identity card (*carnet de sanidad*), and permit police inspections of licensed houses and raids on unlicensed ones.[84]

The La Paz 1906 reglamento specified that brothels could not be in the middle of the city, nor on any block on which there was a church or a school. Nor could there be more than one such establishment in any given block. All windows and doors that faced the street had to be made of opaque glass so that it was not possible to see into any of the rooms. There could be no lights or signs indicating what type of business was conducted on the premises, and no alcoholic beverages could be served in the houses.[85] If the regulations attempted to make licensed houses of prostitution as joyless and sterile as possible, city council records indicate that the rules were frequently ignored. In 1923 all of the casas de tolerancia were in the same La Paz neighborhood of Chijini, and three were on the same block. The rule against selling liquor was generally flaunted. Also, rivalries among the houses caused public spectacles, guaranteeing that anyone could easily detect which buildings were brothels.[86]

Women who worked in the houses were required to have gynecological exams twice weekly, but the manner in which this was to take place changed over the years. Sometimes they were supposed to report to a special clinic run by the Office of Hygiene, while other times the doctors came to them. Generally the prostitutes themselves were required to pay for the visits, but sometimes they were free of charge, and occasionally the madams of the houses were supposed to pay. When they were told to report twice a week for checkups, there was always debate about the locale. In 1929 the gynecology dispensary was moved to the same building as the public maternity clinic, but with a separate entrance around the corner so that there would be no confusion of the prostitutes with the "poor but honest women" coming for medical attention. Before this move the gynecology office had been in the town hall, "very close to a school," where children were subject to the "pernicious influence of the constant coming and going of loose women."[87] The argument for having doctors go to the houses was that it was a way of avoiding prostitutes traveling the streets in groups on the specified days.[88] In the early part of the twentieth century women confined to brothels had to wear special, modest clothing when they left the houses. They dressed all in black with their legs and arms completely covered and wore close-fitting shawls on their heads that were not supposed to allow any hair to escape.[89] Since not even most widows went about so completely swathed, the uniform must have been as effective as a scarlet letter for identifying the women's profession.

There was occasionally some recognition by doctors and local politicians, who wanted to keep prostitutes hidden from sight as much as possible, that even women involved in commercial sex had some rights. A doctor who reported to the municipal council in 1923 on ways to prevent women from brothels from jeopardizing the morals of the public by going in groups to city clinics, still rhetorically proclaimed that "the freedom to walk through public thoroughfares should not be limited for anyone" and that even "women alienated from their social roles deserve the support and guarantees that the law accords them as people."[90]

Yet the trend in the 1920s was certainly to control and isolate women who traded sex for money. Public health officers and politicians devoted most of their efforts to fighting "clandestine" prostitutes, that is, women who were not confined in casas de tolerancia. Many agreed with Dr. Manuel Ergueta, who said in 1923 that the source of venereal disease was not the women who lived in the official brothels, who were subjected to regular exams, but the clandestine prostitutes, "who, besides being innately dirty, were stubborn about any hygienic or prophylactic prescriptions."[91] A year later, the director of the Office of Hygiene concurred that the "percentage of venereal diseases was extremely high among the clandestine element and in that element resides the true origin of venereal contamination."[92] Although medical knowledge had advanced beyond the be-

Official photo of a registered prostitute showing the garments prostitutes were supposed to wear when they went out in public. Credit: Julio Cordero, Foto Cordero, La Paz, Bolivia.

Official photo of a registered prostitute. Credit: Julio Cordero, Foto Cordero, La Paz, Bolivia.

lief that women (particularly prostitutes) were the origin of venereal disease and that men did not infect the prostitutes, in some ways these physicians seemed to be operating on this principle. There was much concern about "the best of our young men" who contracted venereal diseases and became "incapable of propagation of the species," but city councillors and public health doctors never mentioned that these same young men also gave syphilis and gonorrhea to prostitutes and rarely mentioned that the men spread it to their wives or other sexual partners.[93]

Dr. Ergueta and others claimed that most registered prostitutes were effectively cured of syphilis with compounds of arsenic (such as Salvarsan) and mercury. Since there was not any truly effective cure for the disease until the 1940s, when penicillin began to be widely used, his conviction that the registered prostitutes who received treatment were less contagious than clandestine ones was probably more related to issues of control than health. The police frequently conducted roundups of *clandestinas* and made them officially register themselves as prostitutes with the Office of Hygiene, where they were supposed to report for regular checkups. Ergueta admitted that of ninety-one women registered with the Office of Hygiene, and who were supposed to come for gynecological checkups, only twenty-two were from the regulated houses while twenty-six clandestinas reported regularly.[94] Since there were far more than twenty-two prostitutes in the official brothels, even if the treatment the registered women received was effective, they could hardly have been less likely to have venereal diseases than the women who were not isolated in the houses in Chijini.

Women were resistant to being registered in the Office of Hygiene. In addition to enduring the humiliation of the physical exams, the women knew that even if they stopped working as a prostitutes they could never get their names and photographs removed from the list of registered sex workers, but could only get permission to dispense with the obligatory visits to the clinic.[95] In this respect La Paz's law was far more draconian than those in other countries, which at least allowed some possibility for redemption for "fallen" women and permitted them to remove their names from the registry. In fact, registered women who wanted to escape the control of the authorities generally were forced to leave town in order to live under different names elsewhere.[96]

Prostitutes unfortunate enough to require hospitalization for venereal disease commonly ended up in the lazareto. In 1924 the director of the Oficina de Higiene reported that those sent there generally did not receive adequate treatment and furthermore were exposed to all types of serious contagious diseases such as measles, smallpox, and tuberculosis. What usually happened, according to him, was that the women were either released before they were completely well or they stayed indefinitely, becoming victims of chronic diseases, particularly tuberculosis.[97] Although there were periodic efforts in the 1920s and '30s to find new places to hospitalize prostitutes with venereal diseases, there was no similar concern in isolating men who had syphilis or gonorrhea, who were simply assigned beds in regular hospital wards.[98] This approach was in keeping with the outmoded belief that women, particularly prostitutes, were the carriers of venereal diseases and men the victims, who were not going to infect anyone else. It also reflected the assumption that women (especially working-class women) who worked as prostitutes were deviant and needed to be locked up, while the men who patronized them were normal.

The security issue loomed large for public health officials as they tried to relocate hospitalized prostitutes. Without guards to police them, women simply walked out of the lazareto; on one occasion a group of prostitutes in a special section of the lazareto broke down the doors of their ward during the night and fled.[99] In 1931, Councilman Waldo Belmonte Pool proposed that an annex of the Panóptico Nacional (federal prison) be converted into a special infirmary for prostitutes.[100] This was reminiscent of the nineteenth-century French hospital-prison model: in Paris prostitutes were treated in special wards in the Saint-Lazare Prison.[101] The common linguistic root of Saint-Lazare and lazareto symbolically associated these institutions both with repulsive disease (specifically leprosy) and begging, emphasizing the abject, contaminated condition of the women sent to them.

By the late 1920s and early 1930s, it became apparent that the city government was losing the battle to confine prostitution to officially regulated brothels. The 1929 *Memoria* of the municipal council maintained that the growth of the city's population and "the arrival of new elements" had contributed to the increase in the number of illegal places of prostitution. These were said to be in all the neighborhoods of the city, and prostitutes of all classes and social conditions were said to be "legion."[102] If they were of all classes and conditions, the councillors seemed particularly concerned about unregistered prostitutes in working-class neighborhoods; they associated such prostitutes with disorder and danger. They focused particularly on *chicherías*, taverns where the fermented corn beverage *chicha* was sold and that were the scene of lower-class entertainment with Andean popular music and dancing. These establishments were usually run by cholas and were particularly vexing to the city fathers because the cholas escaped their control. In 1930 a group of newspaper reporters took a nighttime tour of La Paz chicherías with the inspector of police and one of the municipal councilors. The journalist from *La Razón* reported visiting numerous places on the edge of the city (Calle Maximiliano Paredes, Calle Tumusla, Avenida Ernest, Avenida 14 de Septiembre), where, he said, chicha was served with total neglect for hygiene and couples danced to the music of pianolas. The nightspots were said to attract numerous women of ill-repute who lived in "inconceivable promiscuity."[103] A report in the 1931 *Memoria* of the city council referred to chicherías as the origin of "moral and physical perversion of the low people." There people were said to get drunk and "satisfy their biological necessities in the worst moral and physical conditions" and to contract venereal diseases.[104] Chicherías were also said to be frequented by domestic servants on their days off, and upper-class employers believed that as a result their maids brought contagious diseases into their homes.[105]

The city council's concern about lower-class prostitution coincided with an upsurge in working-class organization in La Paz. Improved communications, the consolidation of the tin-mining industry, and the availability of work in the nitrate fields on the Chilean coast contributed to greater mobility of the population (the arrival of "new elements" that the city councillors had referred to) and encouraged the formation of unions and other working-class associations. With the economic crisis of 1929 labor militancy increased as Bolivia's export economy virtually collapsed, causing the recently unemployed to be more open to socialist and anarchist appeals. Among the unions formed in the late 1920s and early 1930s were those of female cooks and market venders that were incorporated in the anarchist Federación Obrera Femenina.[106] By the mid-1930s, with the popular repudiation of the political elite as a result of the Chaco War, radical parties began to collaborate with labor unions and with peasants who were organizing to reclaim usurped lands. The struggle against clandestine prostitutes and efforts to close chicherías must be seen as part of the effort by the oligarchy to re-establish control over groups that the governing class increasingly perceived as dangerous and subversive. In February 1930 the police ordered the closing of chicherías in working-class neighborhoods that the city council maintained had become scenes of binges and scandal. However, authorities reassured "gente de tono" (people of social standing), who frequented better establishments where chicha was served, that they would not be affected by the ordinance.[107]

Yet, at the same time that the La Paz city government was try-ing to contain or recontain commercial sex in licensed brothels, some doctors, influenced by the democratic politics of the period, began to acknowledge that women working in so-called casas de tolerancia were being denied basic freedoms and civil rights. They also hoped to find more effective means (than regulated prostitu-tion) for limiting the spread of venereal disease. In 1929 Dr. Isidoro Aramayo, the director of the Office of Hygiene, Health, and So-cial Security (Oficina de Higiene, Salubridad y Previsión Social), made one of the first public criticisms of the system of government-controlled brothels that referred to the welfare of the women who worked in them. He said that while clandestine prostitution was a danger, so were the casas de tolerancia because in them women were forced by the owners to drink with the clients, and alcoholism among the prostitutes was common. Also, in a rather neat exonera-tion of men who devised the regulation system and frequented the brothels, Dr. Aramayo blamed the madams who ran the brothels for turning the prostitutes into "true slave[s]." Next he went on to dis-cuss a project presented to the municipal council by the Dirección General de Sanidad Pública that would have eliminated all sanitary and police control over prostitutes, proposing instead the multipli-cation of antivenereal clinics that would provide treatment free of charge. The project was founded on "scientific opinion and humani-tarian sentiments" because the periodic gynecological exams and the limits on individual freedom that regulation entailed were now con-sidered "an attack on human dignity." The project went on to say that deregulation had been tried in various European and American countries and that its efficacy was being discussed.[108]

Aramayo concluded, however, that this type of approach would not work in Bolivia because of "the special characteristics of our people, their absolute ignorance of hygiene and prophylaxis, their low cultural level and their neglect of anything concerning health."[109] Instead of proposing decriminalization, Aramayo went back to the old system augmented by free nighttime service at the present gynecology dispensary, home visits for microscopic exams and Wassermann tests (for syphilis), and most significantly special hospital rooms for paying patients (high-class prostitutes) where "along with the most careful medical attention and all the modern comforts, the precepts of hygiene would be a reality."[110]

In 1933 Juan Manuel Balcázar, then secretary-general of the Dirección General de Sanidad Pública, again proposed the elimination of regulated prostitution, saying that the greatest cause of venereal disease was not clandestine prostitutes but lack of free medication and laws that made treatment obligatory. He maintained that it was necessary to create dispensaries in cities that did not have them and to acquire large quantities of antivenereal drugs that could be distributed free of charge. The government should outlaw legal prostitution but replace it with compulsory treatment. "The government should not go on promoting prostitution using the pretext that by doing so it was guaranteeing the health of those who frequented the so-called 'casas de tolerancia'." He pointed out that as early as 1923 a presidential decree had ordered the closing of all official brothels, but the decree had never been put into effect.[111]

Although by the 1930s physicians were turning against regulated prostitution, primarily because it did not appear to be the most effective means of fighting venereal disease, there did not develop in Bolivia a movement opposed to licensed brothels on either eugenic or feminist grounds as happened in this period in Mexico. Nor did working-class organizations rally against the system as they did in England, where police roundups were seen as attacks on honest working-class women and as affronts to civil liberties.[112] In La Paz although female working-class activists of the Federación Obrera Femenina often eschewed marriage as a bourgeois institution that could operate to the detriment of working women, they did not see regulated prostitution as limiting women's rights or as an insult to their dignity. In fact, far from expressing solidarity with prostitutes as members of the working class, the anarcho-syndicalist women fought a 1935 law that required cooks to get official health cards specifically because they would be issued by the Oficina de Higiene, which also was responsible for prostitutes' checkups. In the newspaper *La Calle* the organized women maintained: "This place (la Oficina de Higiene) is for women who don't work with their hands and that fact is an attack on the honesty of proletarian women."[113]

If radical unionized women did not support prostitutes as sister workers, other women of the popular sectors were not likely to do so either. In fact many mestizas and cholas were busy vigorously defending their respectability and particularly denying accusations that they traded sex for money. Women in La Paz frequently went to court to defend their honor against various creative insults that they claimed damaged their reputations. They took legal action to refute accusations such as being *peseteras* (the cheapest kind of prostitute), "living in the Calle Bueno" (a center of prostitution), and "being rotten and escaping from the lazareto."[114] Laura Gotkowitz, who has extensively studied insult and slander court cases in late nineteenth- and early twentieth-century Cochabamba, hypothesizes that the courts were a forum where upwardly mobile women not only defended their reputations but also asserted their rights at a time when women were not legally full citizens.[115] Looked at one way, this insistence on personal morality can be understood as an effort to prove the rectitude necessary for citizenship; from another standpoint, the vigorous, legal defense of society's values could also prevent solidarity among working-class people in general and women in particular.

Preventing solidarity and making women abjectly dependent on the state seemed also to be the main objectives of one of the only government efforts to provide housing and help for single women so that they wouldn't fall into prostitution. As late as 1941, with all the populist rhetoric about helping women and children, the public residence for single women in La Paz was still run like a prison. Dormitorio Popular No. 2, "Pabellón General Quintanilla," required that any woman applying for accommodations be totally without financial resources, be absolutely alone, be more than sixteen years old, and have a certificate of good conduct and morality. There were

numerous rules about everything, from what kind of reading matter the residents could introduce into the *dormitorio* to the procedure for arranging to have a visit from a relative. The women were
not allowed to "commit acts contrary to good morals or conduct"
or "criticize or protest against functionaries in the hierarchy [of the
establishment]." Rules and schedules were strictly enforced. For instance, any resident under fifty years of age who did not take a bath
twice a week would be denied breakfast for eight days for the first
infraction and would be expelled from the dormitorio if she was a
recidivist.[116] It is not explained why women over fifty were exempt
from this rule; perhaps they were considered too old to bathe. The
Patronato Nacional de Menores and Huérfanos de Guerra, which
ran the dormitorio, attempted to help the women find work that was
"suitable for their aptitudes." Some women were said to have saved
some money and to have rented modest accommodations "where
they lived honest and moral lives."[117]

Single women who did not live with family members were considered more in need of supervision and discipline than were unmarried mothers; social policy was more kindly disposed toward the
latter by the late 1930s and 1940s. A single mother, after all, had
"fallen" and paid the price and would presumably be redeemed by
motherhood. Furthermore, motherhood placed a series of restric-
tions on a woman's activities that meant she probably would not be
able to enjoy herself too much in the future. Also, although official
publications don't say so, when government officials talked about
poor young women they generally meant daughters of Indian peasant families who had immigrated to the city and formed part of the
growing cholo-mestizo population of La Paz. Even though life was
certainly hard for any single woman who was alone, and many cholas
and mestizas were at pains to publicly establish their respectability,
the *paceño* elite was fixated on the idea of the chola as libidinous and
rebellious. Remember that the chichería, usually run by a chola, was
seen as a particularly dangerous site of lower-class entertainment.

Both Marcia Stephenson and Lesley Gill have written about
present-day, upper-class perceptions of the urban chola, who is considered a threat because of her apparent economic and personal independence. Even the chola's distinctive style of dress—full layered
skirt (pollera), elaborate shawl, and men's hat perched jauntily on
the top of the head—has been interpreted as an affront because it so

directly rejects the hegemonic values of the elite with respect to what is fashionable and desirable.[118] Their not having the slim body silhouette approved for creole women, and the fact that they frequently work as cooks or selling fruits and vegetables in public markets, have both contributed to the idea that cholas are gluttonous (rejecting prescribed female abstemiousness), and by extension sexually insatiable as well.[119] These images of the present, but likely carried over from the past, probably have more to do with upper-class repression and fantasy than they do with the reality of working women's lives. Yet, even if only a minority of cholas joined radical, anarchist unions that actually challenged the elite's economic position, there is enough history of chola economic and personal independence, to fuel upper-class anxieties and give impetus to various ordinances that attempted to control the lives of single women.

Conclusion

There were some undeniable changes in attitudes toward women's and children's health in Bolivia between the 1920s and the 1940s. By the 1940s more doctors and government officials realized that many women had to work outside the home; some authors, like Dr. Emilio Fernández, even applauded these contributions. Furthermore, it was generally accepted in policy circles that the well-being of citizens was too important to the nation to be left in the hands of charitable institutions and rather should be the responsibility of the government. Yet, these new approaches were far from a thoroughgoing overhaul of accepted gender ideologies. Women still did not have full political rights, and the ideal female "citizen" remained the self-sacrificing mother. Women who for one reason or another did not measure up to this ideal were still seen as the cause of population decline: they either neglected their children, aborted unwanted fetuses, or as prostitutes spread diseases that caused infertility and infant mortality. In revolutionary Mexico attempts at reforming men's behavior and encouraging more openness about sexuality may have fallen short of their objectives, yet these modest efforts at changing gender relations would have been radical in Bolivia in this period. Even arguments for eliminating state-regulated prostitution in Bolivia primarily focused on the exploitation of female prostitutes by female brothel managers; they did not mention men as pimps or customers. Nor was there any institution in Bolivia such as the Mexican *Escuela Correccional*, which, however imperfectly, attempted to reform young prostitutes. Although it deprived young women of their freedom and limited family rights in the conviction that reformers could better shape miscreants' lives, the Escuela Correccional at least considered education, cultural activities, and a sense of community important parts of the reform effort.[120] For Bolivian prostitutes there were only the casa de tolerancia and the lazareto. For those poor, single women who the city government thought might slip into prostitution, the prisonlike Dormitorio Popular No. 2 was available.

What is evident in the medical discourse on gender of the late 1930s and '40s is that class analysis was increasingly accepted as a means of understanding women's positions in Bolivian society. Although women were still expected to be exemplary mothers for the good of the nation, there was more recognition that many were also wage earners and were exploited as such. However, none of the writers on health in this period spoke out against the ethnic discrimination that women faced. Far from denouncing racism as preventing native women from receiving good care, experts attributed to "Indianness" many of the health problems that plagued Bolivian infants, and blamed the libertine chola for perpetuating vice and spreading venereal disease. If women in general were still seen as the cause of infant mortality and of lack of population growth, at least for some working women there was now recognition of extenuating circumstances. In the case of Indian women, their very ethnicity caused them to be seen as more liable to be unhealthy and likely to fail to provide appropriately for their children.

Consciously or not, this attack by doctors on Andean women may have been linked to their ongoing efforts to establish their medical superiority. Doctors blamed Indian women for their children's deaths, yet the doctors themselves were far from able to save children's lives from the infectious diseases that decimated the population every year. In addition to pediatrics it was in obstetrics, a field dominated by women and in most of the country by Indian women, that doctors were having the most difficulties asserting their medical superiority. Ironically, it was by maintaining that health care was a right that should be guaranteed by the government that doctors

managed to consolidate their position vis-à-vis other medical practitioners, yet that progressive stance also gave them the opportunity to
demand new forms of social regulation. For instance, doctors used
their new influence in the 1930s and '40s to have the government
prohibit Kallawaya herbalists from practicing in some places. In the
case of women's health, the sphere where doctors arguably were still
the most challenged by various empirics, consolidating professional
control was not just about the practice of medicine but included the
control of women more generally.

5

---•◦ ⋟◉⋞ ◦•---

MENTAL ILLNESS AND DEMOCRACY

The Manicomio Pacheco, 1935–1950

In 1948 an advertisement appeared on the last page of the published proceedings of a major national medical conference that had been held the previous year.[1] It was for the Manicomio Nacional "Pacheco," Bolivia's only true mental hospital, which was located in the city of Sucre. It said the manicomio offered the latest in treatment for psychiatric disorders: Cardiazol, electroconvulsive therapy, even psychoanalysis. The ad proclaimed that "mental diseases are curable. As perfectly curable as any other illness that is *opportunely* treated." It went on to stress that all mental or nervous conditions should be treated by specialists and urged the readers to eschew charlatans, whether they were Bolivians or foreigners. It also announced that the Manicomio Pacheco had special accommodations for male and female patients who could afford to pay for treatment.

Six years earlier Dr. Miguel Levy, the chief health officer for the

Department of Chuquisaca, in which the city of Sucre is located, published an article entitled "La declinación mental del indio" in a respected national medical journal.[2] Levy combined Social Darwinist conceptions about the survival of the fittest and Lamarckian ideas on the inheritance of acquired characteristics with Freudian notions of emotional development, to attempt to prove that Bolivia's Indian population was mentally deficient and that it was "a utopia to [think that] the present Indian or his next descendent [could be] a citizen in the strict sense of the word."[3] According to the article, both intellectual inactivity and the small brain size of Bolivian Indians contributed to their primarily vegetative existence. A stunted emotional development resulted in a simplification of all psychic functions: The Indian maintained a childish egotism throughout life and was incapable of real love or any complex emotions. An absence of imagination and of intellectual curiosity, minimal memory, a short attention span, and the paucity of words in the Aymara, Quechua, and Guarani languages—these factors made the native Bolivian in general unsuited for education. However, according to Levy, when an Indian did achieve some minimal schooling he became a tyrant, abusing and victimizing other illiterate Indians.[4]

There are several important things about the advertisement and Miguel Levy's treatise that make them representative of 1940s Bolivia. It is significant that the ad was placed in a medical publication that would primarily be read by doctors. Clearly it was a statement by psychiatrists and the authorities at the Manicomio Pacheco of their professional expertise and a call for their colleagues in other specialties to defer to them in matters of mental health. In fact it was in the 1940s that doctors who attended the mentally ill in Bolivia began to feel that rather than simply confining patients, they could affect considerable improvement in some people's conditions by using new types of treatment. During the 1940s more patients were admitted to the hospital than in any other decade between 1884, when the hospital was founded, and 1960. Perhaps this was because of greater consciousness of mental illness on the part of doctors and other health officials, and somewhat more confidence in the curability of mental diseases on the part of the public. It was probably also due to the fact that by the 1940s there was better transportation from various parts of the republic to the hospital than had existed earlier.[5]

The advertisement also was a defense of the facilities of the state-run hospital at a time when the first private sanatoria in Bolivia were beginning to treat some people with mental disorders. The manicomio's new special pavilions for those who could afford to pay were intended to attract wealthier families who might have had qualms about sending their relatives to an institution that was in a chronic state of indigence. In fact, before the 1940s (when special quarters for paying patients, or *pensionados*, were introduced) reports by hospital directors consistently detailed horrendous conditions in the manicomio due to lack of funds.[6] The hospital's administration may have hoped to use pensionados fees to subsidize improvements in the manicomio, improvements that would eventually serve to enhance the prestige of mental health professionals and psychiatry in general.

Miguel Levy's treatise, was representative of the era in a different respect because it was an extreme, but not atypical, reaction by a doctor concerned with mental health against a new democratic political discourse that was developing in Bolivia in 1940s that rejected discrimination and inequality. Particularly concerned to refute those who favored education as a right for all Bolivians, Levy specifically took exception to the writings of José Antonio Arze, a sociologist who proposed the recuperation of stolen lands, the end of forced labor, and educational opportunities as the best ways of helping Indians to realize their potential.[7]

This chapter examines mental illness in Bolivia in the 1940s by studying the records of the country's only public mental hospital, the Manicomio Pacheco, and the writings of physicians on psychiatry and related social issues. It asks how thinking about mental health changed as a result of new treatments for psychiatric disease that became available in the 1940s, and as a result of the new democratic and populist politics of the period. It also examines how the new possibilities for treating the mentally ill affected medical professionalization; psychiatry, because of its very limited success rate, was for a long time the stepchild of biomedicine. Most important, it studies the impact that class, gender, and ethnicity had on diagnosis and treatment. In so doing it reveals that the contradictions evident in the elite's views about the correct social roles of Indians and women also influenced doctors' analysis of the causes of mental alienation.

The essential irony of the elite's position on ethnicity was that Indians were exhorted to abandon backward customs and become civilized, while at the same time ruling groups used various means to prevent their access to fundamental cornerstones of liberal "civilization": political rights, education, land ownership, access to markets. A similar approach was taken toward women: their ignorance was believed to be the cause of infant mortality and the lack of population growth, yet they were often criticized for being overeducated, ignoring their duties as mothers, and trying to assume the rights of full citizens. This tortured thinking is seen with especial clarity in doctors' conceptions of emotional stability and intellectual ability. On the one hand, women and Indians were considered "different" and inferior in their psychological makeup, and that difference from non-Indian men could be the basis for their being considered mentally ill. On the other hand, their behavior could also be labeled as aberrant if it was not sufficiently "other," that is, if emotionally and intellectually they were too much like the normative creole male.[8] Strikingly, this type of thinking persisted despite the increasing appeal of democratic and socialist ideas in the 1940s.

The political radicalization that occurred in the late 1930s and the 1940s has been discussed in some detail in previous chapters. The changing political climate also brought new initiatives in public health. For one thing, the government finally recognized the importance of health by giving it ministerial status. In 1936 health was linked to labor and social welfare in the Ministerio de Trabajo, Previsión Social y Salubridad, whose very name indicates a social commitment by the government that was lacking when Sanidad Pública was simply a section of the Ministry of Government. Then in 1938 a separate Ministerio de Higiene y Salubridad was created. The populist-socialist politics that was gaining acceptance was also often evident in the discourse of medical professionals during these years. But as a sector of the population, including doctors, moved to the Left, the country also became more politically polarized. Contesting Marxist-inspired analyses were others that suggested alternatives to socialized medicine based on private initiative; that favored various eugenicist solutions, including sterilization of the criminal and the demented; or that argued the innate inferiority of Indians as Miguel Levy did.[9]

The Manicomio Pacheco, circa 1897. Credit: Francisco Argandoña, ed. *Sucre, Capital de Bolivia, 1897* (Paris: Phototypie Riché et Co., 1897).

The Manicomio Pacheco, an Overview

Bolivia's first and only mental asylum was founded in 1884 on the initiative of Gregorio Pacheco, a leading silver industrialist who was president of Bolivia from 1884 to 1888. By the 1910s the building endowed by Pacheco was too small to accommodate the increased number of patients in the manicomio, but it wasn't until 1926 that a new hospital was opened alongside the original one. This new building became the *manicomio de varones* (men's hospital), while the hospital constructed in 1884 became the *manicomio de mujeres* (women's asylum).[10]

Psychiatry was certainly the most slow-to-progress medical specialty in the country. Although chairs in psychiatry were established in the medical schools in Sucre and La Paz in 1890s, through the first half of the twentieth century the professorships were held by doctors who specialized in other fields and there were no physicians specifically trained in psychiatry to staff the Manicomio Pacheco.[11] Nicolás

Ortiz, who was director of the hospital from 1884 to 1923, was a gynecologist and may have accepted the position as director because he was the son-in-law of Gregorio Pacheco. Jaime Mendoza, director from 1923 to 1926, was actually a general practitioner who had specialized in obstetrics and been a professor of pathology and pediatrics before coming to the manicomio. Miguel Levy, whose article on Indian mental capacity was discussed in the preceding section, was an internist who primarily worked in public health. Alberto Martínez, head of the men's section of the hospital from 1944 to 1970, was the first director with a specialization in psychiatry, completed in Argentina between 1942 and 1944.[12] Several other doctors joined the ranks of trained psychiatrists in the 1940s and 1950s, the most notable of whom was José María Alvarado, who wrote on mental health issues. However, just how poorly developed the field was can be gauged by much more recent statistics on psychiatrists and mental health professionals in the country. A 1989 report prepared by the Sociedad Boliviana de Salud Pública stated that there were only twenty-seven psychiatrists practicing in the country's cities in that year.[13] According to the World Health Organization, in 2001 there were fewer than one psychiatrist, 6.43 psychologists, and 0.16 psychiatric nurses for every 100,000 people in the country.[14]

While hospital statistics are not entirely reliable, it seems clear that there were never enormous numbers of patients in the manicomio. Alfredo Caballero, who has studied the institution, estimates that between 1884 and 1984 perhaps 20,000 people passed through the hospital.[15] That figure may be high: Emilio Fernández, who was director of the men's section of the manicomio from 1937 to 1943, calculated that between its founding and 1943 there had been a total of 1,609 patients in the hospital.[16] In 1942, according to Fernández, there were 124 men and 114 women in the hospital.[17] In the first years of the institution, the vast majority of patients were simply diagnosed as "incurable" and their only treatment was "indefinite confinement."[18] By the 1940s, however, virtually the same diagnostic terms were used in the records of the Manicomio Pacheco as appeared in statistics on psychiatric patients in the United States or in western European countries. Nevertheless, an examination of the most commonly diagnosed conditions in Bolivia demonstrates some key differences. For instance, while in both the United States and Bolivia the most common reason for admission to mental hospitals was schizophrenia, the second most frequent cause for admission in Bolivia was epilepsy.[19] Yet, by the 1930s epilepsy was no longer considered a mental disease in either country, a fact that the hospital's director, Julio C. Fortún, commented on in 1930 when he wrote to the president of the municipal council of the city of Sucre requesting that the city not send epileptics who did not have symptoms of mental illness to the hospital, because they could more appropriately be treated elsewhere.[20] On the other hand, manic depression, the second most common reason for admissions to mental hospitals in the United States, was quite rare in the statistics of the Manicomio Pacheco,[21] while in Bolivia a small but significant number of patients were hospitalized because of psychosis related to untreated malaria.[22] Thus, a large number of people were in the manicomio for conditions essentially related to poverty: lack of other treatment options for those with seizure disorders and inadequate public health measures against malaria.

The patient population of both the men's and women's sections of the hospital was quite young. The largest group of the men in the manicomio in 1937 and in 1941 was that between the ages of 21 and 30, and two-thirds of the patients were 40 or under. Among 454 women admitted in the 1940s for whom ages are available the largest ten-year cohort (105) was between 21 and 30, and almost three quarters were 40 or under.[23] Most men in the hospital in 1937 and in 1941 were listed as being single. In 1937, only 17 percent were married; in 1941, only 12 percent were. Among the women admitted in the 1940s, 33 percent were married. However, since many couples in Bolivia at this time were not legally married, people listed as single may in fact have had companions and families.[24]

The Manicomio Pacheco was the only hospital in Bolivia that dealt exclusively with mental illness, so in terms of social class and race or ethnicity the population of the hospital was diverse. However, race was inconsistently entered in intake records and clinical histories, so it is not possible to establish even approximate percentages of how personnel categorized patients ethnically. According to 1941 records, of the 177 male patients in the hospital in that year, 67 were said to be white, 76 mestizo, and 34 Indian. This is a relatively small number of Indians compared to this group's probable representation in the population at large, which was recorded as 63 percent in the 1950 census, without taking into account a number of small lowland ethnic groups.[25] In any event, as is evident later (see the section "Society, Inside and Out") the category of race could change in the hospital records, reflecting a fluidity typical of the society at large.

In terms of occupation, the largest number of men were peasants or farm laborers (60), but there were also 22 students, 13 merchants, various craftsmen, 1 doctor, 1 accountant, and various white-collar workers. The occupations of the male patients seem to be consistent with general demographic trends, since Bolivia was an overwhelmingly agrarian country at the time. Among the women admitted to the hospital during the 1940s, the vast majority (206) were listed as working in their homes (*labores de casa*), a description that included women of greatly varied economic circumstances. Of the women who gave other professions, there were 28 seamstresses, 13 teachers, 29 servants, 14 students, 24 women involved in commercial activities, 19 cooks, and 12 *palliris* (women who worked in mining areas sorting ore according to quality).

With respect to treatment at the hospital, Cardiazol and insulin were often used to treat schizophrenia and manic depression. Insulin, which was first used in treating schizophrenics in Austria in the 1930s, produced hypoglycemic comas in patients which seemed to alleviate their symptoms, at least in the short run.[26] However, it also was extremely dangerous, causing death in almost 1 out of 100 patients in those U.S. hospitals where it was extensively used.[27] Cardiazol, a drug similar to camphor, induced convulsions without coma. Although it was said to produce remarkable improvement in some patients, it had unpleasant side effects, including anxiety, nausea, and vomiting, and severe muscle pain in the area of the injection.[28] In 1944 the director Alberto Martínez for the first time treated patients with electroconvulsive therapy (ECT) in the Manicomio Pacheco. Of ten female patients in the experiment (nine schizophrenics and one manic depressive), four were said to experience complete remission; four others (including the manic depressive) were significantly improved; and two did not respond favorably to the treatment.[29]

In addition to receiving Insulin, Cardiazol, and ECT, patients were also dosed with a variety of other medicines, including bismuth and mercury for syphilis. It is interesting that the manicomio continued to rely on these two drugs long after the arsenic-based compound, Salvarsan, became the treatment of choice for the disease and that even in the late 1940s, hospital physicians did not administer penicillin to its patients with syphilis. Patients in the manicomio also sometimes received Phenobarbital for seizures, quinine for malaria, and various vitamins and "tonics" for general revitalization. There are rare references in hospital records to psychoanalysis and psychotherapy, sometimes in conjunction with ECT, but there are no indications of which doctors practiced these therapies or notes indicating the patients' progress. Entries in records indicate that some patients received "praxitherapy," which usually meant helping out with the work of maintaining the hospital: cleaning, cooking, possibly gardening.

Despite greater possibilities for prescribing medication or therapy for mental patients than had existed in earlier decades, it was still a minority of the ill who received treatment in the 1940s. Monthly summaries for the male patients for 1947 and 1948 indicate that on average 35 percent received some form of treatment (including vitamins) while 59 percent were in "simple confinement," 3 percent were under observation, and 3 percent were discharged.[30]

While medication offered some the hope of improvement, the prognosis for many patients was not particularly good. Of all the women admitted to the hospital in the 1940s for whom exit condition was recorded, 44 percent died (128 out of 288), while 54 percent were discharged and said to be cured or improved. Of those who were discharged in positive conditions, the largest percentages were among those diagnosed with schizophrenia (67 percent) and psychosis (64 percent); fully 62 percent of those listed as suffering from epilepsy left the hospital dead. Of those women recorded as leaving the hospital well or alleviated, most had been in the manicomio one year or less (79 percent); the longer a patient was in the hospital, the more likely she was to leave in a coffin. But a considerable number of those who died (44 percent) had been in the hospital a year or less. For those who had been in the hospital for a short time, the cause of death was usually a serious complicating medical problem such as malnutrition, malaria, typhoid, or enteritis.

Although the statistics for men are not precisely comparable (since they are for all the men present in the hospital during two years), they still indicate the same trends. Of the 50 men who left the hospital in 1937, 2 were "cured" and 10 were "improved," while

31 died and 7 had escaped. Of the 51 men who left in 1941, 15 were listed as "cured or improved," 29 had died (57 percent), and 7 had escaped.

The Doctors in Their Writings

Although doctors in Bolivia could not strictly be considered psychiatrists by educational specialization, a number of those associated with the manicomio and a few other physicians who worked in the mental health field published articles in the 1930s and 1940s about psychiatry and related social issues. Not all of their writings are specifically about mental illness, but they nonetheless are significant because they reflect the type of social philosophy these doctors brought to the treatment of their patients. In fact there was far less emphasis on mental illness as a problem that should be addressed by a new democratic state than there was on other types of disease. This may be in part because throughout the world psychiatry did not have the prestige of other medical specialties, since, despite much experimentation, doctors in general were not particularly effective in curing those with serious mental illness. Also, to many doctors and policy makers, mental illness may have seemed of secondary importance compared to diseases such as typhoid, or tuberculosis, or malaria because it apparently affected far fewer people. In Bolivia, furthermore, treatment for mental illness until the 1940s was exceptionally rudimentary, and there may have been a tendency on the part of doctors to avoid calling attention to the deficiencies in care and the fact that the training of physicians in the field did not meet international standards.

The most prolific of the doctors who wrote on psychiatric subjects, Jaime Mendoza, was a firm believer in the physiological origins of psychiatric disease. In an article on schizophrenia published in 1938, Mendoza characterized the illness as a progressive, destructive brain disease which began with lesions in the thalamus and then gradually spread to other areas. He held out little hope for a cure but maintained that certain treatments, such as insulin shock, seemed to be the most effective when used in the early stages of the disease.[31] Mendoza also was the only Bolivian physician to attempt to make a theoretical contribution to the understanding of the human psyche.

In 1937 he published "El trípode psíquico" (The Psychic Tripod) in the *Revista del Instituto Médico "Sucre"* (RIMS), in which he combined his belief in the physical (rather than emotional) causes of mental illness with categories similar to Freud's id, ego, and superego (although he did not acknowledge the similarity). Mendoza pointed out that by looking at the inside of a skull, one could see that the human brain was divided into three sections: the occipital lobe, the temporal lobe, and the frontal lobe. He then hypothesized that different aspects of human consciousness were associated with these different areas of the brain. According to Mendoza instinct was controlled by the occipital area, affect located in the temporal region, and intellect associated with the frontal lobe.[32]

Although a physician, Jaime Mendoza is better remembered today as a novelist and essayist. Much of his early work that does not specifically deal with medicine is marked by an apparently contradictory combination of social criticism and voluntarism. On the one hand he pointed to exploitative working conditions and lack of government regulation as the cause of the horrible living conditions of working-class families; on the other he often blamed the poor, especially Indian, women for infant mortality and poor health.[33] Even in a late article on infant mortality (1937) written after the Chaco War, Mendoza still discussed mestizos in terms of racial degeneration in a manner similar to Alcides Arguedas. He wrote: "The cholo, originally the offspring of the Indian and the Spaniard, lost much of the organic resistance of the Indian to destructive agents. . . . Then there is the moral or educational factor. The fact that the cholo finds himself in direct contact with his social superiors has caused him to more easily assimilate than the Indian the defects and vices [of the upper classes] instead of their good qualities."[34]

Yet Mendoza was also aware of the dire economic conditions and hardships of the postwar period that negatively affected infant and child health. He called on individual philanthropists to take actions to protect women and children and stressed the need for the government to support these private initiatives,[35] concluding "And now that socialism is being promoted so much, the necessity [to protect the nation's children] is even greater. The future of the nation is with the children. To abandon them is an anti-social act, or if you will, an anti-socialist act."[36]

In 1943 Emilio Fernández, then the director of the manicomio, wrote an article entitled "Asistencia médico-social de la alienación en Bolivia." In it he stressed economic and social conditions as contributing to mental illness, saying "[We must] struggle against attitudes of fear, ridicule or curiosity with respect to the 'loco,' because the life of a mentally ill person is a reflection of psychic poverty, which generally originates in economic poverty," and "the crowding, the unhealthiness . . . fatigue and misery related to many jobs directly influence insanity." [37] He also favored the establishment of *ligas de higiene mental* (mental hygiene leagues) that would be dedicated to educating people about mental health: explaining that mental illness should not be a cause for shame, that seeking expeditious treatment was a family and societal responsibility, and that not all mentally ill people were totally out of touch with reality—many could be lucid and intelligent. The proposed leagues would also help former mental patients find work and initiate campaigns against "vices" that contributed to mental illness such as alcoholism, abuse of coca and tobacco, and venereal diseases. In addition, Fernández advocated the training in mental hygiene of a corps of *visitadores sociales* who would go to people's homes to help establish domestic conditions that were conducive to mental health and also detect early signs of psychiatric disease in children so they could be promptly treated.[38]

Fernández also wanted changes in the manicomio. According to him, the men's section was run as a "neuro-psychiatric clinic" and the women's according to a "semi-prison model." [39] Presumably the difference between the two facilities was at least partly related to the fact that women were housed in the original building of the Manicomio Pacheco, which dated from 1884, but it may also have been due to the fact that the two buildings had different staffs and sometimes separate directors. Furthermore, the different approaches to treatment could conceivably have been due to gendered understandings of mental health and illness in men and women, which will be discussed in this section and the next one. Fernández favored getting rid of both sections and turning the entire institution into what he called an "asylum and agricultural colony." The asylum would be for chronic patients, who doctors assumed would never leave the institution; and the colony for the acutely ill, who Fernández believed would benefit from productive labor that they could also do when they were released. He stressed this should not be busywork: men would work outside growing crops, tending gardens and orchards;

women would cook, wash clothes, sew, spin, and weave. Fernández also advocated the establishment of departmental psychiatric clinics where people could be treated without the expense and inconvenience of being sent to Sucre, and the establishment of a school to train psychiatric nurses.[40] As we will see later in the chapter, these last two proposals, which were never put into effect, would probably have improved the experience of many patients.

Finally, Fernández outlined legislation on mental health that he hoped the country would adopt. Most important, the proposal established that the treatment of mental illness was the responsibility of the state. But the significant limitations of psychiatric facilities and the lack of awareness about mental illness on the part of most public officials were evident in one of the first clauses of the draft legislation. It stated that in areas where there were hospitals, the mentally ill should be accommodated in them until they could be evaluated or sent to Sucre and that in areas where there were no hospitals, local officials had to make arrangements for appropriate lodging. Under no circumstances, the proposed legislation stated, should "alienated individuals be kept in jails, or transported together with criminals or prisoners." Fernández's legislation went on to stipulate that hospitalization, medicine, and food should be absolutely free in the Manicomio Pacheco, although the institution would continue to have special sections for pensionados. It also specified that the expenses of bringing patients to the hospital in Sucre should be borne by the state, not the patients' relatives.[41]

In general "Asistencia médico-social" expressed the same conviction that the society was responsible for the health of its citizens that Fernández later presented in his 1949 piece on women and children, which was discussed in the previous chapter. Fernández saw both his proposals for bettering the lives of working women and children and for treating and preventing mental illness as having eugenic functions. With respect to the legislation he advocated to protect infants and their mothers, he wrote: "The fundamental principle of the law consists in the defense of human capital, attempting to improve the physical, moral and intellectual qualities of individuals, that is the race, without resorting to euthanasia or the strict selection of progenitors."[42] He also stressed the importance of preventing consanguineous marriages or procreation by people who were either too young or too old, which could cause mental defects. The disruptions of war, poverty, and malnutrition were also said to have deleterious effects on pregnant women that could lead to unhealthy offspring.

In general, Fernández proposed a kind of "social," or "preventive" eugenics, that Nancy Stepan has shown was widely subscribed to about twenty years earlier in many Latin American countries. Based on the Lamarckian assumption that environmental change could cause genetic alteration, this approach considered movements for sanitation and hygiene to be eugenic, that is, contributing to the improvement of the race. Contrary to those who took a "hard" eugenicist position and argued that the "unfit" (which could include Indians or people of mixed race) should not be allowed to reproduce, or should even be allowed to die out through neglect, an environmental eugenicist approach in Bolivia held out the hope of creating a healthy nation through social policy and public health measures. Although by 1949, when Fernández wrote his article on women and children, eugenics had been discredited for many because of its associations with Nazi Germany, in Bolivia a "soft" eugenics, primarily focused on social legislation for women and children, seemed to blend well with populist calls for democracy and social justice.[43]

Not all those who wrote on the issue of mental health subscribed to a "soft" eugenics approach, however. In 1941, Dr. César Adriazola, professor of psychiatry at the medical school in the city of Cochabamba and former general director of health, wrote an article proposing selective sterilization.[44] Maintaining that the majority of social conflicts were caused by the mental disturbance of their perpetrators and that most of these mental disorders were inherited, Adriazola drafted a law for "social" sterilization. This was necessary in Bolivia, he said, precisely because reform measures of the type supported by Fernández could never be successful, because of the "inferior cultural level of the masses and the enormous propagation among them of alcoholism and criminality."[45] Thus he proposed sterilization for (1) habitual or congenital criminals, degenerate criminals, and those suffering from moral insanity; (2) delinquent psychopaths, including those suffering from epilepsy, schizophrenia, dementia praecox, paranoia, or retardation; (3) delinquent alcoholics (without exception); and (4) those mentally ill individuals who, although they were not delinquent, had been institutionalized for violent or aggressive actions.[46]

Weighing in for even more extreme measures was Miguel Levy,

the departmental director of health who had written the article on the mental decline of the Indian in 1942. In 1944, in what must have been a slap in the face to Director Emilio Fernández and the entire staff of the hospital, Levy proclaimed that conditions in the manicomio were so bad that it would be preferable to ameliorate the situation with "selective euthanasia as was done in the most civilized European countries."[47] Levy was careful to say that he was not suggesting that anyone take any actions that were against the law. However, considering Levy's opinions on Indian degeneracy, one cannot but wonder which mental patients he might have selected for elimination if he had been given the chance.

Most of the doctors concerned with psychiatry (other than Jaime Mendoza) tended to write on subjects of a social or political nature that were related to mental illness or emotional development but that were not specifically medical or technical. Although there was some knowledge of Freudian psychology among doctors, as is obvious in the manicomio's records, there was almost nothing written about psychoanalytic theory or psychotherapy in Bolivia. This was in contrast to neighboring Peru, where in the first decades of the century young, left-wing intellectuals, such as José Carlos Mariátegui, had embraced psychoanalysis as a liberating tool for understanding unconscious motivations and desires.[48]

One of the few writings that introduced psychoanalysis to a Bolivian medical audience was a two-part article published in 1926 by Dr. Gregorio Mendizábal. In it he outlined some of the principles of Freudian psychology, including the use of psychoanalysis for the treatment of neurosis.[49] In 1940, in a general article on normal mental and physical functions Dr. Otto Kleinberger, a physician at the Manicomio Pacheco, used the categories "unconscious" and "subconscious" to describe different aspects of human development.[50] Neither of these pieces makes any reference to actual therapeutic practice of psychoanalysis in Bolivia.

Almost all of the writings by doctors associated with mental health issues in Bolivia touch in one way or another on gender. As discussed in the previous chapter, both Jaime Mendoza and Emilio Fernández linked gender, ethnicity, and infant mortality. In several early works Mendoza attributed high infant mortality in the mining areas of Bolivia and among Indians to mothers' drunkenness and neglect.[51] Fernández specifically wanted public health services to reach rural Indian women because he believed that the peasant mothers' Andean birthing and child care practices were responsible for poor maternal and infant health.[52] In the hospital Fernández prescribed household tasks and female crafts as useful work for women patients. While these jobs might have been welcome activities compared to total idleness, the fact that his recommendations for women's work were limited to these indicates that Fernández believed that emotional health would be promoted through reinforcing conventional gender roles.

Several other authors devoted considerable attention to hormonal changes and sexual impulses as causing disturbances in women; in contrast, although some emotional changes were noted in boys during puberty, they were not seen as being the specific causes of mental illness. Kleinberger saw menstruation as a particularly threatening time for women and capable of causing mental disturbances. He also viewed menopause as a potential relief, after which women "returned to a physical and psychic equilibrium that until then had been disturbed by menstruation."[53] For one who believes in the unconscious, perhaps this statement of Kleinberger's could be interpreted to mean that women were more likely to be normal emotionally if they were more like men or if they were pregnant all the time (and therefore not menstruating).

Levy in an article on education during puberty expressed various seemingly contradictory views of women.[54] He said that "nature in its wisdom has made woman a weak but active being, with a delicate but fertile organism."[55] Later in the same article, however, he referred approvingly to the ideas of contemporary feminists and said, "Today's woman has a lively intelligence, she is precocious and vivacious not timid or submissive. . . . She is capable of heavy work; only her sex differentiates her from the man."[56] But a little later in the article he referred to the physiological changes girls experience at puberty, especially menstruation, as often being the cause of hysteria in women, especially if their mothers had not adequately prepared them with "delicate and moral" sex education.[57] Also, when discussing the objectives of education for adolescents, he wrote that the goal for a boy was that he develop into "a truly moral man, healthy in body and spirit" while the girl was to become "an affectionate and respected mother."[58]

Certainly Levy's opinions were not unique for the period (nor for more recent times), but they and the ideas about women held by other members of the profession are important, as we shall see later, in influencing how mental disorders were understood in female patients. Some doctors went further in their analysis of what constituted mental illness in women. For instance, Gregorio Mendizábal in his discussion of mental deviants classified "the prostitute" as a psychopathic personality. He believed that most women dedicated themselves to the profession because they enjoyed frivolous diversions, such as going to cabarets, and wanted to adorn themselves and avoid work.[59]

Society, Inside and Out

In March 1928 Lucía Guevara, the mother of a patient, wrote to the manicomio's director asking how much she should send for her son's care. She explained that she was disposed to pay whatever was required so that he would be treated better. In July she wrote again saying "I beg you to give him all the injections necessary to cure him. I will pay all the costs of the treatment." She apparently felt that offering to pay for treatment was not enough to guarantee the best care for her son: at the end of the letter she pathetically added that she was sending three boxes of candy to the hospital, one for the director of the men's section of the hospital, one for the doctor, and one for her son.[60]

While there had always been relatives such as Sra. Guevara, who sent money to hospital administrators to ensure that patients received better treatment, in the 1940s two classes of patients were officially recognized: *pensionados* and *gratuitos*. On the one hand this can be seen as regularizing a situation that was ripe for abuse. It must have been reassuring to relatives to know that they could pay established fees and not have to curry favor with the hospital staff in order for their relatives to receive good care. On the other hand, it was somewhat ironic that at a time when there was an outcry against privilege in Bolivian society, and health care was beginning to be viewed as a right, separate and unequal facilities were institutionalized for the mentally ill. Pensionados had their own sections and better and more plentiful food. There also is evidence that they frequently received treatment while others with the same

diagnoses did not. For instance, in August 1943 two patients diagnosed as schizophrenic were admitted to the hospital. Genaro Se-
rrano, twenty-two, a *chofer*, was admitted on the first of the month
as a *pensionado*. He was treated with insulin therapy and was said to
improve enormously and was released on 17 November 1943.[61] On
12 August Santiago Rivera, an agricultural worker in a poor state of
nutrition, arrived at the hospital as a gratuito. He was given no treatment, "because of lack of drugs." There is no record of the outcome
of his case.[62]

There is also some evidence that measures were not even taken to
save patients' lives if the patients couldn't pay for them. On 8 April
1943 Toribio Márquez, a thirty-year-old miner, was admitted and
diagnosed as having "tubercular psychosis." He was said to be extremely malnourished, and less than a month later he died of "tubercular wasting." The clinical history noted that he had begun to
work in the mines at an early age, "always with inadequate nutrition." The intern who wrote up the history noted that he "eats very
little." There is no indication that he was given any intravenous fluids
or that any actions were taken to improve his emaciated state.[63] In
contrast, Alfredo Rivas Mayorga, a white office employee suffering
from alcoholic psychosis, arrived in June 1942 as a pensionado and
was given all kinds of intravenous serums to build him up, including
an "invigorating sugar serum" and "hepatic stimulants."[64]

Even when pensionados died, they often appear to have received
far more attention than nonpaying patients in similar conditions.
Maximiliano Méndez, a sixty-two-year-old white merchant from
La Paz who entered the hospital in May 1938, was diagnosed with
neurosyphilis, an advanced form of the disease in which spirochetes
invade the lining of the brain or the spinal column. He eventually
died of heart failure in November of 1943, but before that the hospital doctors continued to try various treatments though his condition
was said to be chronic. He was given mercury and bismuth for his
syphilis and a malaria therapy.[65] In contrast, Manuel Camargo, a
forty-year-old miner from Corocoro, with only one month's schooling, entered the hospital suffering from malnutrition on 22 October
1942. He was, like Méndez, diagnosed as having progressive syphilitic paralysis. His case was considered hopeless, and he died on
9 December from intestinal tuberculosis without having received
any treatment.[66]

Class considerations were important even to the extent of determining how patients arrived at the manicomio and the reception they would receive. On 26 September 1932 the president of the Municipal Council of the city of Cochabamba wrote to the director of the hospital explaining that the next day Sr. Selem Abad, a businessman of Syrio-Palestinian nationality, was going to arrive "on one of the planes of Lloyd Aereo Boliviano." Mr. Abad had had the "misfortune of losing his reason," and the council president asked that the director show him all possible consideration because Mr. Abad was "a foreigner with a deep love of Bolivia."[67] The president of the Municipal Council of La Paz had likewise written the director about Héctor Valcárcel Moscoso, who was coming to the hospital because of "mental attacks due to epilepsy." The president asked that the hospital staff "show deference" to Sr. Valcárcel because he was "una persona decente" of La Paz.[68]

Much more common were the mental patients who were brought to the hospital by police agents and who frequently were not accompanied by relatives, because family members could not afford to make the trip. A letter from the head of the Hospital Viedma in the city of Cochabamba in December 1928 explained that "every one of the 'alienados' that I am dispatching was sent to me by the police who rounded them up in the countryside."[69] Sometimes the records of newly admitted patients included letters from local authorities or notarized documents from relatives or employers explaining that they were violent and dangerous and could not remain in their homes. A particularly sad one was from Rafaela Ramírez of Sucre, who requested the confinement of her Indian servant, Alejandro N., a minor and an orphan. She said he suffered from "mental alienation" and "couldn't remain in the street," suggesting that she had thrown him out of the house because of his aberrant behavior.[70] Frequently, there would also be a letter from a local doctor explaining that he had treated the ill person but that the gravity of the condition required internment in the manicomio.

For the poor, being in the hospital, even as a gratuito, could be expensive because the loss of the income of an adult member of a family could be a significant hardship. Such was the case of Jorge Plaza Ponce who on 9 August 1943 wrote to Miguel Levy, who was then chief health officer of the Department of Chuquisaca asking to be discharged from the manicomio. He said he had been in the hospital for two months and that thanks to the attentions of the director and doctor he was now in a perfect state of health. He went on to explain that his wife had come to Sucre to take care of him, his young children were abandoned in his home in Vilacaya, and his small harvest was going to be ruined as a result of his absence. He begged the authorities to let him go home. The fact that Plaza's wife was in Sucre with him indicates that patients who could not afford to pay for better care might be attended by family members who presumably brought food and clean clothing to the hospital. Clearly his wife's absence from home was another financial burden for the family to bear.[71] Yet once a patient was released from the hospital, getting home could also be a considerable expense. In January 1933 an intern wrote to Sra. Tomasa C. viuda de Chamorro in the city of Tarija saying that the medical director of the manicomio had found her son, Luis, to be sane and that he had not shown any mental disturbance during his stay in the hospital. He then went on to explain that for her son to be released, his mother had to forward the hospital money for his trip home and also pay for someone else to accompany him.[72] Luis Chamorro was actually one of many soldiers admitted to the hospital due to war psychosis during the Chaco conflict. Usually after they were released, they were sent home instead of back to the front.[73]

Class difference is evident in the hospital not only in the treatment of patients but also between the few professional employees of the manicomio and the greater number of attendants or servants who really were in contact with the patients on a regular basis. Generally the professional staff included the director (sometimes two: one for the men's section and one for the women's), one or two doctors, and one or two interns. In 1937 there were twenty-six nonprofessional employees in the men's section of the hospital and nineteen in the women's section.[74] Directors habitually complained about the attendants and servants and accused them of abusing the patients but apparently without much success in changing the situation. During Jaime Mendoza's tenure (1923–1926) he complained of the various means of control or punishment of the patients that were "to the liking of the servants," such as straitjackets, confinement cells, or cold baths at six in the morning.[75]

In 1937 Director Emilio Fernández asked:

What could one do with subalterns who didn't do their jobs and committed abuses that showed an absolute lack of dignity and respect for the institution, such as the servant who satisfies his perverse sexual instincts with the patients, or another who mistreats them, showing up for work drunk and then rents out the patients for construction work in the neighborhood, or another who at night steals food from the hospital pantry or sells the patients' bread for his own profit, or one who on the pretext of searching patients for sharp objects robs them of the little money their relatives have sent, or finally the employee who takes the clothing that patients receive in the mail.[76]

Hospital employees were paid extremely low wages compared to the doctors, and then frequently did not receive what was owed them because the federal government failed to regularly send funds to the manicomio's administration. In 1940 the director's salary was bs. 1,100 a year. Each of the medical interns received bs. 800 annually, while the male aides who worked with the patients on a daily basis received bs. 160.[77] The aides were given no training in how to deal with the mentally ill; in fact, some of the employees were patients who were put to work in what was referred to as "praxitherapy." So poor, untrained workers, some of whom had mental problems themselves, were on the front lines in the madhouse. For a person with sadistic tendencies or fears for his or her own sanity, the possibilities for loss of control and violence were obvious. For others, ignorance and the lack of respect and appreciation they received as employees could lead to callousness and brutality. As Fernández commented, "It seems that with time and constant contact with human pain, sensibilities became anesthetized and the servants adjusted to the pain of their fellow beings until they became indifferent."[78] Still, one wonders if there wasn't a tendency for the upper-class professionals to blame their subordinates for conditions in the institution when in fact the problems were structural and ultimately the responsibility of the administration.

In hospital records, class and race were closely related. As in Bolivian society at large, racial categories could be flexible. Not all intake forms recorded race, but on the ones that did there was sometimes, in addition to a place to indicate race, also a space for "color."[79] Thus a person could be of the white "race" but have his or her color listed as *blanco* (white) or *trigueño* (olive skinned), or on occasion *moreno* (dark). Likewise, mestizos could be moreno or trigueño but Indians seemed to be always listed as moreno. The ethnic labeling of patients in the hospital often seemed to follow Alcides Arguedas's principle that race in Bolivia was determined by social position rather than how a person looked.[80]

Not only were race and color somewhat independent variables in the hospital records, but sometimes a patient's race could change, apparently because of social or economic considerations. For instance, on an intake form Nelly Liscano Barrancos, a twenty-two-year-old student from Cochabamba, was first listed as *mestiza*, but this word was erased and replaced by *blanca* (*mestiza* is still clearly evident on the form although erased).[81] Further down the form, it is indicated that her uncle lived in Sucre and was a judge of the Supreme Court. One can imagine that when the person recording the information found out about the uncle, he or she went back to the beginning of the form and changed the racial category. Another patient, Santiago Almafuerte, also seemed to change racial category according to the information hospital staff had about his education and occupation. The earliest information on Almafuerte says he was a mine worker from Oruro and listed him as mestizo. Later records indicate that he was a twenty-two-year old university student who worked part time for a mining company and label him as white.[82]

Although ethnicity seemed to be considered a relevant piece of information for mental health purposes, almost nothing was published by doctors about Andean cultural factors that might have been important for understanding illness and considering treatment. The one article by a psychiatrist that deals with the issue at all does so in the context of discussing what was known about mental health during the Inca state and in the colonial period. In "La psiquiatría en Bolivia" Dr. José María Alvarado accepted very questionable interpretations of events and phenomena from the pre-Columbian and colonial periods. For instance, he mentions that a Peruvian psychiatrist, Hermilio Valdizán, considered the colonial, messianic religious movement, Taki Onqoy (sometimes translated as "dancing sickness"), to have been an outbreak of Sydenham's chorea, because of the jerky arm and leg movements of people who participated. He also quoted the Peruvian chronicler Garcilaso de la Vega as saying that there was a group of women who inhabited the altiplano who were prostitutes. Alvarado accepted that these women were in fact prostitutes (not shepherds), and he posited that they probably had hormonal imbalances and were mentally ill because under the Inca there were no economic reasons for women to sell their bodies.[83]

Alvarado did mention that when he worked in the men's section of the manicomio, family members of Indian patients often attributed their relatives' alienation to possession by malevolent spirits, especially in a laughing sickness called *ttucu*.[84] In fact, Andean people attributed mental derangement to a variety of causes. Relatively mild emotional problems (depression, loss of appetite, nervousness, etc.) might be caused by *susto* (see chapter 1), a condition that developed when a great fear or trauma caused a person (usually a woman) to lose her *ajayu*, or spirit. The most frequent solution for this common condition was feeding the earth shrines so that they would release the person's ajayu. It is unlikely that people with mild symptoms of susto ever arrived at the Manicomio Pacheco; rather, they were treated within their communities.[85] More severe forms of mental illness could also be blamed on malevolent spirits that had to be propitiated. Again, feeding and hunger are important in understanding the causes and cures for psychic disorders. In a case in an Aymara community near La Paz analyzed by Libbet Crandon-Malamud, a man's insanity was interpreted by one *yatiri* (Andean spiritual healer) as the result of the Pachamama (the earth mother) being displeased and neglected and therefore allowing an *anchanchu* (a malevolent spirit) to send a serious illness. The solution the yatiri proposed, which turned out to be ineffective, was appeasing the Pachamama with a special *mesa* (table of offerings) to bring things back into balance. Ultimately, the patient ended up in the mental ward of the Hospital General in La Paz, but neither confinement there nor ritual and herbal remedies in his home community cured his delusions, mania, and paranoia.[86]

It is probably safe to assume that it was only the most extreme cases from Andean communities that ended up in the manicomio. Chronically ill or mentally defective people were most likely incorporated into village life, as was the case with a number of individuals in Kachitu, the fictitious name Crandon-Malamud chose for the town she studied. The intervention of nonindigenous people sometimes may have been instrumental in bringing people in, as the case

of the alienados who had been rounded up by the police in Cochabamba and sent to the hospital in Sucre suggests. Or when behavior
became so aberrant that life was severely disrupted and local experts
could provide no cures, people might be interned in the manicomio.

Evaristo Balmaceda, an Indian peasant in the grips of an acute
mental disorder, entered the Manicomio on 1 August 1942. In his
case the clinical history indicates that although doctors were conscious of his ethnicity and recorded many fascinating details about
Balmaceda, they didn't seem to have much grasp of Andean beliefs
that might have helped them interpret his case.[87] Balmaceda's intake form said he was a married, thirty-five-year-old Indian peasant,
and he was described by the intern who interviewed him as wearing
"unusual clothing." In fact, Balmaceda wore three berets and a large
hat over them, which was adorned with flowers, two jackets, and
a neck tie. He carried a bag with various items the intern thought
were useless: wire, an oxtail that he said was the cause of his illness,
and cutting tools. On his left foot he wore several stockings and a
rubber gaiter. On his shoes he had various nails and horseshoes. His
wrists were wrapped in rubber bands as if they were bracelets.

Balmaceda (who was apparently bilingual) spoke incoherently,
with great animation and many hand gestures. He smoked cigarettes
and chewed coca constantly. Claiming to be completely sane, he
said he had been brought to the manicomio because of people's false
accusations. He said he had seen and continued to see angels and
devils and that they were under his power. The wind was his com-
padre and if he wanted to, he could tell the wind to turn the world
upside down. He claimed to know everything that happened in the
world, things due to both internal and external forces. For Balmaceda the sun was his God, his doctor, and his master; the moon was
his Virgin Mary. He was diagnosed as suffering from schizophrenia
and the recommended treatment was Cardiazol shock. Although
there are no records of any such treatment, he was discharged on the
5 April 1943 and said to be cured.

In the clinical history there is no indication that the hospital professionals understood that some of Balmaceda's statements reflected
Andean religious beliefs. For instance, in Andean cosmology the sun
is indeed a god and creator of life and the moon is considered the
sun's queen, a female leader-deity frequently identified with the Virgin Mary in Christianity. Yet, Balmaceda's references to these spiri-

tual concepts are simply treated in the clinical history as evidence of his insanity. There is no doubt that Balmaceda was deluded, but clinicians who paid attention to the cultural content of the delusions might have been better able to relate to him.

One also wonders if delusions of grandeur and excessive loquaciousness might be seen as particularly aberrant in Indians, who were believed by many to be naturally stolid and unimaginative. Megan Vaughan, has pointed out that in Nyasaland (now Malawi) in the 1930s, English psychiatrists considered that African patients were suffering from "European type" delusions if they expressed power and strength ("I am God," "I am wealthy"), as opposed to "African type" delusions that the Europeans thought were in keeping with their culture ("My wife is committing adultery," "I want to eat people"). She argues that part of what made Africans "crazy" by European standards was that they were insufficiently "other," that is, they exhibited symptoms thought not to be characteristic of their emotional development.[88] In a similar manner, Evaristo Balmaceda may have disconcerted doctors with his delusions that turned the world upside down, making an Indian peasant the master of the universe. Even Balmaceda's eccentric clothes were not those normally associated with native Bolivian dress; instead they seem almost a caricature of a European gentleman's outfit.

The doctors also were puzzled by thirty-year-old Carmelo Balsa, an Indian peasant from Muyupampa, who was admitted in 1943. Diagnosed as schizophrenic, Balsa claimed to be able to speak English, French, German, Greek, and Turkish and said he was a "Hitlerista" from the party of Germán Busch. The doctor doing the interview was apparently surprised at Balsa's sophistication, because he asked Balsa how he knew about Hitler. Balsa replied that he had been told about him by the wind and the sun.[89]

Even if doctors had been inclined to take cultural difference into account, the forms used for the clinical histories discouraged them from doing so. By the 1940s the Manicomio Pacheco had adopted questionnaires modeled on those used in similar institutions in the United States and in Europe. This was an effort toward standardizing information, professionalizing psychiatric practice; most important, it was a step toward treating all patients equally by asking each of them (or a relative if the patient was unable to speak) the same questions, questions that apparently did not make clinical assumptions based on social position or ethnicity. However, unlike psychiatric interviews today in which the physician generally begins by asking the patient's assessment of the situation,[90] the manico-mio's forms, with their questions about the patient's age at denti-tion or length of menstrual periods, tended to force everyone into the same mold and leave little or no room for the patient's or rela-tive's thoughts on the illness. Nor was there space (except in the margins) for significant information about a person's life, such as the fact that Hipólito Caldas, a peasant from Valle Grande in Santa Cruz, had been working from dawn to dark every day in the fields since he was eight or nine years old (a detail the doctor doing the interview squeezed in, apparently thinking it might be relevant).[91] In fact, when doctors didn't use forms but simply conducted the interview and wrote up the results, there tended to be much more anecdotal information about the person and his or her problems and greater attention to social and personal situations. While this makes for a more complex description, sometimes this additional informa-tion is as revealing of the doctor's attitudes as it is about the patient's condition, as in 1939 when a doctor (who is not identified) wrote of twenty-six-year-old Emma Almagro of La Paz: "She uses expressions and styles very superior to her station and education."[92]

In the hospital records, race and class are never independent of assumptions about gender. The gendering of the information be-gins with the questionnaires, which differ in some important ways for men and women. While both ask similar questions about family history of illness, alcohol consumption, family temperament, the patient's childhood diseases, and so on, in the section on sexual history there are significant differences in the information elicited. Most of the questions for women have to do with menstruation: age at onset, length of menstrual period, discomfort during men-strual periods. These questions are in keeping with several doctors' writings that stressed the psychic dangers linked to menstruation. Another question asked: "Have your sexual relations been normal or abnormal?" (The answer is uniformly "Normal.") Yet another one inquires: "Before or after your first period have you had any little vice? Masturbation, lesbianism, etc?" (No one admits to any.) The men's section on sexual history begins by asking if the patient was "a womanizer, an onanist or a pederast." On the forms this was either left blank or the patient said he was a womanizer. The section goes on to ask about sexually transmitted diseases, whether the patient enjoys sexual contact and under what circumstances, and whether he has ever been impotent.

Given the wording of the questions on sex, it is not surprising that for both men and women the questions elicited virtually no information. Everyone said their sexual relations were normal; most men said they had never had a sexually transmitted disease even when their blood tests showed otherwise; none admitted that they had ever been impotent. Yet the questions themselves reveal important assumptions both about the differences between men and women and about the causes of their mental problems that are evident in other sections of the clinical histories.

Many of the men in fact do suffer from venereal diseases, and a good number are in the hospital because of the paralysis and dementia of neurosyphilis. Also among the men there is considerable emphasis placed on alcoholism as a precipitating factor in their illnesses. Patients diagnosed as schizophrenic, manic, demented, or psychotic are often said to have at least aggravated their conditions by drinking. For instance in 1942 Manuel J. Barreta Cáceres, a forty-two-year-old merchant, was diagnosed as schizophrenic. He reported that he heard voices that told him to pray because he was a sinner, had seen fires that didn't exist, and claimed to have only married a few weeks before although he had been married for many years. Dr. Otto Kleinberger, who examined him, attributed the illness to excessive abuse of alcoholic beverages.[93] Bolivia was not alone in having numbers of patients whose mental disorders were caused by alcoholism or syphilis. Since the late nineteenth century, western European countries and the United States had seen increases in the numbers of people (overwhelmingly men) who were admitted to asylums for insanity related to these conditions.[94]

While women sometimes were said to suffer mental symptoms because of alcohol abuse, it was far rarer than in male patients. Although some also had venereal diseases, I did not encounter a single example of neurosyphilis among women patients in the manicomio. Sex had a different significance in mental illness for women: illicit sexual relations, jealousy, prostitution, inappropriate gender roles—these were all thought to be important in causing mental derangement. In other words, the doctors seemed to take a rather crude psychoanalytic approach to women while with men emotional conflicts about sex were not mentioned. This analysis of the causes of mental illness in women was a slightly more complicated version of theories, such as those expressed by Otto Kleinberger and Miguel Levy, that directly linked female reproductive functions to insanity.[95] Even in the cases of male patients in which there was no clear physiological cause for the presenting problem, the doctors did far less psychologizing. Hospital staff seemed considerably less constrained by the questions on the clinical history forms for women and more likely to fill several extra pages to discuss sexual experiences and even amorous adventures.

The examples abound. Emma Almagro's schizophrenia seemed to have resulted from her complicated personal life about which she was said to feel a great deal of guilt. Admitted to the hospital in 1939 when she was twenty-six years old, she had been living for five years with an army officer to whom she was not married. Although her mother approved of their relationship, Emma herself had serious misgivings about it because she was deeply religious. Nonetheless, while she was living with the officer she began to have sexual relations with a young acquaintance of his. She was terrified of being caught by her companion and this caused her considerable, distress which increased when she became pregnant and had an abortion. It was after this that she began to exhibit symptoms of paranoia, accusing her family of talking about her behind her back and instigating her lover to turn against her.[96]

Raquel Banzer Santander was twenty-three years old when she was admitted to the hospital in 1940 suffering from epilepsy. She was illiterate and single, and she worked as a laundress. Abandoned by her family at an early age, she had "since then . . . lived a miserable life both materially and morally." As a result of her situation, she began to practice prostitution and this was believed to contribute to her breakdown.[97] However, the doctors also treated her for syphilis and found that the medication cleared up the symptoms of the disease, which she had recently contracted, as well as alleviating her seizures. The doctor who examined Bertha Juárez believed that guilt for past transgressions was an important factor in her illness. The thirty-six-year-old housewife from Oruro entered the manicomio in July 1940 suffering from visual and auditory hallucinations. The doctor noted in the medical history, "She is an illegitimate child; before marrying she reportedly lead a dissipated life, beginning sexual relations very early, at approximately ten years of age. Possibly the worry she has had about this life has a role in her mental disturbance."[98]

The fact of having deviated from acceptable social roles for women also was considered a contributing factor in mental breakdown. Hilda Guerra was a dental student from 1947 to 1951, when she was told to stop studying by her physician who thought it was contributing to her nervous condition. According to her mother, she was one of the best students in her class before becoming ill.[99] Even more deviant was Constantina Béjar Meriles, whose age was not recorded. She was an excellent student and athlete, participating in cycling and equitation. She was said to be of an affable and generous disposition and had written a textbook for primary school students. The problem with Constantina which led her parents to take her to the hospital was that she liked to wear masculine clothes and rejected men's amorous advances.[100]

"A woman with considerable experience of the world" was the description given for Clorinda Gutiérrez, a sixty year old from Oruro who ran a bar that was patronized by soldiers. She herself drank a good deal and in June 1933 while she was intoxicated, she apparently insulted the local prefect, who then had her seized by the police, taken to the local hospital, and eventually sent to the manicomio in Sucre. To their credit the doctors there did not consider her mentally ill. She was treated for alcoholism and released.[101]

For some of the female patients, jealousy because of their husbands' real or imagined infidelities was said to be one of the first signs or symptoms of their disease. Estefania Calderón Herrera, a weaver who entered the hospital in June 1941, was said to be extremely jealous of her husband, even imagining that he had sex with animals.[102] Likewise for Lily Restrepo de Justiniano, the first indication of insanity was her jealousy of her husband.[103] But if some were jealous, a larger number were abused by their husbands. Many women dated their first episodes of illness to blows received from their spouses. This was the case with Isabel Almazán, a forty-three-year-old widow from Cochabamba.[104] In fact she was said by her relatives to have been too humble and submissive to her husband when he was alive. Another patient, Celia Almeida de Alcázar, was reported to be "too resigned" because she had put up with the hostility and aggression of her mother-in-law and her sister-in-law, who were said to have instigated the mistreatment by her husband.[105] For other women, the roots of their disorders were traced to the loss of a lover. For example, Benedicta Alvarado, a single laundress, had had only one lover who had ultimately married another woman. Benedicta, now forty and said to be in menopause, was described by doctors as distraught because of her failure to have a family.[106]

Finally, in the women's records there is still considerable emphasis on female biology as causing psychosis, specifically emotional distress related to menstruation. For instance, Ofelia Gondra Siles, a nineteen-year-old student in a convent, was believed by the nuns to have become ill because she bathed during her period.[107] Another patient, Pura Correa de Kagel, went mad after there had been a series of robberies near her home in the countryside. At one point she lay on the bed, clutching her husband's revolver and waiting for intruders. When she did this, it was noted, her husband said she emitted a strong smell and that he saw a stream of blood running between her legs.[108]

Conclusion

By the 1940s, although most people still would not have been pleased to be admitted, the Manicomio Pacheco was no longer a dungeon where patients ate cats or where in the men's section there were only thirty spoons for sixty patients, as had been the case in 1918.[109] The hospital had attempted to augment its meager resources by charging patients who could afford to pay for care. Doctors had experimented with some new forms of treatment, most notably electroshock therapy. Many physicians there, like Alberto Martínez, probably felt gratified to be able to say that more of their patients had now returned to their homes and were "socially rehabilitated."[110] There is evidence in clinical histories that the professional staff was at least attempting (even if in a rather heavy-handed manner) to take emotional factors into account when analyzing patients' problems. By using the same intake forms for everyone, physicians were making an effort to professionalize practice and to treat everyone the same, not jumping to conclusions based on class position or ethnicity. In general the post–Chaco War consensus that health care was a right had an impact on mental health as it did in other medical fields; it helped to raise the quality of care in the manicomio and boost the recognition of the professionals who worked there.

Still, many factors prevented doctors who treated the mentally ill from having the same professional prestige that other Bolivian physicians had acquired by the 1940s. Despite new approaches to patient care, real cures for psychiatric disease were elusive. The lack of doctors specifically trained in psychiatry meant that practitioners did not have the experience and international credentials possessed by clinicians in other fields. At the same time, the fact that virtually no doctors chose to specialize in psychiatry reflected the low esteem in which the field was held. Perhaps, in fact, doctors found it less demoralizing to take turns working at the manicomio and then return to other types of medical practice than to dedicate their entire professional lives to a field that was underfunded and often unsuccessful. Ultimately, many people, both indigenous and otherwise, resisted sending relatives to the hospital until their problems were so severe that they became dangerous to themselves or to others. And it was certainly possible to argue that because Andean healing techniques built on community understandings of illness and means of restoring health, *yatiris*, and other practitioners might bring more relief for some patients than the methods used in the manicomio.

In their political and medical opinions, the doctors who wrote about mental health seem to have been fairly representative of the situation in the country, reflecting the social conflicts and contradictory ideas of the period. Miguel Levy still openly maintained that the Indian was not ready for full citizenship, a position that was beginning to sound anachronistic in the radical 1940s. Yet, other more progressive doctors, such as Emilio Fernández, who favored many social programs to ameliorate the situation of the working class, also saw the backwardness of the Indian population as preventing their complete social integration. Although, ironically, Levy could wax eloquent on modern women's equality with men, none of the doctors in their writing about human development or the welfare of women and children went so far as to suggest full citizenship for women.

Because of the social diversity of the patients in the hospital, the same types of hierarchies existed inside the manicomio that were found in the country at large. Those with money received more treat-

ment and better food and lodging, and local officials intervened
for them with the hospital administration. Poor people, who constituted the majority, received little or no treatment; if they were
lucky, their relatives brought them food and clothing. It was also the
poor who ended up working in the hospital in various menial capaci-
ties. Although few doctors would have agreed with Miguel Levy's
proposal of selective euthanasia for mental patients, in a way it was
taking place. Because of lack of care, many patients, most particularly the poor ones, were dying from tuberculosis, seizures, malaria,
enteritis, and so on.

Despite the uniformity of the questionnaires used for intake interviews, the manicomio's physicians still clearly had difficulty treating indigenous patients the same as non-Indians admitted to the
hospital. In the clinical histories there are indications that certain
kinds of behaviors did not fit with the physicians' understandings
of Indian nature: delusions of grandeur, clothing that was not considered "Indian," too much knowledge of current events. Assumptions about women seem to have been just as deeply ingrained as
those about Indians. They were rhapsodized as mothers of the nation, yet seen as the bearers of backward Indian practices. With
few exceptions, their psychiatric ailments were attributed in various ways to sex. This appears to have been due to the influence
of a superficial Freudian psychology that nicely validated beliefs
about women's biological destiny. Tellingly, despite doctors' apparent familiarity with some psychoanalytic interpretation, male patients in the manicomio were never said to have sexual conflicts that
contributed to their illnesses.

During this period in Bolivia, under increasing pressure from
popular mobilization, suffrage laws were liberalized somewhat: men
only had to prove literacy to vote (property requirements were eliminated); in 1945 literate women were given the right to vote in municipal elections. Also in 1945, informal consensual unions were given
the legal status of marriage. So at a time when women and lower-
class men (some of whom were Indians) were beginning to acquire
some political rights, doctors at the manicomio were still insisting
on their "difference."

Women, Indians, and workers (clearly not exclusive categories)
were often viewed as insubordinate "others" when they demanded
citizenship rights. The insane were commonly also viewed as people

outside the bounds of the human community; those who had "lost their minds" were considered profoundly, frighteningly "other." Yet ironically, a symptom of insanity in an Indian might be not acting "Indian" enough; some of the women in the mental hospital were also seen as insufficiently feminine. These patients in a sense became "others" when their behavior did not conform to what was expected of them. However, for women, going crazy was also commonly associated with their very female being: reproduction and sexuality. And Indians were still considered congenitally, emotionally immature and intellectually inferior.

Turning finally to the doctors' mental processes: their writings and attitudes toward patients show just how complicated changes in consciousness are. Some doctors were swept up in the movement for democracy that developed in the post–Chaco War period. Certainly many of Emilio Fernández's proposals for restructuring mental health services and educating the general population about mental illness reflected democratic, humanitarian sentiments as well as current international thinking about treatment. Yet in a society that was so profoundly unequal economically, where native people and women were still not full citizens, doctors fell back on older assumptions about racial and sexual difference that seemed "natural" to them. Perhaps it is unfair to expect that doctors in Bolivia in the 1940s would, or could, have done otherwise. Changing this orthodoxy would require years of successful struggle by Bolivia's disenfranchised for equal rights, education, and decent living standards. A more equal society alone would not be sufficient but would be an essential precondition for the emergence of new physicians and researchers who could theorize a new psychiatry. And a new psychiatry might have helped to accomplish what some early proponents of psychoanalysis, such as José Carlos Mariátegui, hoped for: liberate people by helping them understand the mental and emotional forces that shaped their lives.

CONCLUSION

From 1900 through the 1940s cemetery records for the city of La Paz remained shockingly the same, showing only minor variations according to season and fluctuations when epidemics were particularly severe. Children and infants were carried off by whooping cough, dysentery, and various other gastrointestinal disorders, while people of all ages died of typhoid, typhus, pneumonia, smallpox, and tuberculosis.[1] Yet these statistics were less discouraging than those for other areas of the country where malaria, yaws, hookworm, and yellow fever were common. In the early 1950s infant mortality for the entire country was estimated at 176 deaths per 1,000 live births; life expectancy was forty-two years for women and thirty-eight for men.[2]

Throughout the period of this study doctors and politicians offered varying explanations for the nation's ill health, some of them, especially in the 1940s, focusing on social and economic inequities. Yet most experts who suggested causes and solutions never could totally escape Alcides Arguedas's metaphor of the "pueblo enfermo." In one way or another they linked physical sickness to ethnicity as he had connected race to national malaise.

We have seen that in the first decades of the twentieth century, doctors—as members of Bolivia's educated, political class—were eager to offer solutions for the so-called Indian problem. Specifically, they grappled with the question of whether native Bolivians could be made healthy and "civilized" so they could work more efficiently and not present a danger of contagion to other social sectors. Jaime Mendoza and Néstor Morales made different medical proposals, yet both found the nub of the problem in the "culture" of indigenous people. They both believed that Indians' lifestyles made them particularly susceptible to disease and also resistant to conventionally prescribed treatments. Morales's solution for dealing with this was a special cure (the vacuno-therapy for typhoid) that he felt was suited to the Indians' backward, cultural practices. Jaime Mendoza did not prescribe different treatment for indigenous people; rather, he believed that "Indianness" not only made them unhygienic and likely to fall ill, but also unable to organize in their own interests as workers. Although seemingly more aware of the structural causes of ill health than Morales, Mendoza was perhaps more pessimistic about the possibilities of change as well. Acculturation would not create new, civic-minded citizens but only produce ignorant cholos who would be no more conscious of the means of promoting good health than Indians.

Like Arguedas and other writers on Bolivia's problems, in considering the role of the Indian in the country Mendoza and Morales consciously or unconsciously touched on questions of their own personal identity. This was problematic: if they could clearly distinguish themselves from Indians because of their culture and education, it was less obvious how to separate themselves from cholos or mestizos, who may have been too close for comfort. Bolivia's upper class could have found some glue for the nation, as well as personal affirmation, in declaring Bolivia a mestizo nation. Nevertheless, at least in the first decades of the twentieth century, the country's elite generally maintained that culture made them white.

The Chaco War, combined with the political mobilization of workers and peasants, changed the political landscape in the country. Like many other wars initiated by leaders to rally patriotic support, the Chaco adventure was a calamity for President Salamanca and the entire nation. A good portion of the disaster was medical. Soldiers died of disease, hunger, and thirst; the public health system effectively ceased to function, as diseases that formerly had been localized spread to greater sectors of the population as a consequence of the mobilization for war. Coming out of the war, and in keeping with international ideological trends, there was a new emphasis on the need for equal access to medical care and the principle that health was a basic right of all Bolivians. Yet, even with this new rhetoric, women and native people still did not enjoy full citizenship. Also, looked at more closely, doctors' writing still reflected an uncertainty that native Bolivians could be equal members of the nation. There was much postwar speculation as to whether Indians had particular resistance or susceptibility to certain diseases, and the old mantra that their habits and lack of culture made them more likely to fall ill was frequently repeated. There was a curious blind spot in many of the writings on medicine in the 1930s and '40s: authors recognized that poverty and inequality were structural causes of ill health, yet still gave racial explanations for particular groups' diseases.

Apparently even more automatic and "natural" than associating health problems with ethnicity was the way writers linked them to gender. It is possible, however, that male writers' insistence on associating women with ill health was a reaction to the fact that women were taking a more active role in public life. Doctors struck out verbally in all directions, blaming upper-class women's frivolity and lower-class women's slovenliness for a variety of health problems. Better-educated women were constantly accused of knowing about everything except their primary patriotic function of motherhood. Indigenous women were singled out as negligent mothers and cholas as promiscuous libertines who spread disease. Indian women were also the ones doctors usually associated with what they considered useless native cures, even though the most famous Andean medical practitioners were men. This special effort to discredit women healers may have been due to the fact that well into the twentieth century, obstetrics was a field dominated by female midwives, with doctors encountering much resistance from their female patients to hospital births or to male physicians delivering babies. Doctors often accused the Western-style, urban midwives of practicing medicine without licenses and performing abortions, while the rural indigenous birth attendants were said to cause infant and maternal death through unhygienic practices.

We also have seen in physicians' writings about psychiatry and treatment of the mentally ill the assumption that normal women and Indians were intrinsically different from and inferior to white men. In keeping with the idea that for women biology was destiny, women's mental problems were often associated with menstruation and reproduction. Indians were often considered to be childlike, stoic, and incapable of abstract or idealistic thought. At the same time, both women and Indians could be considered deviant if they did not conform to what was psychically expected of them. In the 1940s, doctors had greater knowledge of psychoanalytic theory, yet they tended to apply it only to women, who were believed to suffer emotional breakdown due to sexual or emotional conflicts. For men these conflicts were never mentioned as contributing causes of illness. Emotional conflicts were feminine; men simply went crazy from syphilis or alcohol. In some ways this was ironic because it implied that (white) men were not introspective and did not experience guilt, longing, rejection, love, that is, the full range of emotions that they were supposed to have and women and Indians were said to lack.

Breakthroughs in medical research in the twentieth century made possible the first widespread campaigns against yellow fever, malaria, and other epidemic diseases that particularly plagued tropical areas. When the Rockefeller Foundation (RF) began a yellow fever program in Bolivia in 1932, at the beginning of the Chaco War, despite its representatives' authoritarianism and condescension, they were welcomed by the government and doctors. Between then and the early 1950s, Rockefeller not only expanded its activities in the country but also changed its approach in keeping with new thinking in international public health circles. In the more populist 1940s and early 1950s, when there were also other non-Bolivian medical organizations operating in the country, Bolivian politicians became more critical of Rockefeller programs, though they more closely matched the type of assistance Bolivian public health officials had requested. However, even with the more confrontational attitudes on the part of Bolivians, there was still a striking agreement between foundation representatives and national physicians about indigenous people.

The RF was accused by the government and doctors of not doing its job efficiently, but the foundation's medical model and the racial assumptions of its personnel were not questioned.

In the early 1900s, when this book begins, academically trained physicians were making a concerted effort to prove they were more effective doctors than Andean herbalists, spiritual healers, and various Western-style "empirics." By the 1940s because of worldwide improvements in medical science, and doctors' active lobbying efforts, their prestige had increased, though the health of the nation was not much improved and many people still patronized other types of practitioners. The doctors were also given a significant boost by the government's commitment to provide health care to all Bolivians. In the post-Chaco period, the government took on many of the medical and sanitary projects that doctors had been arguing for in medical journals. This effort, aided by programs established by the Rockefeller Foundation and other foreign health organizations, made modern medicine a major national project (despite the campaigns' limited success) and contributed to raising doctors' professional authority. Significantly, it was the populist politics of the 1930s and '40s and the conviction that health care was a right — like education or a living wage — that raised the status of the doctors. Whether they supported the new progressive politics from conviction or self-interest, biomedical doctors benefited from having Western medicine become central to the country's reform effort.

Postscript

Despite the gradual ascendancy of biomedicine over the course of the twentieth century, today people in other countries frequently associate Bolivia with alternative medicine. Almost invariably when I told people I was going to Bolivia to do research on the history of medicine, they responded with interest, thinking I was studying Andean herbal or spiritual healing. In the beginning of the twenty-first century, Bolivian doctors have firmly established their expertise, there have been improvements in national health indicators,[3] and Western medicine is much more widely available throughout the country. Nonetheless, many people still use Andean medicine.

And while most of those who rely on traditional medicine, or combine it with various forms of Western medicine, are Andean themselves, increasing numbers of middle- and upper-class nonindigenous Bolivians are exploring indigenous forms of treatment or are interested in the pharmaceutical potential of herbs used by the Kallawaya. Today although some medical doctors still belittle native medicine or think it is dangerous, others, now secure in their medical hegemony, are more willing to consider the effectiveness of different medical approaches or the possibility of combining healing strategies. For several decades there have been various organizational efforts to promote the collaboration of Western and Andean medical practices, including Western-style offices where patients can consult both medical doctors and yatiris or Kallawaya.[4]

At the same time that doctors trained in the Western tradition have been expressing more interest in, or at least tolerance toward, native Bolivian medicine, there have been a number of children of Kallawaya who have become university-trained physicians. Some of them are actively working with Andean healers. Furthermore, political groups that represent indigenous people have made access to modern medical care one of their demands. The Movimiento al Socialismo (MAS), the Left-of-Center party whose indigenous leader, Evo Morales, was elected president in 2005, lists equal health care for all citizens as a central point of its program along with the defense of all of Bolivia's native cultures and the return of lands to Bolivia's first peoples.[5] Health is also important for the indigenous-led Federación de Juntas Vecinales (FEJUVE) of El Alto, a city adjacent to La Paz whose population is mostly made up of people of Aymara background and recent indigenous immigrants. The federación has become one of the most militant and vocal groups opposing the neoliberal economic policies of successive Bolivian governments, demanding the nationalization of the country's natural resources and a new political system that represents the Bolivia's indigenous majority. Nonetheless in April 2005, volunteers from FEJUVE, including Abel Mamani, the president of organization, joined the minister of Public Health in inaugurating a campaign to vaccinate 25,000 children in El Alto against a number of serious diseases. Mamani himself administered drops of oral polio vaccine to waiting children. The Bolivian representative of the Pan-American Health Organization praised the FEJUVE volunteers, saying it would allow the campaign to reach more children because "there are occasions when people are afraid of the nurses who do the vaccinations."[6]

In the 1930s and 1940s, health care was promoted as part of a nationalist agenda that recognized the class-based inequalities in Bolivia, but either ignored ethnic discrimination or actually saw indigenous people as part of the reason the country was not more healthy and modern. In the twenty-first century, more people are considering the medical merits of Andean medicine while social movements led by native Bolivians are raising the demand for universal, modern health care. If these movements survive and achieve some of their goals, in addition to creating a more equal society, they may also contribute to forging a new understanding of health and well-being.

NOTES

Introduction

Unless otherwise noted, translations of quotations are my own.

1. Nemesio Torres Muñoz, "Informaciones respecto a los tópicos en el proyecto de agenda para las deliberaciones sobre la importancia económica de la medicina preventiva," Rockefeller Foundation (hereafter RF), Record Group 1.1, Series 303, Box 1, Folder 6, included in letter from George Bevier to George K. Strode, 19 March 1952; Sociedad Boliviana de Salud Pública, *Historia y perspectivas de la salud pública en Bolivia*, 118.

2. *Boletín de la Dirección General de Sanidad Pública* (hereafter BDGSP), año 3, no. 5 (1931), 442.

3. For example, David Sowell, *The Tail of Healer Miguel Perdomo Neire*; Steven Palmer, *From Popular Medicine to Medical Populism*.

4. On modern Andean medicine and its connections with Western biomedicine, see Joseph Bastien, *Healers of the Andes*; Libbett Crandon-Malamud, *From the Fat of Our Souls*; Joan Koss-Chionino, Thomas Leatherman, and Christine Greenway, *Medical Pluralism in the Andes*.

5. Marcos Cueto, *Excelencia científica en la periferia*, and "Andean Biology in Peru"; Nancy Stepan, *Beginnings of Brazilian Science*, and "The Interplay between Socio-economic Factors and Medical Science"; Marilia Coutinho, "Tropical Medicine in Brazil."

6. Julyan Peard, *Race, Place and Medicine*, and "Tropical Disorders and the Forging of a Brazilian Medical Identity, 1860–1890."

7. David Arnold, *Imperial Medicine in Indigenous Societies*; Roy MacLeod and Milton Lewis, *Disease, Medicine and Empire*; T. O. Ranger and P. Slack, *Epidemics and Ideas*; Megan Vaughan, *Curing Their Ills*; Teresa Meade and Mark Walker, *Science, Medicine, and Cultural Imperialism*.

8. Ronn Pineo, "Misery and Death in the Pearl of the Pacific," and *Social and Economic Reform in Ecuador*; Juan César García, *Pensamiento social en salud en América Latina*; Kenneth Kiple, "Cholera and Race in the Caribbean." In one of the articles most clearly influenced by dependency theory and the modes of production debate, David McCreery argued that the government system of registering prostitutes and confining them to brothels in Guatemala City was an example of labor coercion, not necessary in a capitalist society but similar to the methods of acquiring an agricultural workforce in the country. McCreery, " 'This Life of Misery and Shame.' "

9. An example of this is seen in the Rockefeller campaign against yellow fever in Peru in the 1920s. See chap. 2, "Sanitation from Above," in Cueto, *The Return of Epidemics*.

10. See the essays in Cueto, *Missionaries of Science*.

11. Teresita Martínez-Vergne, *Shaping the Discourse on Space*; Hugo Vezzetti, "El discurso psiquiátrico."

12. I take the term *linguistic turn* from Bryan Palmer's critique of relativism and the practice of literary deconstruction in the writing of history. Palmer, *Descent into Discourse*.

13. Diego Armus, "El viaje al centro," in Armus, *Entre médicos y curanderos*. Also using a literary approach is an article by Zandra Pedraza Gómez in the same volume: "La difusión de una dietética moderna en Colombia."

14. Jeffrey Needell, "The *Revolta Contra Vacina* of 1904"; Meade, "Civilizing Rio de Janeiro"; Palmer, *From Popular Medicine to Medical Populism*; Armando Solorzano, "The Rockefeller Foundation in Revolutionary Mexico"; María Eugenia Módena, "Combinar recursos curatives"; Sowell, *The Tale of Healer Miguel Perdomo Neire*; Alexandra Stern, "Buildings, Boundaries, and Blood"; Carl J. Murdock, "Physicians, the State and Public Health in Chile, 1881–1891"; María Silvia Di Liscia, "Viruela, vacunación e indígenas en la pampa argentina del siglo XIX." The Cuban government embraced modern biomedicine after the revolution of 1959, yet many other healing traditions continued to exist. Some of these now being promoted by the government as financial exigencies make it more difficult to maintain a First World medical system. See Julie Feinsilver, *Healing the Masses*.

15. Donna Guy, *Sex and Danger in Buenos Aires*; Katherine Elaine Bliss, *Compromised Positions*; McCreery, " 'This Life of Misery and Shame' "; Ann Blum, "Dying of Sadness"; Anne-Emanuelle Birn, "Skirting the Issue"; Nancy Stepan, *The Hour of Eugenics*; Stern, "Responsible Mothers and Normal Children"; Pedraza Gómez, "El debate eugenésico."

16. Exceptions are Stepan, *The Hour of Eugenics*; Peard, *Race, Place and Medicine*; Cueto, "Indigenismo and Rural Medicine in Peru"; Kiple, "Cholera and Race in the Caribbean"; Needell, "The *Revolta Contra Vacina* of 1904"; Sidney Chalhoub, "The Politics of Disease Control."

17. For the purposes of this book, I use Peter Wade's definition of the difference between ethnicity and race. According to Wade, ethnicity is connected to geography and a particular local history. It is "cultural difference spread over geographical space by virtue of the fact that social relations become concrete in spatialised form." He has maintained that to refer to race (usually associated with blackness) is to invoke a long history of slavery and colonialism. Working from this rough differentiation, it is most appropriate to use the term *ethnicity* when discussing indigenous peoples of Bolivia, even though in the period I study intellectuals used the term *race*. *Ethnicity* (as opposed to *ethnic group*) did not come into usage until the post–World War II period. See Wade, *Race and Ethnicity in Latin America*, esp. 5–24. Quote on 18.

18. Recently *mestizo* has replaced *white* or *criollo* to designate those at the top of the racial hierarchy. See Rossana Barragán, "Identidades indias y mestizas"; Silvia Rivera Cusicanqui, "La raíz," esp. 55–96. For the complex meanings of the term *mestizo* in Peru, see Marisol de la Cadena, *Indigenous Mestizos*. De la Cadena reports that in the 1940s in Cuzco neo-Indianist intellectuals used the term *cholo* to denote the pride and masculinity of the true *cuzqueño*. See 145–152.

19. Peard, *Race, Place, and Medicine*, 10.

20. An essential synthetic overview of the process of creating nations in the Andes in the nineteenth century is Brooke Larson, *Trials of Nation Making*.

21. David Brading, *The First America*; John Lynch, *The Spanish American Revolutions, 1808–1826*; Benedict Anderson, *Imagined Communities*.

22. Silvia Rivera Cusicanqui, *"Oprimidos pero no vencidos"*; Florencia Mallon, *Peasant and Nation*; Mark Thurner, *From Two Republics to One Divided*; Larson, "Indios redimidos, cholos barbarizados"; Seemin Qayum, "Creole Imaginings."

23. Elizabeth Dore, "One Step Forward, Two Steps Back," esp. 17–25; Carmen Diana Deere, "Liberalism and Married Women's Property Rights in Nineteenth Century Latin America."

24. Kristin Ruggiero, *Modernity in the Flesh*.

25. Rivera Cusicanqui, *"Oprimidos pero no vencidos"*, esp. chaps. 1 and 2; Charles Hale, *The Transformation of Liberalism in Late Nineteenth-Century*

Mexico, and *Mexican Liberalism in the Age of Mora, 1821–1853*; Eric Langer, "El liberalismo y la abolición de la comunidad indígena en el siglo XIX"; Joseph Love and Nils Jacobsen, *Guiding the Invisible Hand*; Tristan Platt, "Liberalism and Ethnocide in the Southern Andes," and "The Andean Experience of Bolivian Liberalism, 1825–1900."

26. Cusicanqui Rivera, *"Oprimidos pero no vencidos"*; Laura Gotkowitz, *Within the Boundaries of Equality*; Larson, "Indios redimidos."

27. Platt, *Estado boliviano y ayllu andino*.

28. Mallon, *Peasant and Nation*.

29. Carlos Mamani Condori, *Taraqu, 1866–1935*; René Danilo Arze Aguirre, *Guerra y conflictos sociales*; Gotkowitz, "Revisiting the Rural Roots of the Revolution"; Roberto Choque, "Las rebeliones indígenas de la postguerra del Chaco"; Taller de Historia Oral Andino, *Mujer y resistencia comunaria*. Also see Rivera Cusicanqui, *"Oprimidos pero no vencidos."*

30. Zulema Lehm A. and Rivera Cusicanqui, *Los artesanos libertarios y la ética del trabajo*; Ana Cecilia Wadsworth and Ineke Dibbits, *Agitadoras de buen gusto*; Dibbits, Elizabeth Peredo, Ruth Volgger, and Ana Cecilia Wadsworth, *Polleras libertarias*; Guillermo Lora, *Historia del movimiento obrero boliviano*, esp. vols. 2–4.

31. This point is made by Larson, "Capturing Indian Bodies, Hearths and Minds." Also see Sinclair Thomson, "La cuestión india en Bolivia a principios de siglo"; Marta Irurozgui, "La democracia imposible," and *La armonía de desigualdades*; Marie Danielle Demelas, "Darwinismo a la criolla." The early twentieth-century writers themselves are discussed later in the book.

32. Gotkowitz, "Revisiting the Rural Roots of the Revolution"; Irma Lorini, *El movimiento socialista "embrionario" en Bolivia, 1920–1939*; Larson, "Indios redimidos, cholos barbarizados."

33. Joan Scott, "Gender: A Useful Category of Historical Analysis."

34. For a selection of work of this type, see June Nash and Helen Safa, *Women and Change in Latin America*.

35. See Gilbert M. Joseph and Daniel Nugent, *Everyday Forms of State Formation*, and Mallon, *Peasant and Nation*. This approach to the state is the theoretical offspring of older writing about power and hegemony, including Michel Foucault, *Discipline and Punish*; *The Birth of the Clinic*; *The History of Sexuality*, vol. 1. However, for many Latin Americanists, whose inclinations and training are more Marxist, the works of Antonio Gramsci and Raymond Williams are probably more influential. Williams, *Marxism and Literature*; Gramsci, *Selections from the Prison Notebooks*. Also see Philip Corrigan and Derek Sayer, *The Great Arch*.

36. Sueann Caulfield, "The History of Gender in the Historiography of Latin America," 481. A selection of the works on gender and the state include Caulfield, *In Defense of Honor*; Susan Besse, *Restructuring Patriarchy*; Dore and Maxine Molyneux, *Hidden Histories of Gender and the State in*

Latin America; Karin Rosemblatt, *Gendered Compromises*; Eileen Findlay, *Imposing Decency*; Heidi Tinsman, *Partners in Conflict*. For an overview of historical studies on gender in Latin America, see Sueann Caulfield, "The History of Gender in the Historiography of Latin America," and the articles in the issue.

37. For instance, there is the series Protagonistas de la Historia published by the Ministerio de Desarrollo Humano in La Paz in 1997, which includes Silvia Arze, Magdalena Cajías, and Ximena Medinaceli, *Mujeres en rebelión*; Magdalena Cajías de la Vega and Iván Jiménez Chávez, *Mujeres en las minas de Bolivia*; Qayum, María Luisa Soux, and Barragán, *De terratenientes a amas de casa*; Florencia Durán Jordán and Ana María Seoane Flores, *El complejo mundo de la mujer durante la Guerra del Chaco*. Also Beatriz Rossells, *La mujer*; Luis Oporto Ordóñez, *Las mujeres en la historia de Bolivia*; Ximena Medinaceli, *Alterando la rutina*.

38. Dibbits, Peredo, Volgger, and Wadsworth, *Polleras libertarias*; Wadsworth and Dibbits, *Agitadoras de buen gusto*.

39. Lesley Gill, *Precarious Dependencies*; Marcia Stephenson, *Gender and Modernity in Andean Bolivia*.

40. Barragán, "Miradas indiscretas a la patria potestad"; Gotkowitz, "Trading Insults," and "Commemorating the Heroínas."

1   Hygiene and the "Indian Problem"

1. Irurozqui, "La democracia imposible," esp. 174–78; Larson, "Capturing Indian Bodies, Hearths and Minds," 187–190.

2. Rivera Cusicanqui, *"Oprimidos pero no vencidos,"* 25–42.

3. Klein, *Bolivia*, 319, 153.

4. Irurozqui, "La democracia imposible," 178–179.

5. Ramiro Condarco Morales, *Zarate, el "temible" willka"*; Demelas, "Darwinismo a la criolla"; Rivera, *"Oprimidos pero no vencidos,"* 14–16.

6. On indigenous motivations for joining the Liberals, see Platt, "The Andean Experience of Bolivian Liberalism, 1825–1900."

7. On varying approaches of liberals to the land question, see Langer, "El liberalismo y la abolición de la comunidad indígena en el siglo XIX." Much recent work on liberalism in Latin America has demonstrated that despite the rhetoric of assimilation, liberals were ambivalent about eliminating caste and racial distinctions. See Hale, *The Transformation of Liberalism in Late Nineteenth-Century Mexico*; Love and Jacobsen, *Guiding the Invisible Hand*; Platt, "Liberalism and Ethnocide in the Southern Andes."

8. Rivera Cusicanqui, *"Oprimidos pero no vencidos"*; Elizardo Pérez, *Warisata*.

9. Gabriel René-Moreno has quoted Nicomedes Antelo as saying in 1882 "El indio y el mestizo incásicos radicalmente no sirven para nada en

la evolución progresiva de las sociedades modernas. Tendrán tarde o tem-
prano, en la lucha por la existencia, que desaparecer bajo la planta soberana
de los blancos puros o purificados" ("The Indian and the 'Incaic' mestizo
at root don't serve any purpose in the progressive evolution of modern
societies. Sooner or later in the struggle for survival they will have to disappear under the sovereign sole of the pure whites or the purified whites.")
He does not explain what a "blanco purificado" was. See Gabriel René-
Moreno, *Nicomedes Antelo*, 53. Rivera Cusicanqui quotes the authors of the
1900 national census as commenting favorably on the decline of the percentage of Indians in the population, saying that Indians were the cause
of Bolivia's backwardness since they were resistant to all innovation and
progress. *"Oprimidos pero no vencidos,"* 17.

10. On Lamarckism in Latin America, see Stepan, *The Hour of Eugenics*,
esp. 63–76. For Bolivia see Irurozqui, *La armonía de las desigualdades*, 151.
According to Demelas ("Darwinismo a la criolla," 64), even Social Darwinist Sabino Pinilla held out the hope of mental improvement based on
the inheritance of acquired characteristics. Less specifically Lamarckian but
more inclined to find environmental causes for ethnic differences than Social Darwinists were Alcides Arguedas and Franz Tamayo. See Arguedas,
Pueblo enfermo, and *Raza de bronce*, and Tamayo, *La creación de la pedagogía*
nacional. Examples of the more prevalent cultural/environmental approach
common among doctors include Luis Isaac L. Landa, *Problemas políticos*;
Jaime Mendoza, *En las tierras del Potosí*, and *Apuntes de un médico*; Ernesto
Navarre, *La tuberculosis en el departamento de La Paz*.

11. *Revista Médica* 3:21–22 (La Paz, March–April, 1902), 426.

12. *Revista de Bacteriología e Higiene* (hereafter *RBH*) (La Paz, 15 May
1912), 61–63.

13. Balcázar, *Historia de la medicina en Bolivia*, 252, 545; Sociedad Boliviana de Salud Pública, *Historia y perspectivas de la salud pública en Bolivia*,
57. In fact until the 1950s, vaccination campaigns were launched only after
epidemics had already broken out. The disease remained endemic in the
country until 1958, when the Servicio Cooperativo Interamericano de Salud
Pública began a consistent campaign. Ibid.

14. *RBH* (15 April 1912), 34.

15. *RBH* (December 1913–January 1914), 121, 125–127.

16. Rockefeller Archive Center (hereafter RF), Record Group 1.1, Series
303, Bolivia, "Report on Medical Education in Bolivia."

17. *RBH* (July 1918), 1236–1237.

18. Stepan, "The Interplay between Socio-economic Factors and Medi-
cal Research," and "Initiation and Survival of Biomedical Research in a
Developing Country"; Cueto, "La ciudad y las ratas," 1–26; Thomas Glick,
"Science and Society in Twentieth-Century Latin America."

19. The cities of Oruro, Sucre, and Cochabamba and the department
of La Paz. In contrast, there were 818 lawyers in the same places. *Boletín de*

la Oficina Nacional de Inmigración, Estadística y Propaganda Geográfica (La Paz, 30 June 1901), 728, 792, 821, 851.

20. See Arnold, *Colonizing the Body*, and *Imperial Medicine in Indigenous Societies*; Roy MacLeod and Milton Lewis, *Disease, Medicine and Empire*; Ranger and Slack, *Epidemics and Ideas*; Vaughan, *Curing Their Ills*.

21. The best-known Bolivian *indigenista* novels are probably *Wuata Wuara* and *Raza de bronce*, by Arguedas; *Utama*, by Alfredo Guillen Pinto; and *Yanakuna*, by Jesús Lara, although many novels have indigenista elements. See Josefa Salmón, *El espejo indígena*; Echevarría, "Panorama y bibliografía de la novela social boliviana."

22. Bautista Saavedra, *El ayllu*.

23. "Proceso de Mohoza: Defensa del abogado Bautista Saavedra. Pronunciada en la Audiencia de 12 de Octubre de 1901," in Bautista Saavedra *El ayllu*, pt. 2, 135–157.

24. Manuel Rigoberto Paredes, *Provincia de Inquisive*, and *La altiplanicie*; Thomson, "La cuestión india en Bolivia a principios de siglo"; Larson, "Indios redimidos, cholos barbarizados," 30–34.

25. Angel Rama, "El área cultural andino"; Gonzalo Aguirre Beltrán, "Indigenismo y mestizaje"; Alan Knight, "Racism, Revolution and Indigenismo"; Irurozqui, "La democracia imposible," 173.

26. Georges Parrenin and Jean Pierre Lavaud, *Pour une approche sur l'indigénisme en Bolivia, 1900–1932*; Salmón, *El espejo indígena*.

27. Arguedas, *Pueblo enfermo* (1910), esp. chap. 2. This emphasis on mestizos' lack of political principles was in keeping with the elite's opposition to the clientelism of both Liberal and Conservative Party bosses in the first decades of the twentieth century.

28. Arguedas, *Pueblo enfermo*, 3rd ed. (1936). Quote on 74. Discussion of mestizos is primarily in chap. 3, "Psicología de la raza mestiza," 73–83.

29. Barragán, "Identidades indias y mestizas," 22.

30. Tristan Marof, *La justicia del Inca*. Also see "Proceso de un escritor," excerpt from *La verdad socialista en Bolivia*. On another radical indigenista, Alipio Valencia Vega, see Thomson, "Revolutionary Memory in Bolivia," 126–129.

31. Gotkowitz, "Commemorating the Heroínas."

32. On *susto* and emotional causes of illness, see Maria Tapias, "Disease and Dis-Ease," esp. chap. 4.

33. Bastien, *Healers of the Andes*, 38–42.

34. Ibid.

35. For a recent comprehensive historical account of the Kallawaya, see Carmen Beatriz Loza V., *Kallawaya*.

36. Crandon-Malamud, *From the Fat of Our Souls*, esp. 119–120.

37. Bastien, "Qollahuaya-Andean Body Concepts."

38. George M. Foster, *Hippocrates' Latin American Legacy*, 1–7.

39. Ibid. Esp. in chaps. 8 and 9 Foster makes the case for the Old World

origins of the ideas of hot and cold in American medicine. Bastien contends that the Andean hydraulic model, including ideas about the qualities of the fluids, predated the Europeans' arrival but that the Andean healers incorporated some Greek humoral concepts into their practice. *Healers of the Andes*, 45–52.

40. Bastien, *Healers of the Andes*, 58–60.

41. Ibid., 52, 97–99; Louis Girault, *Kallawaya curanderos itinerantes de los Andes*, 30.

42. Carmen Beatriz Loza interviewed a number of Kallawaya, who recounted their apprenticeships traveling throughout South America with experienced healers. *Kallawaya*, 80–81.

43. Ranaboldo, *El camino perdido*, 43.

44. Girault, *Kallawaya curanderos itinerantes de los Andes*, 31–33; Enrique Oblitas Poblete, "La lengua secreta de los Incas"; Saignes, "¿Quiénes son los Callahuayas?"

45. Belisario Díaz Romero, "Farmacopea Callaguaya"; Salmón Ballivián, "Los Callahuayas, médicos ambulantes."

46. Paredes, "Ideas médicas indígenas," 90–91.

47. Ibid., 91–100.

48. Bastien, *Healers of the Andes*; Girault, *Kallawaya curanderos itinerantes de los Andes*, 23–33; Jean Vellard, "Conducto de la población frente a la medicina moderna," 365.

49. Jaime Zeballos Pasten, "Los Callahuayas"; Carlos Ponce Sangines, "Los Callahuaya."

50. Rolando Costa Ardúz, "Revista de Bacteriología e Higiene," 20.

51. *RBH* (15 April 1912), 34.

52. Ibid., 35.

53. *Boletín de Estadística y Demografía* (La Paz, January, February, March 1913), 15; (April, May, June 1913), 13; (October, November, December 1914), 8; (January, February, March 1915), 17.

54. Sandra Lauderdale Graham, *House and Street*; Mary Douglas, *Purity and Danger*; Meade, "Civilizing Rio de Janeiro"; Vaughan, *Curing Their Ills*.

55. An unforgettable materialization of Morales's anxieties is found at the end of José María Arguedas's novel *Deep Rivers*, when plague-infected Indians from haciendas stream into the Peruvian town of Abancay demanding the bishop's blessing.

56. *RBH* (15 April 1912), 36.

57. Ibid., 37.

58. Michael Worboys, "The Emergence and Early Development of Parasitology"; Peard, "Tropical Disorders and the Forging of a Brazilian Medical Identity, 1860–1890," 25.

59. R. L. Huckstep, *Typhoid Fever and Other Salmonella Infections*; Charles Le Baron and David Taylor, "Typhoid Fever."

60. It may be significant that as late as the 1940s, the vaccine was also said to be particularly effective as a cure for the African population of Kenya. See Huckstep, *Typhoid Fever and Other Salmonella Infections.*

61. RBH (15 September 1913), 715.

62. Dr. Hermógenes Sejas in ibid., 713.

63. Néstor Morales in ibid., 706.

64. Arguedas, *Pueblo enfermo* (1910), 40.

65. However, Arguedas did not only adhere to a cultural explanation; he also believed that skin color was the result of climate and that Bolivian "whites" from the highlands had darker complexions than those from valley zones, who were more likely to be fair. *Pueblo enfermo* (1910), 40.

66. RBH (15 November 1913), 792.

67. RBH (15 September 1913), 689.

68. RBH (15 October 1913), 760.

69. RBH (15 September 1913), 691.

70. RBH (15 October 1913), 760.

71. Article from the La Paz daily, *El Norte*, reprinted in RBH 15 October 1913, 763. The photos were not published with the article.

72. RBH (September 1918), 1331–1333, 1341. By the mid-nineteenth century, careful studies of people with typhoid fever in France and England had shown that these conventional treatments did not alleviate the symptoms or shorten the course of the disease. Leonard G. Wilson, "Fevers."

73. Bastien, *Healers of the Andes*, 16; Loza V., *Kallawaya*, 73.

74. Balcázar, *Historia de la medicina en Bolivia.*

75. Armed conflict with Brazil over the rubber-producing Acre territory resulted in Bolivia losing this Amazonian region in 1903.

76. Mendoza, *En las tierras del Potosí*, 61.

77. Ibid., 72.

78. Ibid., 120.

79. Ibid., 197.

80. Ibid., 61.

81. Ibid., 127.

82. Ibid., 157.

83. Ibid., 161.

84. Gunnar Mendoza Loza, "Jaime Mendoza," 5.

85. Mendoza, *En las tierras del Potosí*, 203.

86. For a more recent discussion of women as being associated with Indianness that shows how a group of Peruvian peasants have internalized dominant ideology about ethnicity and gender, see De la Cadena, "Women Are More Indian."

87. Honorable Consejo Municipal de La Paz (hereafter HCMLP), *Memoria del Presidente Señor Adolfo González, Año 1923* (La Paz: Imprenta "Artística," 1924).

88. HCMLP, *Memoria del Presidente Dr. Vicente Mendoza López, 1928* (La Paz: Imprenta "Artística," 1929).

89. Ibid.; HCMLP, *Memoria, 1923*; HCMLP, *Memoria del Presidente Señor Adolfo González, Año 1924* (La Paz: Imprenta "Artística," 1925); HCMLP, *Memoria del Presidente Dr. Abel Iturralde, 1927* (La Paz: Imprenta Atenea, 1928); HCMLP, *Memoria y anexos del Presidente Sr. Ezequiel Jáuregui, Año 1931* (La Paz: Imprenta "Renacimiento," 1931).

90. A. Flores, "El paludismo en Mizque."

91. Ernesto Navarre, *La tuberculosis en el Departamento de La Paz*, Archivo de La Paz (ALP)/MC (Municipalidad de Coroico), Obitos, Coroico, Sepolturas Gratuitas, 1928, 1929.

92. Rivera Cusicanqui, *"Oprimidos pero no vencidos,"* 25–38.

2   The Medical Crisis of the Chaco War

1. Aurelio Melean, *La sanidad boliviana en la campaña del Chaco (1933–1934)*.

2. A recent essay on the causes of the 1952 revolution is James Dunkerley, "The Origins of the Bolivian Revolution in the Twentieth Century."

3. Bruce Farcau, *The Chaco War: Bolivia and Paraguay, 1832–1935*, 8–9; Roberto Querejazu Calvo, *Masamaclay*, 465–466.

4. Farcau, *The Chaco War*, 138–139.

5. Klein, *Bolivia*, 181–185.

6. Farcau, *The Chaco War*, 71, 146.

7. Arze Aguirre, *Guerra y conflictos sociales*, 40–42.

8. Querejazu Calvo, *Masamaclay*, 472.

9. Dunkerley, "The Origins of the Bolivian Revolution in the Twentieth Century," 144.

10. Melean, "Organización científica," 14–16.

11. Melean, "Organización de Sanidad en Vanguardia," 93, 96–98, 111–113.

12. Melean, "Organización científica," 11–20.

13. The following are from Melean, *La sanidad boliviana en la campaña del Chaco (1933–1934)*: "Estadística de enfermedades atendidas en el Hospital Militar de Villa Montes en 1933," 137–139; "Estadística de fallecimientos del Hospital Militar de Villa Montes — 1933," 142; "Causas de evacuación de heridos y enfermos del 1 de enero al 31 de diciembre de 1933." Quote from Ovidio Suárez Morales, "La enterocolitis del ejército en el Chaco," 387.

14. Emilio Fernández M., "Vitaminas y avitaminosis," 321–340. Statistics from Villa Montes Hospital in Melean, "Estadística de enfermedades atendidas en el Hospital Militar de Villa Montes en 1933," in Melean, *La sanidad boliviana*, 137–139.

15. Fernández M., "Vitaminas y avitaminosis," 296. Chuño is freeze-dried dehydrated potatoes.

16. "Estadística de enfermedades atendidas en el Hospital Military de Villa Montes en 1933," in Melean, *La sanidad boliviana*, 138; "Causas de evacuación de heridos y enfermos del 1 de enero al 31 de diciembre de 1933," in Melean, *La sanidad boliviana*, 151.

17. Néstor Orihuela, "Anotaciones sobre paludismo en el Chaco," 210–211.

18. Francisco Cernadas, "Cuidado a enfermos y heridos evacuados al interior de la república," 204–205.

19. Melean, "Organización científica," 14–15.

20. Cernadas, "Cuidado a enfermos y heridos evacuados al interior de la república," 206.

21. J. Mejía Gandarillas, "Enterocolitis toxi-infecciosas," 224–225.

22. Ricardo Arze Loureiro, "Enfermedades venéreas," 406. Arze Loureiro claimed that healthy soldiers used "la inoculación manual o instrumental de flujo uretral" to produce gonorrhea and thereby be hospitalized before reaching the front lines, 406.

23. In addition to using published interviews and memoirs, in 1996 I interviewed a number of Chaco War veterans in La Paz. Several I met at the office of the Organización de Ex-Combatientes de la Guerra del Chaco in La Paz, and several others I was introduced to by friends or relatives of the veterans. I also managed to talk to two nurses who served in the Chaco by approaching them at the government office where they had to line up to collect their pension checks. Most of the veterans I spoke with were working class and told similar stories of deprivation. I am indebted to Cecilia Arauco de Machicao for helping me set up most of these interviews. Claudia Heckl arranged for me to speak with Francisco Iporre Valdez. Everyone I interviewed, without exception, was gracious and more than willing to talk about their experiences.

24. Carlos Herbas Cabrera, *El Cristo de Tarairi*, 54–58.

25. Eduardo Salinas Valdivieso, "Intoxicaciones," 379–380.

26. Farcau, *The Chaco War*, 158.

27. Interviews with Melaneo Sánchez Rodríguez, Desiderio Poquechoque, and Florencio Vásquez published in Arze Aguirre, *Guerra y conflictos sociales*, 211–254.

28. Interview conducted by author with Daniel Macuaga, La Paz, 26 March 1996.

29. Interview conducted by author with Víctor Campos, La Paz, 27 March 1996.

30. Interview with Melaneo Sánchez Rodríguez, in Arze Aguirre, *Guerra y conflictos sociales*, 212–213.

31. Interview with Daniel Macuaga, La Paz, 26 March 1996.

32. Interview with Florencio Vásquez in Arze Aguirre, *Guerra y conflictos sociales*, 248–249.

33. Interview with Luis Michel in Arze Aguirre, *Guerra y conflictos sociales*, 176.

34. Interview with Melaneo Sánchez Rodríguez in Arze Aguirre, *Guerra y conflictos sociales*, 214.

35. Interview conducted by author with Eduardo Aruaco, La Paz, 29 April 1996.

36. Interview conducted by author with Francisco Iporre Valdez, La Paz, 22 April 1996; Iporre Valdez, "Fragmento de sus memorias del Ingeniero de Minas Francisco Iporre Valdez."

37. Melean, "Organización de Sanidad en Vanguardia," 107.

38. Interview with Iporre Valdez, La Paz, 22 April 1996; and "Fragmento de sus memorias del Ingeniero de Minas Francisco Iporre Valdez."

39. Interview with Eduardo Arauco, La Paz, 29 April 1996.

40. Boletín de la Dirección General de Sanidad Pública (hereafter BDGSP), año 3, no. 5 (1931), 437–441. Number of employees in "Informe anual de la Dirección General de Sanidad" (Renato A. Riverin), 25 July 1931 in BDGSP, año 3, no. 6 (1931), 868.

41. BDGSP, año 3, no. 5 (1931), 442.

42. "Informes de las Direcciones Departamentales," Cochabamba (Dr. Pablo Lavayen), BDGSP, año 5, no. 8 (1935), 4.

43. BDGSP, año 3, no. 5 (1931), 441.

44. "Informe de la Dirección de Sanidad" (Dr. E. Lara Q.), BDGSP, año 4, no. 7 (1934), 126–127.

45. Ibid., 145.

46. "Informe de la Dirección General" (J. M. Balcázar), BDGSP, año 4, no. 7 (1933), 70.

47. "Informe de la Dirección General de Sanidad Pública" (J. M. Balcázar), BDGSP, año 4, no. 7 (1933), 68–70; Dr. E. Lara Quiróz al Ministro de Estado en el despacho de Instrucción, BDGSP, año 5, no. 8 (1935), 40; Decreto de José Luis Tejado Sorzano, Presidente Constitucional de la República, 17 June 1935, reprinted in BDGSP, año 5, no. 8 (1935), 152.

48. "Informe de la Dirección de Sanidad" (Dr. E. Lara Q.), BDGSP, año 4, no. 7 (1934), 126–127.

49. "Informes de las Direcciones Departamentales" (Dr. J. de Sierra), BDGSP, año 5, no. 8 (1935), 82.

50. "Informe de la Dirección General," BDGSP, año 4, no. 7 (1933), 70.

51. "Informe de la Dirección de Sanidad," BDGSP, año 4, no. 7 (1934), 139.

52. "Informe del Director General de Sanidad Pública," BDGSP, año 5, no, 8 (1935), 7.

53. Claudia Ranaboldo, *El camino perdido*, 62, 70; Loza V. *Kallawaya*, 129–130.

54. Informe de la Dirección General, BDGSP, año 4, no. 3 (1933), 80.

55. "Informe del Director General de Sanidad Pública, 1934–1935," BDGSP, año 5, no. 8 (1935), 4.

56. Bernardo Cadario, "Informes de las Direcciones Departamentales," Santa Cruz, BDGSP, año 5, no. 8 (1935), 74–76.

57. "Liga Nacional contra la Tuberculosis," BDGSP, año 1, no. 1 (1929), 54–56; "Informe de la Dirección de Sanidad" (Juan Manuel Balcázar), BDGSP, año 3, no. 7 (1933), 85.

58. "Liga Nacional contra la Tuberculosis," BDGSP, 55.

59. "Informe de la Dirección de Sanidad," BDGSP, año 4, no. 7 (1934), 136.

60. Ibid., 130.

61. "Informe de la Dirección General," BDGSP, año 4, no. 7 (1933), 80. The mortality rate for untreated typhus (there was no treatment before the introduction of broad-spectrum antibiotics in the late 1940s) is generally between 5 percent and 25 percent but can be as high as 40 percent. Victoria Harden, "Typhus, Epidemic," 1081.

62. "Informes de las Direcciones Departamentales," Potosí (Dr. Trifón Quiróz F.), BDGSP, año 5, no 8 (1935), 50, 59.

63. Interview with Sra. Elsa Echalar, La Paz, 2 April 1996.

64. "Informes de las Direcciones Departamentales," Potosí (Dr. Trifón Quiróz F.), BDGSP, año 5, no. 8 (1935), 52.

65. "Informe de la Dirección General" (J. M. Balcázar), BDGSP, año 4, no. 7 (1933), 79.

66. Also, during the Chaco War Argentina, although officially neutral, supported Paraguay, and its government may have been looking for any pretext to discredit Bolivia.

67. "Informe de la Dirección de Sanidad" (Dr. E. Lara Q.), BDGSP, año 4, no. 7 (1934), 137.

68. "Informes de las Direcciones Departamentales," Oruro (Dr. R. Rivera), BDGSP, año 5, no. 8 (1935), 69.

69. "Informe del Director General de Sanidad Pública" (Dr. E. Lara Q.), BDGSP, año 5, no. 8 (1935), 5; "Informes de las Direcciones Departamentales," La Paz (Dr. Fuentes Alcoreza), BDGSP, año 5, no. 8 (1935), 43–44.

70. "Informes de las Direcciones Departamentales," Tarija (Dr. A. Baldivieso), BDGSP, año 5, no. 8 (1935), 77.

71. "La epidemia de Santa Cruz (Informe del comisionado doctor Juan Manuel Balcázar, Director Interino de Sanidad Pública)," BDGSP, año 3, no. 6 (1931 and first half of 1932), 1186–1195.

72. Donald Cooper and Kenneth Kiple, "Yellow Fever," 1100–1107. Ironically, the fact that adults who have not been exposed to yellow fever before generally get more severe cases meshed with racial politics in a contrary fashion in Brazil. In that country, at the time of transition from slavery

to free labor (late nineteenth century), government and public health officials were most concerned about eliminating yellow fever, which was most severe among nonimmune European immigrants. Hoping to "whiten" the nation by importing a workforce, they were correctly concerned that yellow fever would frighten Europeans who were thinking about emigrating. On the other hand, they paid almost no attention to diseases such as tuberculosis and cholera, which were decimating the black population. Sidney Chalhoub, "The Politics of Disease Control."

73. "La epidemia de Santa Cruz," año 3, no. 6 (1931 and first half of 1932), 1186–1195.

74. "La fiebre amarilla y la Fundación Rockefeller en Bolivia," BDGSP, año 3, no. 6 (1931 and first semester of 1932), 1227–1228.

75. RF, Record Group 1.1, Series 303, Box 2, Folder 14, F. L. Soper to Dr. Russell, 20 June 1932.

76. "Informes parciales de los directores de sanidad departamental," Tarija (Juan Ramírez), BDGSP, año 3, no. 6 (1931 and first half of 1932), 900.

77. At the end of the Chaco War, researchers believed that the only mosquito that spread malaria in Bolivia were varieties of the *Anopheles* mosquito. This may not have been the case, since other vectors were known to spread the disease in neighboring Brazil, esp. *A. darlingi*. Germán Orosco P., "Lucha antipalúdica," 242; Stepan, " 'The Only Serious Terror in These Regions.' "

78. "Paludismo en Bolivia," BDGSP, año 3, no. 5 (1931), 512–518.

79. Flores, "El paludismo en Mizque," 52.

80. Ibid., 50–52.

81. "Jefatura Sanitaria de Mizque" (Dr. Demetrio Frontaura A., jefe de Zona Sanitaria Mizque), BDGSP, año 5, no. 8 (1935), 85.

82. Ibid., 89–90.

83. Ibid., 91.

84. Ibid., 85.

85. Ibid., quotes on 88, 91.

86. Querejazu, *Masamaclay*, 108–109; Farcau, *The Chaco War*, 74.

87. Tabera R., *Apuntes para la historia de la Guerra del Chaco-Picuiba*, 300.

88. Arze Aguirre, *Guerra y conflictos sociales*, 83–115; Mamani Condori, *Taraqu, 1866–1935*, 134–139.

89. Joseph Bastien, *Healers of the Andes*, 11, 23.

90. José Antezana Estrada, "Proyecto de Código Sanitario de Bolivia," 2.

91. *Boletín del Ministerio de Higiene y Salubridad* 2:2 (1939), 142.

3   Rockefeller Foundation in Bolivia

1. Williams, "Nationalism and Public Health"; Solorzano, "The Rocke-feller Foundation in Revolutionary Mexico"; Steven Palmer, "Central American Encounters with Rockefeller Public Health, 1814–1921."

2. Cueto, "Visions of Science and Development," 3, 4, 12.

3. "International Health Division" in *The Rockefeller Foundation Annual Report, 1932*, 36–37.

4. RF, Record Group 5, Series 1.2, Box 28, Folder 433, "Conference on Educational Needs of Bolivia," 1916.

5. RF, Record Group 5, Series 1.2, Box 28, Folder 433, "Medical Educa-tion in Bolivia, 1926."

6. Between 1913 and 1916 the medical programs of the RF were coordi-nated by the International Health Commission; in 1916 it was renamed the International Health Board and in 1927 the International Health Division. Raymond Fosdick, *The Story of the Rockefeller Foundation*, 24.

7. See Cueto, "Visions of Science and Development."

8. Ibid., 12.

9. RF, "Conference on Educational Needs of Bolivia," 1916, 1.

10. Ibid., 2–4.

11. Cueto, "Visions of Science and Development," 6.

12. RF, "Medical Education in Bolivia, 1926," 15.

13. Ibid., 6–8, 9, 10. Quote on 8. Number of volumes in libraries in Buenos Aires and Montevideo in Cueto, "Visions of Science and Devel-opment," table 2, p. 8.

14. It is now known that the mortality rate from yellow fever is lower than it was often believed, because many people had mild cases that were not diagnosed. Cooper and Kiple, "Yellow Fever."

15. RF, Record Group 12.1, A. M. Walcott Diary, 20–27 June 1932.

16. Ibid.

17. Cueto, "Sanitation from Above," 29–31; Fred Soper et al., "Yellow Fever without *Aedes aegypti*."

18. RF, Record Group 12.1, A. M. Walcott, Diary, 17 July 1932.

19. "Informe del Director General de Sanidad Pública," BDGSP, año 4, no. 7 (1933), 86; RF, Record Group 12.1, A. M. Walcott Diary, 1 Septem-ber 1932.

20. RF, Record Group 12.1, A. M. Walcott Diary, 11 October 1932; A. M. Walcott Diary, 22 October 1932.

21. RF, Record Group 12.1, A. M. Walcott Diary, 10 October 1932.

22. RF, Record Group 12.1, A. M. Walcott Diary, 18 October 1932.

23. Ibid., 7 October 1932.

24. The directors of public health in 1933 and 1935 in their official pub-

lication went out of their way to praise the work of the RF. Juan Manuel Balcázar in 1933 said that the foundation was doing "una labor verdaderamente transcendental" ("a truly transcendent effort"). Dr. E. Lara Q. also praised the RF and its Bolivian head of the Yellow Fever Service. "Informe del Director" (J. M. Balcázar), BDGSP, año 4, no. 7 (1933), 86; "Informe del Director General de Sanidad Pública" (Dr. E. Lara Q.), BDGSP, año 5, no. 8 (1935), 5–6.

25. Dr. Angel Claros, "Informe del Servicio de Fiebre Amarilla en Bolivia (27 de junio de 1932 a 31 de diciembre de 1935)," BDGSP, año 5, no. 8 (1935), 172; Dr. René Valda, Diary, 6 February 1933. Included in Walcott diary for 16 March 1933.

26. BDGSP, Angel Claros, "Informe," 170.

27. RF, Diary of L. W. Hackett, 25 January 1941.

28. BDGSP, Angel Claros, "Informe," 156–157.

29. RF, Record Group 12.1, A. M. Walcott Diary, 8 August 1932; "The work done by the inspectors is terribly rotten, almost unbelievably so," 27 August 1932; "The work of the inspectors is pretty rotten," 29 August 1932.

30. RF, A. M. Walcott Diary, 7 September 1932, 27 September 1932, 24 October 1932, 7 November 1932, 7 December 1932.

31. Dr. Angel Claros, "Informe del Servicio de Fiebre Amarilla en Bolivia (27 June 1932 to 31 December 1935)," BDGSP, año 5, no. 8 (1935), 173.

32. Cooper and Kiple, "Yellow Fever," 1106.

33. Angel Claros, "Informe del Servicio de Fiebre Amarilla en Bolivia," 168.

34. Larson, "Capturing Indian Bodies, Hearths and Minds."

35. Fosdick, "President's Review," in *The Rockefeller Foundation Annual Report, 1942*, 10.

36. RF, Diary of L. W. Hackett, 23 January 1941.

37. Ibid., 22 January 1941.

38. Cueto, "The Rockefeller Foundation's Medical Policy and Scientific Research in Latin America."

39. RF, Diary of L. W. Hackett, 28 October 1941.

40. Ibid., 25 January 1941.

41. RF, Record Group 1.1: Projects, Series 303: Bolivia, Box 1, Folder 2, "Contract approved by the Supreme Government of Bolivia," legalized copy, no. 41, 26 February 1943.

42. Ibid., Diary of L. W. Hackett, 28 October 1941.

43. RF, Diary of L. W. Hackett, 10 March 1941.

44. RF, "Contract approved by the Supreme Government of Bolivia."

45. Cueto, "The Rockefeller Foundation's Medical Policy and Scientific Research in Latin America," 132.

46. RF, Diary of L. W. Hackett, 22 October 1941, 358.

47. Ibid., 10 March 1941, 181.

48. Ibid.

49. Ibid., 22 October 1941.

50. Quoted in Larson, "Capturing Indian Bodies, Hearths and Minds," 200. Original source: SCIDE, *Rural Education in Bolivia*, 8.

51. Larson, "Capturing Indian Bodies, Hearths and Minds," 197–203.

52. RF, Bevier Diary, 27 March 1946.

53. On the Pan-American Sanitary Bureau see Marcos Cueto, *El valor de la salud*.

54. RF, Record Group 1.1, Series 303, Box 1, Folder 6, George K. Strode Diary, 2 April 1951.

55. RF, Bevier Diary, 22 March 1946, 29 September 1949, 15 October 1949.

56. RF, Record Group 1.1, Series 303, Box 1, Folder 5, "L. W. Hackett to G. K. Strode," 16 February 1949.

57. RF, Record Group 1.1, Series 303, Box 1, Folder 6, "Bevier to Strode, March 19, 1951" and attached WHO questionnaire completed by Torres Muñoz.

58. "The Campaign against Malaria in Sardinia," *The Rockefeller Foundation Annual Report, 1950*, 48, 50.

59. RF, Record Group 1.1, Series 303, Box 1, Folder 5, "Control de tifus"; RF, WHO questionnaire.

60. RF, Record Group 1.1, Series 303, Box 1, Folder 6, "George Bevier to A. J. Warren," 20 August 1951; RF, WHO questionnaire.

61. Klein, *Bolivia*, 211–212.

62. Jorge Dandler and Juan Torrico A., "From the National Indigenous Congress to the Ayopaya Rebellion"; Gotkowitz, "Revisiting the Rural Roots of the Revolution."

63. RF, Bevier Diary, 22 March 1946.

64. Ibid., 13 January 1950.

65. Ibid., 13 September 1949, 16 September 1949, quote on 121.

66. *La Razón*, Friday, 24 March 1950.

67. RF, Record Group 1.1, Series 303, Box 1, Folder 5, "G. Bevier to G. K. Strode," 19 April 1950.

68. RF, Bevier Diary, 28 January 1950; *New York Times*, 21 March 1950.

69. RF, Bevier Diary, 11 February 1950, 16 February 1950.

70. Alfredo Augsten Diary, included in Bevier Diary, 14 June 1950.

71. RF, Bevier Diary, 3 March 1950, 4 March 1950.

72. Ibid., 11 February 1950.

73. Ibid., 2 March 1950, 29.

74. Ibid., 3 March 1950.

75. *La Razón*, Saturday, 18 March 1950.

76. Costa Ardúz, "Imponente estirpe en la Dirección del Instituto Nacional de Bacteriología"; Oswaldo Maldonado M., "Félix Veintemillas."

77. *La Razón*, Thursday, 23 March 1950.

78. *Los Tiempos*, 17 August 1950.

79. *Los Tiempos*, 19 August 1950, 6.

80. RF, Record Group 1.1, Series 303, Box 1, Folder 6, George Bevier to A. J. Warren, 30 August 1951.

81. RF, Record Group 12.1, Diary of George Bevier, 13 April 1951, 28.

82. Birn, "Skirting the Issue," 400.

83. Yet in terms of U.S. foreign policy, somewhat ironically, the foundation did not work closely with the SCISP, the U.S.-government-funded health program in Bolivia. Officers of the RF, in fact, suspected that the Bolivian government's attack on the Division of Endemic Diseases was an effort to find a pretext to transfer all RF operations to the SCISP. RF, Record Group 1.1, Series 303, Box 1, Folder 5, "G. Bevier to G. K. Strode," 30 March 1950.

4   Women and Public Health

1. *La Razón* (La Paz), Wednesday, 20 March 1996, 1, A-11.

2. *La Razón* (La Paz), Wednesday, 12 July 2000, A-18.

3. *Chola* is the term generally used for Aymara- or Quechua-speaking urban women in Bolivia. They are known for their attire, which includes a full skirt known as a *pollera*, a shawl held fast with a silver brooch, and a distinctive hat (in La Paz usually a felt bowler hat, but there are regional variations). Cholas today are often conceived of as an intermediate group between Indians and whites/mestizos, but in the period of this study the term *cholo/chola* was often used interchangeably with *mestizo*. Cholas are frequently merchants in city markets or domestic servants, but in the twenty-first century they are found in many different professions. As women they have figured significantly in the country's literary imagination, sometimes being depicted as unhygienic and unfeminine and at other times as hypersexualized. See discussion later in this chapter and Stephenson, *Gender and Modernity in Andean Bolivia*; Gill, *Precarious Dependencies*; Ximena Mejía, *"Mujeres de Pollera."* On cholos more generally, see the introduction to this book.

4. "Anexos a la memoria presentada por el Presidente del Consejo Municipal, Dr. Vicente Mendoza López," in HCMLP, *Memoria del Presidente Dr. Vicente Mendoza López, 1928* (La Paz: Imprenta Artística, 1929), 2:303–315.

5. In 1950 La Paz had a population of 321,073. Klein, *Bolivia*, 319.

6. "Población clasificada según sus oficios y profesiones," in "Anexos a la memoria . . . Dr. Vicente Mendoza López," 313–314.

7. Miguel Levy, "Educación en el período de la pubertad," 58.

8. "La mortalidad infantil," *RIMS*, no. 46 (October 1929), 42. Unsigned introduction to a reprinted paper by Dr. Luis Morquio.

9. "Población clasificada según su instrucción elemental," in "Anexos a la memoria . . . Dr. Vicente Mendoza López," 316.

10. Klein, *Bolivia*, 227.

11. Medinaceli, *Alterando la rutina*, 31–34.

12. Ibid., 153.

13. "Cuadro estadístico de natalidad de la ciudad de La Paz en 1928, según legitimidad, sexo y raza," in HCMLP, *Memoria del Presidente Dr. Vicente Mendoza López, 1928*, vol. 1 (La Paz: Imprenta Artística, 1929).

14. "Cementerio General. Cuadro demográfico de la mortalidad ocurrida en la ciudad de La Paz, desde el día 1 de enero hasta el día 31 de diciembre de 1928 años," in HCMLP, *Memoria, 1928*.

15. Landa L. *Problemas políticos*, 18–28.

16. Medinaceli, *Alterando la rutina*, 21–59.

17. Lehm A. and Rivera C., *Los artesanos libertarios y la ética del trabajo*, 153–181; Dibbits, Peredo, Volgger, and Wadsworth, *Polleras libertarias*; Wadsworth and Dibbits, *Agitadoras de buen gusto*.

18. Juan Manuel Balcázar, *Protección y crianza del niño*, 20–22.

19. Debórah Dwork, "Childhood"; "Pediatrics," in Roderick E. McGrew, *Encyclopedia of Medical History*, 244.

20. Edward Stockwell, "Infant Mortality."

21. *Revista Médica* 3:21–22 (La Paz, March–April 1902): 426; RBH 1:2 (La Paz, 15 May 1912), 61–63.

22. RBH 5:3 (La Paz, July 1918), 1242–1244.

23. Mendoza, "Una indicación (en favor de los niños de las clases obreras)," 461.

24. Ibid., 461–462.

25. Ibid., 463–464.

26. Ibid., 464.

27. Ibid., 465–466.

28. Ibid., 469, 463.

29. Ibid., 466–469. Quotes on 466 and 469.

30. Luis Morquio, "De causas de la mortalidad de la primera infancia y medios de reducirla."

31. Ibid., 43.

32. Ibid., 44–45.

33. Ibid., 46. Quote from Profesora Ernesta dal Co.

34. E. Lara Q., "La lucha contra la mortalidad infantil," 99.

35. Ibid.

36. This idea was commonly held in Europe during the nineteenth century and, as the discussion later in this chapter indicates, was generally accepted in Bolivia well into the 1900s. On Europe see Mary Spongberg, *Feminizing Venereal Disease*.

37. Juan Manuel Balcázar, *Protección y crianza del niño*.

38. Ibid., 2.

39. Stephenson, *Gender and Modernity in Andean Bolivia*, 128–134 and 59–110, passim.

40. "Bajo el puente de la calle yanacocha fue visto el cadáver de un niño," *La Razón*, Friday, 28 March 1930, 12.

41. "Una criatura de 3 días fue arrojado desde un puente," *La Calle*, Friday, 20 November 1936, 5.

42. Ibid.

43. Balcázar, *Protección y crianza del niño*, 7–8.

44. Ibid., 6–7.

45. Ibid., 16–17.

46. Nick and Nora Charles were the glamorous, Martini-swilling sleuths in Dashiell Hammett's novel *The Thin Man* (Knopf, 1934). They were also popularized in an MGM movie starring William Powell and Myrna Loy (1934) and a television series that ran from 1957–59 featuring Peter Lawford and Phyllis Kirk.

47. Emilio Fernández, "Protección a la madre y al hijo," 56–57.

48. Ibid., 63–64.

49. HCMLP, *Memoria del Presidente Señor Adolfo González, Año 1923* (La Paz: Imprenta "Artística," 1924), 263.

50. HCMLP, "Proyecto de ordenanza," in *Memoria del Presidente Señor Adolfo González, Año 1924* (La Paz, Imprenta "Artística," 1925), 96.

51. Ibid., 97.

52. HCMLP, "Proyecto de ordenanza," in *Memoria, 1924*, 97.

53. "Informe de Cirujano en Jefe de los Hospitales de Miraflores" (n.d.), in HCMLP, *Memoria, 1924*, 394; "Informe del Administrado Interventor de los Hospitales de Miraflores, César Saavedra, 30 November 1924," in HCMLP, *Memoria, 1924*, 424.

54. It is not possible to establish infant mortality per 1,000 live births, because birth records are not available. "Demografía: Estadística del Cementerio General," HCMLP, *Memoria, 1923*, 498–499; "Cementerio General: Cuadro demográfico de la mortalidad ocurrido en la ciudad de La Paz, 1928," in HCMLP, *Memoria del Presidente Dr. Vicente Mendoza López, 1928*, vol. 1 (La Paz: Imprenta Artística, 1929); "Anexos a la memoria de 1931," in HCMLP, *Memoria y anexos del Presidente Sr. Ezequiel Jáuregui, Año 1931* (La Paz: Imprenta "Renacimiento," 1931), 259; *Boletín del Honorable Ayuntamiento de La Paz, 1942*, año 42 (La Paz, 1942); *Boletín Municipal*, (February, March, November 1944).

55. Eclampsia is a condition of late pregnancy of unknown etiology that includes hypertension, albuminuria, and adema and can lead to coma or seizures if not treated. Generally once the condition has been stabilized, delivery is induced. See "Preeclampsia and Eclampsia," in *The Merck Manual*, 1764–1765.

56. Dr. Natalio A. Aramayo, "Consultorios de maternidad," quote on 561.

57. "Protección a la maternidad y a la infancia," *Boletín del Ministerio del Trabajo, Previsión Social y Salubridad*, no. 2 (January 1938), 15.

58. Ibid., 16.

59. John M. Riddle, *Eve's Herbs*; Dwork, "Childhood."

60. On midwives' and others' knowledge of the abortifacient properties of herbs see Riddle, *Eve's Herbs*, chap. 6.

61. Irvine S. L. Loudon, "Childbirth"; Jean Donnison, *Midwives and Medical Men*.

62. Lee Penyak, "Obstetrics and the Emergence of Women in Mexico's Medical Establishment"; Birn, "Skirting the Issue"; Brad R. Huber and Alan R. Sandstrom, "Recruitment, Training, and Practice of Indigenous Midwives."

63. Palmer, *From Popular Medicine to Medical Populism*, 139–154.

64. Kristin Ruggiero, "Honor, Maternity, and the Disciplining of Women."

65. Peard, *Race, Place and Medicine*, 107–137.

66. Ismael Montes, Presidente Constitucional de la República, "Decreto Supremo, 6 de mayo de 1916" in BDGSP, año 1, no. 1 (La Paz, August 1929), 17–19.

67. "El ingreso a la Escuela de Obstétrica," *La Razón*, Thursday, 23 January 1930.

68. "Circular de Adolfo Flores, Director General de Sanidad, al Señor Director de Sanidad Departamental y Asistencia Pública," 21 mayo de 1929, BDGSP, año 1, no. 1 (August 1929), 46.

69. HCMLP, *Memoria, 1923*, 195–196.

70. Ibid., 196.

71. Ibid.

72. *Boletín del Honorable Ayuntamiento*, año 28 (La Paz, session of 6 November 1923), 3.

73. Ibid.

74. *La Calle*, Saturday, 23 January 1937.

75. Hospital General, La Paz, Ginecología, Estadísticas, 1942–1949.

76. This is similar to the situation in La Paz more recently, where the incidence of abortion is most common after women have had several children. Rance, "Bolivia," 63.

77. Bliss, *Compromised Positions*. When Mexico finally eliminated registered prostitution, it was replaced by a new law that penalized *both* men and women who spread venereal diseases. Ibid., 203–205.

78. *Boletín del H. Ayuntamiento Municipal*, año 17 (La Paz, 11 July 1922), 5.

79. Ibid.

80. Guy, *Sex and Danger in Buenos Aires*; Mary Gibson, *Prostitution and the State in Italy, 1860–1915*; Bliss, *Compromised Positions*, 2, 27–29, 32, 46.

81. Gibson, *Prostitution and the State*, 39–64; Alain Corbin, *Women for*

Hire, 214–258; Judith Walkowitz, *Prostitution and Victorian Society*, 90–147.

82. Guy, *Sex and Danger in Buenos Aires*, 105–135.

83. Bliss, *Compromised Positions*, chap. 6.

84. Cecilia Patiño C., Doris Cerdeña V., and Sidey Fallas L., *Comercialización de mujeres*, 21, 66–67. Registration cards from the 1980s found in the Archivo Histórico de La Paz (ALP), list women as *copetineras* or *meretrizes*, include their pictures, and indicate that the vast majority worked in establishments on the Avenida de las Américas on the outskirts of town. A few, generally foreigners, lived and worked in upscale, residential neighborhoods.

85. The 1906 reglamento is published in Antonio Paredes Candia, *De rameras, burdeles y proxenetas*, 87–98. The 1927, largely unchanged version is from HCMLP, *Memoria del Presidente Dr. Able Iturralde, 1927* (La Paz: Imprenta Atenea, 1928), 163–168.

86. Honorable Consejo Municipal de La Paz (HCMLP), *Memoria del Presidente Señor Adolfo González, Año 1923* (La Paz: Imprenta "Artística," 1924), 394–396.

87. HCMLP, *Memoria del Sr. Presidente Dr. Serapio Navajas, 1929* (La Paz: Editorial "Renacimiento," 1929), 32.

88. HCMLP, *Memoria, 1923*, 397–398.

89. Paredes Candia, *De rameras, burdeles y proxenetas*, 81, 84, 77.

90. "Informe del Director de la Oficina de Higiene Municipal, Dr. Manuel Ergueta T.," in HCMLP, *Memoria, 1923*, 425.

91. Ibid.

92. "Informe del Director de la Oficina de Higiene," La Paz, 2 December 1924, in HCMLP, *Memoria 1924*, 346–347.

93. *Boletín del Honorable Ayuntamiento de La Paz*, año 26 (Session of July 1922), 6. On the idea that women were the original cause of venereal disease, see Spongberg, *Feminizing Venereal Disease*.

94. "Informe del Director de la Oficina de Higiene Municipal, Dr. Manuel Ergueta T.," in HCMLP, *Memoria, 1923*, 427.

95. "Reglamento de Prostitución," HCMLP, *Memoria del presidente Dr. Abel Iturralde, 1927* (La Paz: Imprenta Atenea, 1928), 163–168.

96. "Informe del Director de la Oficina de Higiene," La Paz, 2 de diciembre de 1924, in HCMLP, *Memoria, 1924*, 347.

97. Ibid.

98. Hospital General, La Paz, Hombres, Estadísticas, 1926.

99. *Boletín del Honorable Ayuntamiento de La Paz*, año 39 (March 1934), 26.

100. HCMLP, *Memoria*, 1931, 48.

101. Corbin, *Women for Hire*, esp. 94–95.

102. "Anexos," in HCMLP, *Memoria, 1929*, 7.

103. *La Razón*, Saturday, 18 January 1930, 8.

104. "Anexos," in HCMLP, *Memoria, 1931*, 236.

105. BDGSP, año 5, no. 8 (1935), 61.

106. Lehm and Rivera, *Los artesanos libertarios*; Klein, *Bolivia*.

107. *La Razón*, Thursday, 13 February 1930, 12 and Thursday, 20 February 1930, 4 (quote in this issue).

108. HCMLP, *Memoria del Presidente Sr. Carlos Zalles* [1929] (La Paz: Imprenta "Atenea," 1930), 46–48.

109. Ibid.

110. Ibid.

111. "Informe de la Dirección General de Sanidad (gestión de 1933)" (Juan Manuel Balcázar, Secretario General), BDGSP, año 4, no. 7 (1933), 84–85. A similar shift to opposition to regulation for public health reasons rather than because of liberal principles occurred among doctors in Italy around the turn of the century. Gibson, *Prostitution and the State in Italy*, 90.

112. Walkowitz, *Prostitution and Victorian Society*, esp. 102–103 and 141–142.

113. Cited in Dibbits, Peredo, Volgger, and Wadsworth, *Polleras libertarias*, 24. Walkowitz has also pointed out that in England opposition to the Contagious Disease Acts was mostly among middle-class women and working-class men. Working-class women, she maintains, were less involved in the movement because they "clung to a social respectability based on shakier material foundations." *Prostitution and Victorian Society*, 146.

114. "Querella correccional contra las personas que indica por los delitos que refiere; Rosa Solares Millan y Bernadina Arriague de Millan con Dolores de Fernández," Archivo Histórico de La Paz (ALP), CSD, 1923 #1955; ALP, Policía, Libro de Sección Garantías y Compromisos-Denuncias, 11 February 1947.

115. Gotkowitz, "Trading Insults."

116. "Reglamento Interno del Dormitorio Popular No. 2, 'Pabellón General Quintanilla'," *Boletín del Ministerio de Trabajo, Previsión Social y Salubridad*, no. 6 (1941), 141–142.

117. "Albergues," *Boletín del Ministerio del Trabajo, Previsión Social y Salubridad*, no. 6 (1941), 129.

118. Gill, *Precarious Dependencies*.

119. Stephenson, *Gender and Modernity in Andean Bolivia*, esp. 173–175.

120. Bliss, *Compromised Positions*, 116–119. In his film *Los olvidados de siempre* (1950), Luis Buñuel presented a romanticized view of another reform effort of the revolutionary period in Mexico: the reformatory for delinquent youth. His depiction is in keeping with the convictions of social workers and mental-hygiene experts in Mexico that the reformatory offered young boys real alternatives but ultimately could not overcome the poverty and bad influence of their families.

5 Mental Illness and Democracy

1. *Actas de las Segundas Jornadas Médicos-Quirúrgicas Nacionales,* 410.
2. Miguel Levy, "La declinación mental del indio," 15–33.
3. Ibid., 16–17.
4. Ibid., 19–22, 25–31. Many of these points had been made by Bolivian intellectuals earlier in the century. See chapter 1.
5. Emilio Fernández M., "Asistencia médico-social de la alienación en Bolivia," 159–160.
6. Juan Manuel Balcázar, *Historia de la medicina en Bolivia,* 521.
7. Levy, "La declinación mental del indio," 32–33. For a sampling of José Antonio Arze's thought on native Bolivians, agrarian reform, and education, among other subjects, see "Panorama de sociografía de Bolivia," esp. 139–150.
8. This conclusion is similar to Megan Vaughan's for Africa. See *Curing Their Ills,* esp., 100–128.
9. E. L. Osorio, "El ejercicio de la medicina ante los actuales problemas de reforma del orden social"; César Adriazola, "Ley de Esterilización Social," 48–50. On eugenics in Latin America, see Stepan, *The Hour of Eugenics.*
10. José María Alvarado, "La psiquiatría en Bolivia," 151–152.
11. Ibid., 154–156. Alvarado lists the doctors who held the psychiatry chairs. I have compared them to biographies of physicians published in Balcázar, *Historia de la medicina en Bolivia*; and in Sociedad Boliviana de Salud Pública, *Historia y perspectivas de la salud pública en Bolivia.*
12. Alfredo Caballero Zamora, *La institucionalización de la locura en Bolivia,* 181–182.
13. Sociedad Boliviana de Salud Pública, *Historia y perspectivas de la salud pública en Bolivia.* Alfredo Caballero Zamora wrote that one year earlier, in 1988, there were twenty-six psychiatrists in Bolivia. Caballero Zamora, *La institucionalización de la locura en Bolivia,* 200.
14. Organización Mundial de la Salud, *Atlas de recursos de salud mental en el mundo,* cited in Guillermo Rivera, "La salud mental en Bolivia y sus tareas pendientes."
15. Alfredo Caballero Zamora, *La institucionalización de la locura en Bolivia,* 146; Archivo Nacional de Bolivia, Sucre (hereafter ANB), Instituto Psiquiátrico Nacional de Mujeres (hereafter IPM), 41, Estadísticas; ANB, Instituto Psiquiátrico Nacional de Varones (hereafter IPV), 75, Estadísticas.
16. Fernández M., "Asistencia médico-social de la alienación en Bolivia," 161.
17. Ibid., 159.
18. Caballero Zamora, *La institucionalización de la locura en Bolivia,* 149.
19. ANB, IPV, 75, Estadísticas (all statistics on men come from this

source); ANB, IPM, 41, Estadísticas (all statistics on women come from this source). Bureau of the Census, *Patients in Hospitals for Mental Disease, 1934*; Bureau of the Census, *Patients in Hospitals for Mental Disease, 1935*; Bureau of the Census, *Patients in Hospitals for Mental Disease, 1936*; National Institute of Mental Health, *Patients in Mental Institutions, 1927*; National Institute of Mental Health, *Patients in Mental Institutions, 1948*; National Institute of Mental Health, *Patients in Mental Institutions, 1949*.

20. ANB, IPV, II, Correspondencia, Julio C. Fortún al Presidente de Honorable Consejo Municipal de Sucre, 14 November 1930. Jerrold Levy, "Epilepsy."

21. Out of 464 women admitted to the hospital in the 1940s for whom diagnosis was recorded, only 4 were said to suffer from manic depression. ANB, IPM, 41. Three of 127 men in 1937 and four out of 177 in 1941 were so diagnosed. ANB, IPV, 75.

22. Of the women in the hospital, 4 percent were diagnosed as having malarial psychosis. ANB, IPV, 75.

23. ANB, IPM, 41, Estadísticas; ANB, IPV, 75, Estadísticas. For the 1,609 patients he reported were in the hospital between 1884 and 1943, Fernández M. calculated 73.4 percent were under forty: "Asistencia médico-social," 162–163.

24. Emilio Fernández M. also makes this point in discussing marital status of patients. Ibid., 163.

25. Rivera Cusicanqui, *"Oprimidos pero no vencidos,"* 15.

26. Edward Shorter, *A History of Psychiatry*, 210–214.

27. Ibid., 212.

28. Ibid., 214–216.

29. J. Alberto Martínez Z., " 'El electro-shock' (electro-plexia): Su aplicación en el Manicomio Nacional 'Pacheco,' " 298–303; Caballero Zamora, *La institucionalización de la locura en Bolivia*, 183–184.

30. ANB, IPV, Resúmenes, 1947, 1948.

31. Jaime Mendoza, "La Esquizofrenia."

32. Jaime Mendoza, "El trípode psíquico."

33. For example, *En las tierras del Potosí*; "Una indicación (en favor de los niños de las clases obreras)." Also see chapters 1 and 4.

34. Jaime Mendoza, "La defensa de los niños," 11.

35. Ibid., 4–5, 12–13.

36. Ibid., 14.

37. Fernández M., "Asistencia médico-social de la alienación en Bolivia," 166, 163.

38. Ibid., 166–167.

39. Ibid., 167.

40. In 1940 the director of Mexico City's public mental hospital made a series of proposals for improving care that were very much like those offered by Fernández. See Cristina Rivera-Garza, "La vida en reclusión," 218–219.

41. Ibid., 172–175. Quote on 173.

42. Fernández, "Protección a la madre y al hijo," 57.

43. See Stepan, *The Hour of Eugenics*, chap. 3, esp., 84–95.

44. Adriazola, "Ley de Esterilización Social."

45. Ibid., 49.

46. Ibid., 50.

47. Speech given by Levy at the Conferencia del Distrito 28 del Rotary Internacional, April 1944. Cited in Caballero, *La institucionalización de la locura en Bolivia*, 180.

48. Augusto Ruiz Zevallos, *Psiquiatras y locos*, esp. 121–137.

49. Gregorio Mendizábal, "Higiene y profilaxis mental."

50. Otto Kleinberger, "El principio y desarrollo de las facultades y actividades mentales y corporales, y consideraciones de la in-y subconsciencia."

51. Mendoza, *El las tierras del Potosí*, 61, and "Una indicación (en favor de los niños de las clases obreras)." On the perception of women as being more "Indian" and maintaining Indian cultural traditions, see de la Cadena, "Women Are More Indian"; Stephenson, *Gender and Modernity in Andean Bolivia*.

52. Fernández, "Protección a la madre y al hijo," 63–64.

53. Kleinberger, "El principio y desarrollo de las facultades y actividades mentales y corporales, y consideraciones de la in-y subconsciencia," 22.

54. Levy, "Educación en el período de la pubertad."

55. Ibid., 56.

56. Ibid., 61.

57. Ibid., 62–63.

58. Ibid., 58.

59. Mendizábal, "Higiene y profilaxis mental," pt. 2, 30–31.

60. ANB, IPV, 9, Correspondencia, Casta L. viuda de Guevara a Antenor de la Vía García, Cochabamba, 29 March 1928 and 19 July 1928 . Patients' surnames have been altered to protect their identity.

61. ANB, IPV, 63, Historias Clínicas.

62. Ibid., 60, Historias Clínicas.

63. Ibid., 59, Historias Clínicas.

64. Ibid., 63, Historias Clínicas.

65. Ibid., 59, Historias Clínicas.

66. Ibid.

67. Ibid., 13, Correspondencia, Guillermo Prudencio al Sr. Presidente de la Sociedad Administradora de Manicomios, Cochabamba, 26 September 1932.

68. Ibid., 12, Correspondencia, Oficial Mayor del H. Consejo Municipal de La Paz al Señor Director del Manicomio Pacheco, La Paz, 3 July 1931.

69. Ibid., 9, Correspondencia, Ysrael Segarra al Director del Manicomio Pacheco, Cochabamba, 7 December 1928.

70. ANB, IPV, 9, Correspondencia, Rafaela Ramírez al Sr. Director del Manicomio Pacheco, Sucre, 31 October 1928.

71. ANB, IPV, 60, Historias Clínicas, Jorge Plaza Ponce al Jefe de Sanidad Departamental, Sucre, 9 August 1943.

72. ANB, IPV, 14, Correspondencia, Practicante interno a Sra. Tomasa C. viuda de Chamorro, Sucre, 19 January 1933.

73. Ibid., 14, Correspondencia, 1933.

74. Caballero, *La institucionalización de la locura en Bolivia*, 234.

75. Cited in Balcázar, *Historia de la medicina en Bolivia*, 521.

76. Cited in ibid., 521–522.

77. ANB, IPV, 75, Estadísticas.

78. Cited in Balcázar, *Historia de la medicina*, 522–523.

79. Interestingly, Emilio Fernández maintained that race was not listed in the books of statistics he used for his analysis. The records that I cite from the Manicomio Pacheco that are now in the ANB do record race for at least some of the patients.

80. Arguedas, *Pueblo enfermo*, 3rd ed., 36.

81. ANB, IPM, 2, Papeletas de Ingreso.

82. ANB, IPV, 59, Historias Clínicas.

83. Alvarado, "La psiquiatría en Bolivia," 130, 131–133.

84. Ibid., 130.

85. Bastien, *Healers of the Andes*, 42–44.

86. Crandon-Malamud, *From the Fat of Our Souls*, chap. 11.

87. ANB, IPV, 59, Historias Clínicas.

88. Vaughan, *Curing Their Ills*, 100–128.

89. ANB, IPV, 63, Historias Clínicas.

90. "The Psychiatric Interview," in *The Merck Manual*, 1458–1462.

91. ANB, IPV, 59, Historias Clínicas.

92. ANB, IPM, 1, Filiaciones.

93. ANB, IPV, 59, Historias Clínicas.

94. Shorter, *A History of Psychiatry*, 53–60.

95. The idea that female genitals and reproductive functions were directly responsible for mental disorders was also common among doctors in the early twentieth century in Mexico. See Rivera Garza, "The Criminalization of the Syphilitic Body."

96. ANB, IPM, 11, Historias Clínicas.

97. Ibid.

98. Ibid.

99. Ibid.

100. Ibid.

101. Ibid.

102. Ibid.

103. ANB, IPM, 12, Historias Clínicas.

104. Ibid., 11, Historias Clínicas.

105. Ibid.

106. Ibid., 1, Filiaciones.

107. Ibid.

108. Ibid.

109. Caballero Zamora, *La Institucionalización de la locura en Bolivia*, 169.

110. Martínez Z., " 'El Electro-shock,' (electro-plexia)," 301.

Conclusion

1. Archivo de la Casa de la Cultura "Rosendo Gutiérrez," La Paz, Cementerio General, Sección Estadística, 1900, 1919, 1933, 1943.

2. United Nations, *Demographic Yearbook: Historical Supplement [1928/1997]*, table 9, cited in Herbert S. Klein, "Social Change in Bolivia since 1952," 236.

3. In 2003 life expectancy at birth was sixty-four years, and the infant mortality rate (under one year) was fifty-three per thousand. UNICEF, "At a Glance: Bolivia," www.unicef.org/infobycountry/bolivia_statistics.html.

4. Bastien, *Healers of the Andes*, 31–32; The Secretariado Arquidiocesano de Pastoral Social (Archdiocesan Secretariat of Social Pastorship) has been working since the 1980s to develop programs that both increase knowledge of traditional medicine and also encourage Andean healers and doctors to work together.

5. Movimiento al Socialismo, "Diez puntos de programa del MAS" available at www.masbolivia.org.

6. *La Razón*, 21 April 2005; link to article found on Bolivia, Biblioteca Virtual en Salud, www.desastre.bvsp.org.bo.

BIBLIOGRAPHY

Archives

Archivo de la Casa de la Cultura "Rosendo Gutiérrez," La Paz
    Cementerio General, Sección Estadística.
Archivo Histórico de La Paz (ALP)
Archivo Nacional de Bolivia, Sucre (ANB)
    Instituto Psiquiátrico Nacional de Mujeres (IPM)
    Instituto Psiquiátrico Nacional de Varones (IPV)
Hospital General, La Paz, Ginecología, Estadísticas.
Hospital General, La Paz, Hombres, Estadísticas.
Hospital General, La Paz, Mujeres, Estadísticas,
Rockefeller Archive Center, Sleepy Hollow, N.Y. (RF)

Interviews

Mario Salcedo, La Paz, 2 March 1996
Madre Aureliana, La Paz, 14 March 1996

Francisco Iporre Valdez, La Paz, 22 April 1996
Daniel Macuaga, La Paz, 26 March 1996
Víctor Campos, La Paz, 27 March 1996
Elsa Echalar, La Paz, 22 April 1996
María Avedoña Guzmán, La Paz, 26 April 1996
María Montaños Saavedra, La Paz, 26 April 1996
Clotilde Lemaitre de Arauco, La Paz, 29 April 1996
Eduardo Arauco, La Paz, 29 April 1996

Periodicals and Journals

Archivos Bolivianos de la Medicina
Boletín de Estadística y Demografía
Boletín de la Dirección General de Sanidad Pública (BDGSP)
Boletín de la Oficina Nacional de Inmigración, Estadística y Propaganda Geográfica
Boletín del Honorable Ayuntamiento de La Paz, name varies slightly in different years
Boletín del Ministerio de Higiene y Salubridad
Boletín del Ministerio del Trabajo, Previsión Social y Salubridad
La Calle
Honorable Consejo Municipal de La Paz (HCMLP), *Memorias y anexos del Honorable Consejo Municipal de La Paz*, name varies slightly in different years; publisher varies over time, and publication information has been included in the notes
El Norte
Primeras Jornadas Médico-Quirúrgicas Nacionales
La Razón
Revista de Bacteriología e Higiene (RBH)
Revista del Instituto Médico "Sucre" (RIMS)
Revista Médica
The Rockefeller Foundation Annual Report
Los Tiempos

Secondary Sources

Actas de las Segundas Jornadas Médico-Quirúrgicas Nacionales. Sucre: Universidad Mayor Real y Pontificia de San Francisco Xavier de Chuquisaca, 1948.
Adriazola, César. "Ley de Esterilización Social." *RIMS*, no. 73 (1941), 48–50.
Aguirre Beltrán, Gonzalo. "Indigenismo y mestizaje: Una polaridad biocultural." *Cahiers d'Histoire Mondiale* 6:1 (1960), 158–171.

Alvarado, José María. "La psiquiatría en Bolivia." *Archivos bolivianos de medicina* 1:3 (1943), 129–157.

Anderson, Benedict. *Imagined Communities: Reflections on the Origin and Spread of Nationalism.* 2nd ed. London: Verso, 1991.

Antezana Estrada, José, "Proyecto de Código Sanitario de Bolivia." *Primer Congreso Médico Nacional (Trabajos Presentados).* La Paz, 1939.

Aramayo, Natalio A., "Consultorios de maternidad." *Boletín de la Dirección General de Sanidad Pública,* año 3, no. 5 (1931), 560–566.

Arguedas, Alcides. *Pueblo enfermo.* 2nd ed. Barcelona: Vda. De Luis Tasso, 1910.

———. *Pueblo enfermo.* 3rd ed. La Paz: Librería Editorial "Juventud," 1991 [1936].

———. *Raza de bronce.* La Paz: Los Tiempos, n.d.

———. *Wuata Wuara.* Barcelona: Imprenta Luis Tasso, 1904.

Arguedas, José María. *Deep Rivers.* Austin: University of Texas Press, 1978.

Armus, Diego. "El viaje al centro: Tísicas, costureritas y milonquitas en Buenos Aires (1910–1940)." In *Entre médicos y curanderos: Cultura, historia y enfermedad en la América Latina moderna,* edited by Diego Armus, 221–158. Buenos Aires: Grupo Editorial Norma, 2002.

Arnold, David. *Colonizing the Body: State Medicine and Epidemic Disease in Nineteenth-Century India.* Berkeley: University of California Press, 1993.

———. *Imperial Medicine in Indigenous Societies.* Manchester: Manchester University Press, 1988.

Arze, José Antonio. "Panorama de sociografía de Bolivia." In *Bosquejo Socio-dialéctico de la Historia de Bolivia,* edited by José Roberto Arze, 95–155. La Paz: Ediciones Camarlinghi, 1978.

Arze, Silvia, Magdalena Cajías, and Ximena Medinaceli, *Mujeres en rebelión: La presencia femenina en las rebeliones de Charcas del siglo XVIII.* La Paz: Ministerio de Desarrollo Humano, 1997.

Arze Aguirre, René Danilo. *Guerra y conflictos sociales: El caso rural boliviano durante la campaña del Chaco.* La Paz: Centro de Estudios de la Realidad Económica y Social, 1987.

Arze Loureiro, Ricardo. "Enfermedades venéreas: Balanopostitis y condilomas acuminatus en el Chaco." In *La sanidad boliviana en la campaña del Chaco (1933–1934),* edited by Aurelio Melean, 405–407. Cochabamba: Imprenta de la Universidad, 1938.

Balcázar, Juan Manuel. *Historia de la medicina en Bolivia.* La Paz: Ediciones "Juventud," 1956.

———. *Protección y crianza del niño (El libro consejero de la madre).* La Paz: Librería e Imprenta Arno Hnos., 1937.

Barragán, Rossana. "Identidades indias y mestizas: Una intervención al debate." *Autodeterminación* 10 (1992), 17–44.

———. "Miradas indiscretas a la patria potestad: Articulación social y conflictos de género en la ciudad de La Paz, siglos XVIII–XIX." In *Más allá del silencio: Las fronteras de género en los Andes*, edited by Denise Arnold, 407–454. La Paz: Centre for Indigenous American Studies and Exchange (CIASE), University of Saint Andrews, Scotland, 1997.

Bastien, Joseph W. *Healers of the Andes: Kallawaya Herbalists and Their Medicinal Plants*. Salt Lake City: University of Utah Press, 1987.

———. "Qollahuaya-Andean Body Concepts: A Topographical-Hydraulic Model of Physiology." *American Anthropologist* 87 (1985), 595–611.

Besse, Susan K. *Restructuring Patriarchy: The Modernization of Gender Inequality in Brazil, 1914–1940*. Chapel Hill: University of North Carolina Press, 1996.

Birn, Anne-Emanuelle. "Skirting the Issue: Women and International Health in Historical Perspective." *American Journal of Public Health* 89:3 (March 1999), 399–407.

Bliss, Katherine Elaine. *Compromised Positions: Prostitution, Public Health, and Gender Politics in Revolutionary Mexico City*. University Park: Pennsylvania State University Press, 2001.

Blum, Ann S. "Dying of Sadness: Hospitalism and Child Welfare in Mexico City, 1920–1940." In *Disease in the History of Latin America: From Malaria to AIDS*, edited by Diego Armus, 209–236. Durham, N.C.: Duke University Press, 2003.

Brading, David. *The First America: The Spanish Monarchy, Creole Patriots, and the Liberal State, 1492–1867*. Cambridge: Cambridge University Press, 1991.

Bureau of the Census. *Patients in Hospitals for Mental Disease*. Washington, D.C.: United States Government Printing Office, 1934–1938.

Caballero Zamora, Alfredo. *La institucionalización de la locura en Bolivia*. Quito, Ecuador: Consejo Latinoamericano de Ciencias Sociales, 1989.

Cajías de la Vega, Magdalena, and Iván Jiménez Chávez, *Mujeres en las minas de Bolivia*. La Paz: Ministerio de Desarrollo Humano, 1997.

Caulfield, Sueann. "The History of Gender in the Historiography of Latin America." *Hispanic American Historical Review* 81:3–4 (August–November 2001), 449–490.

———. *In Defense of Honor: Sexual Morality, Modernity and Nation in Early–Twentieth Century Brazil*. Durham, N.C.: Duke University Press, 2000.

Cernadas, Francisco. "Cuidado a enfermos y heridos evacuados al interior de la república." In *La sanidad boliviana en la campaña del Chaco (1933–1934)*, edited by Aurelio Melean, 201–209. Cochabamba: Imprenta de la Universidad, 1938.

Chalhoub, Sidney. "The Politics of Disease Control: Yellow Fever and Race in Nineteenth Century Rio de Janeiro." *Journal of Latin American Studies* 25 (1993), 441–463.

Choque, Roberto. "Las rebeliones indígenas de la post-guerra del Chaco:

Reivindicaciones indígenas durante la prerevolución." *DATA* 3 (1992) 37–53.

Condarco Morales, Ramiro. *Zarate, el "temible" willka: Historia de la rebelión indígena de 1899 en la república de Bolivia*. 2nd ed. La Paz: Imprenta y Librería Renovación, 1982.

Cooper, Donald B., and Kenneth F. Kiple, "Yellow Fever." In *The Cambridge World History of Human Disease*, edited by Kenneth F. Kiple, 1100–1107. New York: Cambridge University Press, 1993.

Corbin, Alain. *Women for Hire: Prostitution and Sexuality in France after 1850*. Cambridge, Mass.: Harvard University Press, 1990.

Corrigan, Philip, and Derek Sayer. *The Great Arch: English State Formation as Cultural Revolution*. Oxford: Basil Blackwell, 1985.

Costa Ardúz, Rolando. "Imponente estirpe en la Dirección del Instituto Nacional de Bacteriología: Félix Veintemillas." *Crónica Aguda* 2:50 (La Paz, January 1989), 4–6.

———. "Revista de Bacteriología e Higiene." *Crónica Aguda: Tribuna de la Cultura Médica* 2:51 (La Paz, January 1989), 18–20.

Coutinho, Marilia. "Tropical Medicine in Brazil: The Case of Chagas Disease." In *Disease in the History of Latin America: From Malaria to AIDS*, edited by Diego Armus, 76–100. Durham, N.C.: Duke University Press, 2003.

Crandon-Malamud, Libbett. *From the Fat of Our Souls: Social Change, Political Process and Medical Pluralism in Bolivia*. Berkeley: University of California Press, 1991.

Cueto, Marcos. "Andean Biology in Peru: Scientific Styles in the Periphery." *Isis* 80 (1989), 640–658.

———. "La ciudad y las ratas: La peste bubónica en Lima y la costa peruana a comienzos del siglo veinte." *Histórica* 15:1 (Julio 1991), 1–26.

———. *Excelencia científica en la periferia: Actividades científicas e investigación biomedical en el Perú, 1890–1950*. Lima: Tarea, 1989.

———. "Indigenismo and Rural Medicine in Peru: The Indian Sanitary Brigade and Manuel Nuñez Butrón." *Bulletin of the History of Medicine* 65 (1991), 22–41.

———. *The Return of Epidemics: Health and Society in Peru during the Twentieth Century*. Aldershot, England: Ashgate, 2001.

———. "The Rockefeller Foundation's Medical Policy and Scientific Research in Latin America: The Case of Physiology." In *Missionaries of Science*, edited by Cueto, 126–148.

———. "Sanitation from Above: The Rockefeller Foundation and Yellow Fever." In *The Return of Epidemics: Health and Society in Peru during the Twentieth Century*, by Cueto, 29–47.

———. *El valor de la salud: Historia de la Organización Panamericana de la Salud*. Washington, D.C.: Organización Panamericana de la Salud, 2004.

Cueto, Marcos. "Visions of Science and Development: The Rockefeller Foundation's Latin American Surveys of the 1920s." In *Missionaries of Science*, edited by Cueto, 1–22.

Cueto, Marcos, ed. *Missionaries of Science: The Rockefeller Foundation and Latin America*. Bloomington: Indiana University Press, 1994.

Dandler, Jorge, and Juan Torrico A., "From the National Indigenous Congress to the Ayopaya Rebellion: Bolivia, 1945–1947." In *Resistance, Rebellion, and Consciousness in the Andean Peasant World, 18th to 20th Centuries*, edited by Steve J. Stern, 334–378. Madison: The University of Wisconsin Press, 1987.

Deere, Carmen Diana. "Liberalism and Married Women's Property Rights in Nineteenth Century Latin America." Paper presented at the Economic History and Development Workshop, University of Massachusetts, Amherst, 7 April 2004.

De la Cadena, Marisol. *Indigenous Mestizos: The Politics of Race and Culture in Cuzco, Peru, 1919–1991*. Durham, N.C.: Duke University Press, 2000.

———. "Women Are More Indian: Gender and Ethnicity in a Community in Cuzco." In *Ethnicity, Markets, and Migration in the Andes: At the Crossroads of History and Anthropology*, edited by Brooke Larson and Olivia Harris, with Enrique Tandeter, 327–343. Durham, N.C.: Duke University Press, 1995.

Demelas, Marie Danielle. "Darwinismo a la criolla: El darwinismo social en Bolivia, 1880–1910." *Historia Boliviana* 1:2 (1981), 55–82.

Díaz Romero, Belisario. "Farmacopea Callaguaya: Enumeración de las plantas medicinales." In *Compilación de estudios sobre medicina Kallawaya*, edited by Rolando Costa Ardúz, 55–66. La Paz: Convenio Andrés Bello, Instituto Internacional de Integración, 1988.

Dibbits, Ineke, Elizabeth Peredo, Ruth Volgger, and Ana Cecilia Wadsworth. *Polleras libertarias: Federación Obrera Femenina, 1927–1965*. La Paz: Taller de Historia y Participación de la Mujer (TAHIPAMU), 1989.

Di Liscia, María Silvia. "Viruela, vacunación e indígenas en la pampa argentina del siglo XIX." In *Entre médicos y curanderos*, edited by Diego Armus, 29–69. Buenos Aires: Grupo Editorial Norma, 2002.

Donnison, Jean. *Midwives and Medical Men: A History of Inter-professional Rivalry and Women' Rights*. New York: Schoken Books, 1977.

Dore, Elizabeth. "One Step Forward, Two Steps Back: Gender and the State in the Long Nineteenth Century." In *Hidden Histories of Gender and the State in Latin America*, edited by Elizabeth Dore and Maxine Molyneux, 3–32. Durham, N.C.: Duke University Press, 2000.

Dore, Elizabeth, and Maxine Molyneux, eds., *Hidden Histories of Gender and the State in Latin America*. Durham, N.C.: Duke University Press, 2000.

Douglas, Mary. *Purity and Danger*. London: Routledge, 1992.

Dunkerley, James. "The Origins of the Bolivian Revolution in the Twentieth Century: Some Reflections." In *Proclaiming Revolution: Bolivia in Comparative Perspective*, edited by Merilee S. Grindle and Pilar Domingo, 135–163. London: Institute of Latin American Studies, and Cambridge, Mass.: David Rockefeller Center for Latin American Studies, 2003.

Durán Jordán, Florencia, and Ana María Seoane Flores, *El complejo mundo de la mujer durante la Guerra del Chaco*. La Paz: Ministerio de Desarrollo Humano, 1997.

Dwork, Debórah. "Childhood." In *Companion Encyclopedia of the History of Medicine*, vol. 2, edited by W. F. Bynum and Roy Porter, 1072–1092. London: Routledge, 1993.

Echevarría, Evelio. "Panorama y bibliografía de la novela social boliviana." *Inter-American Review of Bibliography* 27:2 (1977), 143–152.

Farcau, Bruce W. *The Chaco War: Bolivia and Paraguay, 1832–1935*. Westport, Conn.: Praeger, 1996.

Feinsilver, Julie. *Healing the Masses: Cuban Health Politics at Home and Abroad*. Berkeley: University of California Press, 1993.

Fernández M., Emilio. "Asistencia médico-social de la alienación en Bolivia." *Archivos bolivianos de la medicina* 1:3 (1943), 159–176.

———. "Protección a la madre y al hijo." *RIMS*, no. 85 (February–April 1949), 53–64.

———. "Vitaminas y avitaminosis." In *La sanidad boliviana en la campaña del Chaco (1933–1934)*, edited by Aurelio Melean, 278–360. Cochabamba: Imprenta de la Universidad, 1938.

Findlay, Eileen. *Imposing Decency: The Politics of Sexuality and Race in Puerto Rico, 1870–1920*. Durham, N.C.: Duke University Press, 1999.

Flores, A. "El paludismo en Mizque." *Boletín de la Dirección General de Sanidad Pública*, año 1, no. 1 (La Paz, August 1929), 50–54.

Fosdick, Raymond B. *The Story of the Rockefeller Foundation*. New York: Harper and Brothers, 1952.

Foster, George M. *Hippocrates' Latin American Legacy: Humoral Medicine in the New World*. Langhorne, Pa.: Gordon and Breach, 1994.

Foucault, Michel. *The Birth of the Clinic: An Archaeology of Medical Perception*. New York: Vintage Books, 1979.

———. *Discipline and Punish: The Birth of the Prison*. New York: Vintage Books, 1979.

———. *The History of Sexuality: An Introduction*, Vol. 1. New York: Vintage Books, 1990.

García, Juan César. *Pensamiento social en salud en América Latina*. Mexico City: Interamericana McGraw Hill, 1994.

Gibson, Mary. *Prostitution and the State in Italy, 1860–1915*. New Brunswick, N.J.: Rutgers University Press, 1986.

Gill, Lesley. *Precarious Dependencies: Gender, Class and Domestic Service in Bolivia*. New York: Columbia University Press, 1994.

Girault, Louis. *Kallawaya curanderos itinerantes de los Andes: Investigación sobre prácticas medicinales y mágicas*. La Paz: UNICEF, 1987.

Glick, Thomas. "Science and Society in Twentieth-Century Latin America." *The Cambridge History of Latin America*. Vol. 6, pt. 1, "1930 to the Present," 463–535. Cambridge: Cambridge University Press, 1994.

Gotkowitz, Laura. "Commemorating the Heroínas: Gender and Civic Ritual in Early Twentieth-Century Bolivia." In *Hidden Histories of Gender and the State in Latin America*, edited by Elizabeth Dore and Maxine Molyneux, 215–237. Durham, N.C.: Duke University Press, 2000.

———. "Revisiting the Rural Roots of the Revolution." In *Proclaiming Revolution: Bolivia in Comparative Perspective*, edited by Merille S. Grindle and Pilar Domingo, 164–182. London: Institute of Latin American Studies, 2003.

———. "Trading Insults: Honor, Violence, and the Gendered Culture of Commerce in Cochabamba, Bolivia, 1870s–1950s." *Hispanic American Historical Review* 83:1 (2003), 83–118.

———. *Within the Boundaries of Equality: Race, Gender and Citizenship in Cochabamba, Bolivia, 1880–1953*. Durham, N.C.: Duke University Press, forthcoming.

Gramsci, Antonio. *Selections from the Prison Notebooks*. New York: International Publishers, 1971.

Guillen Pinto, Alfredo. *Utama*. La Paz: Casa Arno, 1945.

Guy, Donna J. *Sex and Danger in Buenos Aires: Prostitution, Family, and Nation in Argentina*. Lincoln: University of Nebraska Press, 1991.

Hale, Charles. *Mexican Liberalism in the Age of Mora, 1821–1853*. New Haven, Conn.: Yale University Press, 1968.

———. *The Transformation of Liberalism in Late Nineteenth-Century Mexico*. Princeton, N.J.: Princeton University Press, 1989.

Harden, Victoria A. "Typhus, Epidemic." In *The Cambridge World History of Human Disease*, edited by Kenneth F. Kiple, 1080–1084. New York: Cambridge University Press.

Herbas Cabrera, Carlos. *El Cristo de Tarairi: "Dos hermanos en la guerra" (diario de campaña): Bolivia con el Paraguay, 1932–1935 — Una contribución a la historia*. Oruro, Bolivia: Editorial Universitaria, 1977.

Huber, Brad R., and Alan R. Sandstrom, "Recruitment, Training, and Practice of Indigenous Midwives: From the Mexico–United States Border to the Isthmus of Tehuantepec." In *Mesoamerican Healers*, edited by Brad R. Huber and Alan R. Sandstrom, 139–178. Austin: University of Texas Press, 2001.

Huckstep, R. L. *Typhoid Fever and Other Salmonella Infections*. Edinburgh: E. and S. Livingstone, 1962.

Iporre Valdez, Francisco. "Fragmento de sus memorias del Ingeniero de Minas Francisco Iporre Valdez." Typed manuscript in possession of the author.

Irurozqui, Marta. *La armonía de las desigualdades: Elites y conflictos de poder en Bolivia, 1880–1920.* Cuzco: Centro Bartolomé de Las Casas, 1994.

———. "La democracia imposible: 1900–1930." In *Visiones de fin de siglo: Bolivia y América Latina en el siglo XX,* edited by Dora Cajías, Magdalena Cajías, Carmen Johnson, and Iris Villegas, 165–192. La Paz: Institut Française d'Etudes Andines, 2001.

Joseph, Gilbert M., and Daniel Nugent, eds. *Everyday Forms of State Formation: Revolution and Negotiation of Rule in Modern Mexico.* Durham, N.C.: Duke University Press, 1994.

Kiple, Kenneth. "Cholera and Race in the Caribbean." *Journal of Latin American Studies* 17 (1985), 157–177.

Klein, Herbert S. *Bolivia: The Evolution of a Multi-ethnic Society.* 2nd ed. New York: Oxford University Press, 1992.

———. "Social Change in Bolivia since 1952." In *Proclaiming Revolution: Bolivia in Comparative Perspective,* edited by Merilee S. Grindle and Pilar Domingo, 232–258. London: Institute of Latin American Studies, and Cambridge, Mass.: David Rockefeller Center for Latin American Studies, 2003.

Kleinberger, Otto. "El principio y desarrollo de las facultades y actividades mentales y corporales, y consideraciones de la in-y subconsciencia." *RIMS,* no. 72 (1940), 13–22.

Knight, Alan. "Racism, Revolution and Indigenismo: Mexico, 1910–1940." In *The Idea of Race in Latin America, 1870–1940,* edited by Richard Graham, 71–113. Austin: University of Texas Press, 1990.

Koss-Chionino, Joan D., Thomas Leatherman, and Christine Greenway, eds. *Medical Pluralism in the Andes.* London: Routledge, 2003.

Landa, Luis Isaac L. *Problemas políticos.* Antofagasta, Chile: Imprenta Moderna, 1929.

Langer, Eric D. "El liberalismo y la abolición de la comunidad indígena en el siglo XIX." *Historia y Cultura* 14 (1988), 59–95.

Lara, Jesús. *Yanakuna.* Cochabamba: "Los Amigos del Libro," 1952.

Lara Q., E. "La lucha contra la mortalidad infantil." *Boletín de la Dirección General de Sanidad Pública* 4:7 (1933), 99–125.

Larson, Brooke. "Capturing Indian Bodies, Hearths and Minds: The Gendered Politics of Rural School Reform in Bolivia, 1910–52." In *Proclaiming Revolution: Bolivia in Comparative Perspective,* edited by Merilee Grindle and Pilar Domingo, 283–209. London: Institute of Latin American Studies, and Cambridge, Mass.: David Rockefeller Center for Latin American Studies, 2003.

———. "Indios redimidos, cholos barbarizados: Imaginando la modernidad neocolonial boliviana (1900–1910)." In *Visiones de fin del siglo: Bolivia y América Latina en el Siglo XX,* edited by Dora Cajías, Magdalena Cajías, Carmen Johnson, and Iris Villega, 27–48. La Paz: Coordinadora de Historia, 2001.

Larson, Brooke. *Trials of Nation Making: Liberalism, Race, and Ethnicity in the Andes, 1810–1910*. Cambridge: Cambridge University Press, 2004.

Lauderdale Graham, Sandra. *House and Street: The Domestic World of Servants and Masters in Nineteenth-Century Rio de Janeiro*. Austin: University of Texas Press, 1992.

Le Baron, Charles W., and David W. Taylor, "Typhoid Fever." In *The Cambridge World History of Human Disease*. Cambridge: Cambridge University Press, 1993.

Lehm A., Zulema, and Silvia Rivera Cusicanqui. *Los artesanos libertarios y la ética del trabajo*. La Paz: Taller de Historia Oral Andino, 1988.

Levy, Jerrold E. "Epilepsy." In *Companion Encyclopedia of the History of Medicine*, edited by W. F. Bynum and Roy Porter, 713–718. London: Routledge, 1993.

Levy, Miguel. "La declinación mental del indio: Sus procesos mentales." *RIMS*, no. 74 (January–March 1942), 15–33.

———. "Educación en el período de la pubertad." *RIMS*, no. 51 (January 1929), 55–70.

Lora, Guillermo. *Historia del movimiento obrero boliviano*. 5 vols. Cochabamba: "Los Amigos del Libro," 1967–1980.

Lorini, Irma. *El movimiento socialista "embrionario" en Bolivia, 1920–1939: Entre nuevas ideas y residuos de la sociedad tradicional*. La Paz: Editorial "Los Amigos del Libro," 1994.

Loudon, Irvine S. L. "Childbirth." In *Companion Encyclopedia of the History of Medicine*, vol. 2, edited by W. F. Bynum and Roy Porter, 1050–1071. London: Routledge, 1993.

Love, Joseph, and Nils Jacobsen. *Guiding the Invisible Hand: Economic Liberalism and the State in Latin American History*. New York: Praeger, 1988.

Loza V., Carmen Beatriz. *Kallawaya: Reconocimiento mundial a una ciencia de los Andes*. La Paz: Viceministerio de Cultura, La Fundación Cultural del Banco Central, UNESCO, 2004.

Lynch, John. *The Spanish American Revolutions, 1808–1826*. 2nd ed. New York: Norton, 1986.

MacLeod, Roy, and Milton Lewis, eds. *Disease, Medicine and Empire: Perspectives on Western Medicine and the Experience of European Expansion*. London: Routledge, 1988.

Maldonado M., Oswaldo. "Félix Veintemillas: Enfoque sobre su vida y su obra." *Crónica Aguda*, 2:50 (January 1989), 6–9.

Mallon, Florencia E. *Peasant and Nation: The Making of Postcolonial Mexico and Peru*. Berkeley: University of California Press, 1991.

Mamani Condori, Carlos B. *Taraqu, 1866–1935: Massacre, guerra y "Renovación" en la biografía de Eduardo L. Nina Qhispe*. La Paz: Ediciones Aruwiyiri, 1991.

Marof, Tristan. *La justicia del Inca*. Brussels: Falk Fils, 1926.

———. "Proceso de un escritor." Excerpt from *La verdad socialista en Bolivia* (1938). In *La polémica en Bolivia: Un panorama de la cultura de una nación a través de las grandes polémicas*, edited by Edgar Oblitas Fernández, vol. 1, 743–751. La Paz: Druck, 1997.

Martínez Z., J. Alberto. " 'El electro-shock' (electro-plexia): Su aplicación en el Manicomio Nacional 'Pacheco'." In *Primeras Jornadas Médico-quirúrgicas Nacionales*, 298–303. La Paz: Ateneo de Medicina de La Paz, 1946.

Martínez-Vergne, Teresita. *Shaping the Discourse on Space: Charity and Its Wards in Nineteenth Century Puerto Rico*. Austin: University of Texas Press, 1999.

McCreery, David, " 'This Life of Misery and Shame': Female Prostitution in Guatemala City, 1880–1920." *Journal of Latin American Studies* 18:2 (1986), 333–353.

Meade, Teresa. "Civilizing Rio de Janeiro: The Public Health Campaign and the Riot of 1904." *Journal of Social History* 20:2 (1986), 301–332.

Meade, Teresa, and Mark Walker, eds. *Science, Medicine, and Cultural Imperialism*. New York: St. Martin's Press, 1991.

Medinaceli, Ximena. *Alterando la rutina: Mujeres en las ciudades de Bolivia. 1920–1930*. La Paz: Centro de Información y Desarrollo de la Mujer (CIDEM), 1989.

Mejía, Ximena. "*Mujeres de Pollera*: Exploring Gender, Class and Ethnicity in La Paz, Bolivia." Senior Honors' Thesis, Smith College, 2005.

Mejía Gandarillas, J. "Enterocolitis toxi-infecciosas." In *La sanidad boliviana en la campaña del Chaco (1933-1934)*, edited by Aurelio Melean, 416–424. Cochabamba: Imprenta de la Universidad, 1938.

Melean, Aurelio, ed. *La sanidad boliviana en la campaña del Chaco (1933-1934)*. Cochabamba: Imprenta de la Universidad, 1938.

———. "Organización científica: Profilaxis general para las enfermedades contagiosas o febriles." In *La sanidad boliviana en la campaña del Chaco*, edited by Melean, 11–16.

———. "Organización de Sanidad en Vanguardia." In *La sanidad boliviana en la campaña del Chaco*, edited by Melean, 84–123.

Mendizábal, Gregorio. "Higiene y profilaxis mental." *RIMS*, no. 44 (1926), 39–51 and no. 45 (1926), 19–53.

Mendoza, Jaime. *Apuntes de un médico: Ensayos y semblanzas*. Sucre: Escuela Tipográfica Salesiana, 1936.

———. "La defensa de los niños," *RIMS*, no. 65 (1937), 1–14.

———. "La esquizofrenia." *RIMS*, no. 68 (1938), 1–8.

———. "Una indicación (en favor de los niños de las clases obreras)." *RIMS*, no. 38 (February 1920), 455–472.

———. *En las tierras del Potosí*. La Paz: Los Tiempos: 1988 [1911].

———. "El trípode psíquico." *RIMS*, no. 65 (1937), 65–80.

Mendoza Loza, Gunnar. "Jaime Mendoza." *Crónica Aguda* 1:17 (May 1988), 1–16. Originally published as "Jaime Mendoza: Resumen biográfica" in *Presencia* (La Paz, 27 March 1966).

Merck Manual, The. 15th ed. Rahway, N.J.: Merck Sharpe and Dohme Research Laboratories, 1987.

Módena, María Eugenia. "Combinar recursos curativos: Un pueblo mexicano en las últimas décadas del siglo XX." In *Entre médicos y curanderos: Cultura, historia y enfermedad en la América Latina moderna*, edited by Diego Armus, 331–370. Buenos Aires: Grupo Editorial Norma, 2002.

Morquio, Luis. "De causas de la mortalidad de la primera infancia y medios de reducirla." *RIMS*, no. 46 (October 1926), 42–50.

Murdock, Carl J. "Physicians, the State and Public Health in Chile, 1881–1891." *Journal of Latin American Studies* 27 (1995), 551–567.

Nash, June, and Helen Safa, eds. *Women and Change in Latin America.* South Hadley, Mass. .: Bergin and Garvey, 1986.

National Institute of Mental Health. *Patients in Mental Institutions.* Washington, D.C.: United States Government Printing Office, n.d.

Navarre, Ernesto. *La tuberculosis en el departamento de La Paz.* La Paz: Imprenta Artística, 1925.

Needell, Jeffrey. "The *Revolta Contra Vacina* of 1904: The Revolt against 'Modernization' in *Belle-Epoque* Rio de Janeiro." *Hispanic American Historical Review* 67:2 (1987), 233–269.

Oblitas Poblete, Enrique. "La lengua secreta de los Incas." In *Compilación de estudios sobre medicina Kallawaya*, edited by Rolando Costa Ardúz, 286–313. La Paz: Convenio Andrés Bello, Instituto Internacional de Integración, 1988.

Oporto Ordoñez, Luis, ed., *Las mujeres en la historia de Bolivia: Imágenes y realidades del siglo XX (1900–1950).* La Paz: Grupo Editorial Anthropos, 2001.

Organización Mundial de la Salud, *Atlas de recursos de salud mental en el mundo.* Geneva: World Health Organization, 2001.

Orihuela, Néstor. "Anotaciones sobre paludismo en el Chaco." In *La sanidad boliviana en la campaña del Chaco (1933–1934)*, edited by Aurelio Melean, 210–226. Cochabamba: Imprenta de la Universidad, 1938.

Orosco P., Germán. "Lucha antipalúdica." In *La sanidad boliviana en la campaña del Chaco (1933–1934)*, edited by Aurelio Melean 238–247. Cochabamba: Imprenta de la Universidad, 1938.

Osorio, E. L. "El ejercicio de la medicina ante los actuales problemas de reforma del orden social." *RIMS*, no. 81 (1946), 3–11.

Palmer, Bryan D. *Descent into Discourse: The Reification of Language and the Writing of Social History.* Philadelphia: Temple University Press, 1990.

Palmer, Steven. "Central American Encounters with Rockefeller Public Health, 1814–1921." In *Close Encounters with Empire: Writing the Cultural History of U.S.-Latin American Relations*, edited by Gilbert Joseph,

Catherine LeGrand, and Ricardo Salvatore, 311–332. Durham, N.C.: Duke University Press, 1998.

——. *From Popular Medicine to Medical Populism: Doctors, Healers, and Public Power in Costa Rica, 1800–1940*. Durham, N.C.: Duke University Press, 2003.

Paredes, Manuel Rigoberto. *La altiplanicie: Descripción de la Provincia de Omasuyos*. La Paz: Ediciones Isla, 1965 [1914].

——. "Ideas médicas indígenas." From *Mitos, supersticiones y supervivencias populares de Bolivia* (1920). In *Compilación de estudios sobre medicina Kallawaya*, edited by Rolando Costa Ardúz, 89–100. La Paz: Convenio Andrés Bello, Instituto Internacional de Integración, 1988.

——. *Provincia de Inquisive: Estudios geográficos, estadísticos y sociales*. La Paz: J. M. Gamarra, 1906.

Paredes Candia, Antonio. *De rameras, burdeles y proxenetas: Historia y tradición*. La Paz: Ediciones ISLA, 1998.

Parrenin, Georges, and Jean Pierre Lavaud. *Pour une approche sur l'indigénisme en Bolivia, 1900–1932*. Ivry, France: Equipe de recherché sur les sociétés indiennes paysannes d'Amérique Latine.

Patiño C., Cecilia, Doris Cerdeña V., and Sidey Fallas L. *Comercialización de mujeres: Una violación de los derechos humanos. Estudio sobre la prostitución en la ciudad de Oruro*. Oruro, Bolivia: Centro Diocesano de Pastoral Social, 1998.

Peard, Julyan. *Race, Place and Medicine: The Idea of the Tropics in Nineteenth-Century Brazilian Medicine*. Durham, N.C.: Duke University Press, 1999.

——. "Tropical Disorders and the Forging of a Brazilian Medical Identity, 1860–1890." *Hispanic American Historical Review* 77:1 (1997), 1–45.

Pedraza Gómez, Zandra. "El debate eugenésico: Una visión de modernidad en Colombia." *Revista de Antropología y Arqueología* 9:1–2 (1997), 115–159.

——. "La difusión de una dietética moderna en Colombia: La revista *Cromos* entre 1940–1986." In *Entre médicos y curanderos: Cultura, historia y enfermedad en la América Latina moderna*, edited by Diego Armus, 293–329. Buenos Aires: Grupo Editorial Norma, 2002.

Penyak, Lee. "Obstetrics and the Emergence of Women in Mexico's Medical Establishment." *The Americas* 60:1 (July 2003), 59–85.

Pérez, Elizardo. *Warisata: La escuela-ayllu*. 2nd ed. La Paz: HISBOL, 1992.

Pineo, Ronn F. "Misery and Death in the Pearl of the Pacific: Health Care in Guayaquil, Ecuador, 1870–1925." *Hispanic American Historical Review*, 70:4 (1990), 609–638.

——. *Social and Economic Reform in Ecuador: Life and Work in Guayaquil*. Gainesville: University of Florida Press, 1996.

Platt, Tristan. "The Andean Experience of Bolivian Liberalism, 1825–1900: The Roots of Rebellion in Nineteenth-Century Chayanta (Potosí)." In

Resistance, Rebellion, and Consciousness in the Andean Peasant World, 18th to 20th Centuries, edited by Steve Stern, 280–323. Madison: University of Wisconsin Press, 1987.

———. *Estado boliviano y ayllu andino: Tierra y tributo en el norte de Potosí* Lima: Instituto de Estudios Peruanos, 1982.

———. "Liberalism and Ethnocide in the Southern Andes." *History Workshop* 17 (1988), 3–18.

Ponce Sangines, Carlos. "Los Callahuaya: Apuntes para su estudio." In *Compilación de estudios sobre medicina Kallawaya*, edited by Rolando Costa Ardúz, 110–146. La Paz: Convenio Andrés Bello, Instituto Internacional de Integración, 1988 [1950].

Qayum, Seemin. "Creole Imaginings: Race, Space and Gender in the Making of Republican Bolivia." Ph.D. dissertation. Goldsmith College, University of London, 2002.

Qayum, Seemin, María Luisa Soux, and Rossana Barragán. *De terratenientes a amas de casa: Mujeres de la élite de La Paz en la primera mitad del siglo XX*. La Paz: Ministerio de Desarrollo Humano, 1997.

Querejazu Calvo, Roberto. *Masamaclay: Historia política, diplomática y militar de la Guerra del Chaco*. La Paz: Empresa Industrial Gráfica E. Burillo, 1965.

Rama, Angel. "El área cultural andino: Hispanismo, mesticismo, indigenismo." *Cuadernos Americanos* 196 (1974), 136–173.

Ranaboldo, Claudia. *El camino perdido: Biografía del líder campesino Kallawaya Antonio Alvarez Mamani*. 2nd ed. La Paz: Servicios Múltiples de Tecnologías Apropiados, 1992.

Rance, Susanna. "Bolivia: Pushing the Government on Reproductive Health." *Women's Health Journal* 4:94 (October–December 1994), 60–65.

Ranger, T. O., and P. Slack, eds. *Epidemics and Ideas*. Cambridge: Cambridge University Press, 1991.

René-Moreno, Gabriel. *Nicomedes Antelo*. Santa Cruz: Publicaciones de la Universidad Gabriel René-Moreno, 1960 [1901].

Riddle, John M. *Eve's Herbs: A History of Contraception and Abortion in the West*. Cambridge, Mass.: Harvard University Press, 1997.

Rivera, Guillermo. "La salud mental en Bolivia y sus tareas pendientes." *Galenored Internacional*. http://galenored.com, 8 August 2004.

Rivera Cusicanqui, Silvia. *"Oprimidos pero no vencidos": Luchas del campesinado aymara y qhechwa de Bolivia, 1900–1980*. Geneva: Instituto de Investigaciones de las Naciones Unidas para el Desarrollo Social, 1986.

———. "La raíz: Colonizadores y colonizados." In *Violencias encubiertas en Bolivia*, edited by Xavier Albó and Raúl Barrios Morón, 27–139. La Paz: Centro de Investigación y Promoción del Campesinado (CIPCA), 1993.

Rivera-Garza, Cristina. "The Criminalization of the Syphilitic Body: Prostitutes, Health Crimes, and Society in Mexico City, 1867–1930." In *Crime and Punishment in Latin America: Law and Society since Late Colonial Times*, edited by Ricardo D. Salvatore, Carlos Aguirre, and Gilbert M. Joseph, 147–180. Durham, N.C.: Duke University Press, 2001.

———. "La vida en reclusión: Cotidianidad y estado en el Manicomio General La Castañeda (Mexico City, 1910–1930)." In *Entre médicos y curanderos: Cultura, historia y enfermedad en la América latina moderna*, edited by Diego Armus, 179–219. Buenos Aires: Grupo Editorial Norma, 2002.

Roderick E. McGrew. *Encyclopedia of Medical History*. New York: McGraw-Hill, 1985.

Rosemblatt, Karin. *Gendered Compromises: Political Cultures and the State in Chile, 1920–1950*. Chapel Hill: University of North Carolina Press, 2000.

Rossells, Beatriz. *La mujer: Una ilusión. Ideologías e imagines de la mujer en Bolivia en el siglo XX*. La Paz: Centro de Información y Desarrollo de la Mujer (CIDEM), 1987.

Ruggiero, Kristin. "Honor, Maternity, and the Disciplining of Women: Infanticide In Late Nineteenth-Century Buenos Aires." *Hispanic American Historical Review* 72:3 (1992), 353–373.

———. *Modernity in the Flesh: Medicine, Law, and Society in Turn-of-the-Century Argentina*. Stanford, Calif.: Stanford University Press, 2004.

Ruiz Zevallos, Augusto. *Psiquiatras y locos: Entre la modernización contra los Andes y el nuevo proyecto de modernidad. Perú, 1850–1930*. Lima: Instituto Pasado y Presente, 1994.

Saavedra, Bautista. *El ayllu: Estudios sociológicos*. 4th ed. La Paz: Librería Editorial "Juventud," 1971.

Saignes, Thierry. "¿Quiénes son los Callahuayas? Nota sobre un enigma etnohistórico." In *Compilación de estudios sobre medicina Kallawaya*, edited by Rolando Costa Ardúz, 495–528. La Paz: Convenio Andrés Bello, Instituto Internacional de Integración, 1988.

Salinas Valdivieso, Eduardo. "Intoxicaciones." In *La sanidad boliviana en la campaña del Chaco (1933–1934)*, edited by Aurelio Melean, 378–382. Cochabamba: Imprenta de la Universidad, 1938.

Salmón, Josefa. *El espejo indígena: El discurso indigenista en Bolivia, 1900–1956*. La Paz: Plural Editores, Facultad de Humanidades y Ciencias de la Educación, Universidad Mayor de San Andrés, 1997.

Salmón Ballivián, José. "Los Callahuayas, médicos ambulantes: La planta que vuelve valiente a los cobardes." *Boletín de la Sociedad Geográfica de La Paz* 31:57 (second semester, 1925), 81–90.

Scott, Joan. "Gender: A Useful Category of Historical Analysis." *American Historical Review* 91:5 (December 1986), 1053–1075.

Servicio Cooperative Inter-Americano de Educación (SCIDE). *Rural Edu-*

cation in Bolivia: A Study in Technical Cooperation. La Paz: Institute of Inter-American Affairs (IIAA), 1955.

Shorter, Edward. *A History of Psychiatry: From the Era of the Asylum to the Age of Prozac.* New York: John Wiley and Sons, 1997.

Sociedad Boliviana de Salud Pública. *Historia y perspectivas de la salud pública en Bolivia.* La Paz: UNICEF Organización Panamericana de la Salud (OPS), 1989.

Solorzano, Armando. "The Rockefeller Foundation in Revolutionary Mexico: Yellow Fever in Yucatan and Veracruz." In *Missionaries of Science: The Rockefeller Foundation and Latin America,* edited by Marcos Cueto, 52–71. Bloomington: Indiana University Press, 1994.

Soper, Fred L., et al., "Yellow Fever without *Aedes aegypti*: A Study of a Rural Epidemic in Valle do Channaan, Espiritu Santo, Brazil, 1932." *American Journal of Hygiene* 18 (1933): 555–587.

Sowell, David. *The Tail of Healer Miguel Perdomo Neire: Medicine, Ideologies and Power in the Nineteenth-Century Andes.* Wilmington, Del.: Scholarly Resources, 2001.

Spongberg, Mary. *Feminizing Venereal Disease: The Body of the Prostitute in Nineteenth-Century Medical Discourse.* New York: New York University Press, 1997.

Stepan, Nancy. *Beginnings of Brazilian Science: Oswald Cruz, Medical Research, and Policy, 1890–1920.* New York: Science History Publications, 1981.

———. *The Hour of Eugenics: Race, Gender, and Nation in Latin America.* Ithaca, N.Y.: Cornell University Press, 1991.

———. "Initiation and Survival of Biomedical Research in a Developing Country: The Oswaldo Cruz Institute of Brazil 1900–20." *Journal of the History of Medicine and Allied Sciences* 30:4 (October 1975), 303–325.

———. "The Interplay between Socio-economic Factors and Medical Research: Yellow Fever Research, Cuba and the United States." *Social Studies of Science* 8 (1979), 397–423.

———. " 'The Only Serious Terror in These Regions': Malaria Control in the Brazilian Amazon." In *Disease in the History of Modern Latin America: From Malaria to AIDS.* Edited by Diego Armus, 25–50. Durham, N.C.: Duke University Press, 2003.

Stephenson, Marcia. *Gender and Modernity in Andean Bolivia.* Austin: University of Texas Press, 1999.

Stern, Alexandra. "Buildings, Boundaries, and Blood: Medicalization and Nation-Building on the U.S.-Mexico Border, 1910–1930." *Hispanic American Historical Review* 79:1 (1999), 41–82.

———. "Responsible Mothers and Normal Children: Eugenics and Nationalism in Post-Revolutionary Mexico, 1920–1940." *Journal of Historical Sociology* 12:4 (1999), 369–396.

Stockwell, Edward G. "Infant Mortality." In *The Cambridge World History of Human Disease*, edited by Kenneth F. Kiple, 224–229. Cambridge: Cambridge University Press, 1993.

Suárez Morales, Ovidio. "La enterocolitis del ejército en el Chaco." In *La sanidad boliviana en la campaña del Chaco*, edited by Aurelio Melean, 383–389. Cochabamba: Imprenta de la Universidad, 1938.

Tabera R., Félix. *Apuntes para la historia de la Guerra del Chaco-Picuiba.* La Paz: Impresa Don Bosco, 1979.

Taller de Historia Oral Andino. *Mujer y resistencia comunaria: Historia y memoria.* La Paz: Taller de Historia Oral Andina (THOA), 1986.

Tamayo, Franz. *La creación de la pedagogía nacional.* La Paz: Biblioteca Sesquicentenario de la República, 1975 [1910].

Tapias, Maria. "Disease and Dis-Ease: Emotions, Sociality and Illness in Punata, Bolivia." Ph.D. dissertation in Anthropology. University of Illinois, Urbana-Champaign, 2001.

Thomson, Sinclair. "La cuestión india en Bolivia a principios de siglo: El caso de Rigoberto Paredes." *Autodeterminación* 4 (1987–1988), 83–114.

———. "Revolutionary Memory in Bolivia: Anticolonial and National Projects from 1781 to 1952." In *Proclaiming Revolution: Bolivia in Comparative Perspective*, edited by Merille S. Grindle and Pilar Domingo, 117–134. London: Institute of Latin American Studies, 2003.

Thurner, Mark. *From Two Republics to One Divided: The Contradictions of Postcolonial Nation Making in Andean Peru.* Durham, N.C.: Duke University Press, 1997.

Tinsman, Heidi. *Partners in Conflict: The Politics of Gender, Sexuality, and Labor in the Chilean Agrarian Reform, 1950–1973.* Durham, N.C.: Duke University Press, 2002.

United Nations. *Demographic Yearbook: Historical Supplement [1928/1997].* New York: United Nations, 2000.

Vaughan, Megan. *Curing Their Ills: Colonial Power and African Illness.* Stanford, Calif.: Stanford University Press, 1991.

Vellard, Jean. "Conducto de la población frente a la medicina moderna." In *Compilación de estudios sobre medicina Kallawaya*, edited by Rolando Costa Ardúz, 362–370. La Paz: Convenio Andrés Bello, Instituto Internacional de Integración, 1988.

Vezzetti, Hugo. "El discurso psiquiátrico." In *El Movimiento Positivista argentino*, edited by Hugo Biagini, 362–373. Buenos Aires: Editorial Belgrano, 1985.

Wade, Peter. *Race and Ethnicity in Latin America.* London: Pluto Press, 1997.

Wadsworth, Ana Cecilia, and Ineke Dibbits. *Agitadoras de buen gusto: Historia del Sindicato de Culinarias (1935–1958).* La Paz: Taller de Historia y Participación de la Mujer (TAHIPAMU), 1989.

Walkowitz, Judith R. *Prostitution and Victorian Society: Women, Class, and the State.* Cambridge: Cambridge University Press, 1980.

Williams, Raymond. *Marxism and Literature*. Oxford: Oxford University Press, 1977.

Williams, Steven C. "Nationalism and Public Health: The Convergence of Rockefeller Foundation Technique and Brazilian Federal Authority during the Time of Yellow Fever, 1925–1930." In *Missionaries of Science: The Rockefeller Foundation and Latin America*, edited by Marcos Cueto, 23–51. Bloomington: Indiana University Press, 1994.

Wilson, Leonard G. "Fevers." In *Companion Encyclopedia of the History of Medicine*, edited by W. F. Bynum and Roy Porter, 401–406. London: Routledge, 1993.

Worboys, Michael. "The Emergence and Early Development of Parasitology." In *Parasitology: A Global Perspective*, edited by Kenneth S. Warren and John Z. Bowers, 1–18. New York: Springer-Verlag, 1983.

Zeballos Pasten, Jaime. "Los Callahuayas." In *Compilación de estudios sobre medicina Kallawaya*, edited by Rolando Costa Ardúz, 147–162. La Paz: Convenio Andrés Bello, Instituto Internacional de Integración, 1988 [1951].

Zook, David H., Jr. *The Conduct of the Chaco War*. New Haven, Conn.: Bookman Associates, 1960.

Zulawski, Ann. "Hygiene and the 'Indian Problem': Ethnicity and Medicine in Bolivia, 1910–1920." *Latin American Research Review* 35:2 (spring 2000), 107–129.

———. "Mental Illness and Democracy in Bolivia: The Manicomio Pacheco, 1935–1950." In *Disease in the History of Modern Latin America: From Malaria to AIDS*, edited by Diego Armus, 237–267. Durham, N.C.: Duke University Press, 2003.

INDEX

ANN ZULAWSKI

is a professor of history and Latin American studies
at Smith College. She is the author of *They Eat from
Their Labor: Work and Social Change in
Colonial Bolivia* (1995).

✖

Library of Congress Cataloging-in-Publication Data
Zulawski, Ann.
Unequal cures : public health and political change in Bolivia,
1900–1950 / Ann Zulawski.
p. cm.
Includes bibliographical references and index.
ISBN-13: 978-0-8223-3900-7 (cloth : alk. paper)
ISBN-978-0-8223-3916-8 (pbk. alk. paper)
1. Public health—history—Bolivia. 2. Health care—Bolivia. 3. Bolivia—
Social conditions. I. Title. [DNLM: 1. Public Health—history—Bolivia.
2. Delivery of Health Care—history—Bolivia. 3. Health Policy—
history—Bolivia. 4. History, 20th Century—Bolivia.
WA 11 DB6 Z94u 2007]   RA461Z85 2007
362.19084—dc22   2006023688